Researching

Information Systems

and Computing

Briony J Oates

SAGE Publications

London ● Thousand Oaks ● New Delhi

First published 2006

SAGE Publications Ltd
1 Oliver's Yard
55 City Road
London EC1Y 1SP

SAGE Publications Inc.
2455 Teller Road
Thousand Oaks, California 91320

SAGE Publications India Pvt Ltd
B-42, Panchsheel Enclave
Post Box 4109
New Delhi 110 017

British Library Cataloguing in Publication data

A catalogue record for this book is available from
the British Library

ISBN 1-4129-0223-1
ISBN 1-4129-0224-X (pbk)

Library of Congress Control Number: 2005927557

Typeset by C&M Digitals (P) Ltd, Chennai, India
Printed in Great Britain by The Alden Press, Oxford
Printed on paper from sustainable resources

Researching

Information Systems

and Computing

Contents

List of Figures and Tables

List of Abbreviations

ACM	Association of Computing Machinery
AIS	Association for Information Systems
BCS	British Computer Society
CASE	Computer-aided Software Engineering
CERN	European Organisation for Nuclear Research
IEEE	Institute of Electrical and Electronic Engineers
IS	The information systems discipline
IT	Information Technology
LAN	Local Area Network
SD	Standard Deviation
SDLC	Systems Development Life-cycle
SSM	Soft Systems Methodology
UML	Unified Modelling Language
URL	Universal Resource Locator
XP	eXtreme Programming

Preface

This book is an introductory text on research methods for those in the information systems (usually shortened to IS) and computing disciplines. It is suitable for individual study by novice researchers, particularly those embarking upon masters or PhD research. It can also be used by a tutor as a course text for a taught course in research methods for IS and computing at either masters or senior undergraduate level. It can also be helpful to more experienced researchers who want to learn about particular research approaches with which they are not currently familiar.

IS researchers study how information systems are developed and used by individuals, groups, organizations and society. Often those information systems involve the use of computers. IS researchers study the interaction between the social sphere of people and their organizations and the technical sphere of systems based upon information and communication technologies. They study the processes by which systems are analysed and designed, the contributions they make to business effectiveness, the reasons for the failure of some computer systems and the effect information technology has on our modern world.

Computing researchers are also concerned with the development and use of systems based upon information and communication technologies. They include computer scientists who focus on the mathematical underpinnings of computer-based products, software engineers who research into the process of developing high-quality, reliable systems, web developers who specialize in Internet applications, and animators and artists who develop games, virtual reality environments and digital multimedia applications. Unlike IS researchers, computing researchers have tended to concentrate more on the technical sphere than the social. However, there are increasingly calls for computing researchers to pay greater attention to the viability of their computer-based products and processes in the real world away from the lab, to ensure that their theories and systems are properly validated. Some computing researchers are therefore paying greater attention to the social sphere and its interaction with the technological sphere – such as IS researchers.

Since both IS and computing researchers are interested in the development and use of systems based upon information and communication technologies, albeit often from different perspectives, it is appropriate to address them both in this one book. However, the two communities of IS and computing have developed separately, with discrete bodies of literature and differing preferred research approaches. This book therefore makes clear where the two communities differ in approach, includes examples of research from both disciplines and cites work from the literature of both.

It addresses:

- the kinds of research questions addressed in IS and computing;
- the research approaches used in IS and computing;
- examples of previous research from the IS and computing literature;
- the analysis and evaluation of research projects in IS and computing.

The book discusses the nature of research and the research process, and explains how to do a literature review, the starting point for most research projects. It then covers the main research strategies used in IS and computing (surveys, design and creation, experiments, case studies, action research and ethnography) and the main data generation methods (interviews, questionnaires, observation and documents). It addresses both quantitative and qualitative data analysis. It also explains the different underlying philosophical paradigms of research (the scientific method and positivism, interpretivism and critical research) and relates them to the different research strategies. Some guidance is also given on how to present the results of research, whether via an article or thesis, conference paper or software demonstration. Of course, the book also discusses the ethics of research and the need to ensure that the actions of researchers do not cause harm to others (physiological, psychological, social, political or economic).

Since the Internet and World Wide Web are such important technology-based information systems in our modern world, attention is also paid throughout the book to possible research topics *about* the Internet and World Wide Web, and to how they can be used *within* research approaches in IS and computing. Some web addresses are given of useful resources for IS and computing researchers. These were all correct at the time of writing this book but, of course, sites move and change their address or disappear entirely. If a web address no longer seems to be valid, try entering relevant keywords into a search engine – often this will enable you to track down the new address.

How to Use this Book

Here are some suggestions on how to use this book, whether you are an individual novice researcher, a lecturer or instructor using it as a course text, or an experienced researcher.

Individual novice researchers

If you are a novice researcher, probably a newly enrolled masters or PhD student, I recommend that you read all the chapters in this book. Then you will have a good overview of the range of approaches used in IS and computing, and will be able to choose the one(s) most appropriate to your needs and interests. Each chapter includes some practical exercises to help you test your understanding of the concepts explained in that chapter. If possible, discuss your answers to the questions with a fellow student or work colleague – by comparing your answers and exploring any differences you will increase further your understanding of the topics. Use the evaluation guides provided in almost every chapter to help you analyse and evaluate the research of others, particularly the work you read as you study the previous literature in your discipline. Once you have decided your research topic's appropriate strategy, data generation method(s) and underlying philosophical paradigm, you can obtain more detailed information about them by following up each chapter's suggestions for further reading.

Instructors and lecturers

If you are teaching a course in research methods for IS and computing, this book can be an appropriate course text. I have used the material to teach both undergraduates and postgraduates. The chapters average 5000–6000 words and are written in a student-friendly style. Students can therefore be asked to read one or two each week. Some of the practical work suggested in each chapter can be carried out by the students in class. Alternatively they can do the work in their own time and give seminar presentations on their findings. They can also give seminar presentations that discuss the further reading suggestions provided at the end of each chapter. The practical work usually includes an exercise asking students to analyse and evaluate a piece of research based on a particular strategy or data generation method. The intention is to encourage students to read critically, and to recognize where insufficient information about the research process means that we must treat the reported research findings with some caution. There is a variety of ways to tackle this exercise:

- Since each chapter cites published examples of a particular strategy or method being used in IS and computing research, the students can analyse and evaluate one of them. (This requires particular care for undergraduate students. Many IS papers include a lot of social theory with which students may not be familiar and many computing articles include sophisticated mathematical work that some students may find off-putting.)
- The lecturer can require that some other research paper be studied and evaluated – one whose content is known to be relevant and at an appropriate level for the class members.
- The students can be asked to do a literature search to find and evaluate another example of published work based on that strategy or method.
- One group of students can be asked to carry out a small piece of research based on a particular strategy or method, and present their research process and findings to the class. The other class members then analyse and evaluate their colleagues' work.

Experienced researchers

If you are reading this book as an experienced researcher, you can dip into those chapters that explain any research approaches with which you are unfamiliar. I also recommend that you read the first three chapters, to gain an appreciation of the book's structure and style, and its definition of what is meant by 'research'.

Acknowledgements

I wish to thank students and colleagues in the School of Computing, University of Teesside, Middlesbrough, UK. They have used and commented upon much of the material in this book, and helped me refine it. I also want to thank Linda Hockley, of the Centre for Internet Computing, University of Hull, and Frances Bell and her colleagues at the Information Systems, Organisation and Society Research Centre, University of Salford, for suggestions, advice and lively discussions about the nature of research in IS and computing. Finally I must, as always, thank Spider for his constant support and good humour.

Introduction – The Purpose of this Book

In this chapter you will learn about:

- the aims of this book;
- the information systems and computing disciplines;
- what we mean by 'research';
- the 6Ps of research;
- the structure and content of this book.

Aims of this Book

This book is about how to do research in the information systems (usually shortened to IS) and computing disciplines. Its main aim is to help you to undertake a research project, whether you are a research student aiming for an MPhil or a PhD, or a student on a taught course at masters or senior undergraduate level, or a member of academic staff who is uncertain about how to do some research. The book also aims to help you analyse and evaluate research undertaken by others, so that you will come to know what constitutes 'good' (or 'valid' or 'trustworthy' or 'high quality') research, and so that you will be able to assess whether studies carried out by others provide you with the evidence you need.

The IS and Computing Disciplines

IS as a discipline is concerned with the development and use of information systems by individuals, groups, organizations and society, where usually those information systems involve the use of computers. Other degree titles for IS include Business

Computing, Management Information Systems and Informatics, and IS students and lecturers are found in business schools, social sciences and computing departments, as well as in IS departments. IS is particularly concerned with the real-world social and organizational context in which information systems are developed and used.

The computing discipline includes computer science, software engineering, information technology (IT), web development, computer games, computer animation and multimedia. Like IS, it is concerned with the development and use of computer-based products, but it tends to concentrate primarily on the technological rather than the social aspects.

IS and computing have developed as separate disciplines, with independent academic communities and discrete bodies of literature. However, since they are both concerned with the analysis, development and use of computer-based products there is a large area of overlap between them, so it is appropriate to address them together in this one book.

There are many books on how to do research, but they are aimed at researchers in the natural or social sciences or business studies. Very few are aimed at research in IS and computing. This book helps to fill that gap by concentrating on:

- the kinds of research questions addressed in IS and computing;
- the research approaches used in IS and computing;
- examples of previous research from the IS and computing literature.

Evidence-based Practice

IS has a long tradition of carrying out field research (often called *empirical research*) in order to find out what happens when information systems are requested, developed and used by people. This book will help new IS researchers to do such research, and to analyse and evaluate the work of other IS researchers. The findings of IS research can be used as evidence to support the effective development and use of information systems – that is, evidence-based practice in IS.

Until recently, almost all computing research was concerned only with developing computer-based products (for example, data processing systems, websites, artificial intelligence robots, computer games and digital art) and the methods we use to build such products. This book will help new computing researchers carry out such *design and creation* research, and to analyse and evaluate the work of other computing researchers.

Some computing researchers, software engineering researchers in particular, have begun to realize the necessity to go *beyond* designing and creating new computer-based products, to find out what happens when their products are implemented in the real world (often called the *empirical assessment of systems*). There have been many examples of computer-based products with which the developers were happy, but they failed in some way when put into use. Computing researchers are realizing they need to know *why* that happens. Often computing research has offered new technical products, but they have not been taken up and used. Again, some computing researchers want to know why. They have also realized the need to find out what happens when the methods they propose are put into use in the real world. The computing literature, especially that for software engineering, contains many proposals for new ways of designing and developing computer-based systems, for example, information hiding, design patterns, UML (Unified Modelling Language) and agile development methods such as eXtreme Programming (XP). However, surprisingly (and worryingly) little work has so far been done to find out whether and how these methods work in practice. Similarly, consultants and teachers tell systems developers and computer artists about how they ought to develop computer-based products, but few of these prescriptions have been validated – they often amount to little more than someone's opinion.

In short, as illustrated below, little work has been done to find the *evidence* that validates ideas about appropriate technical products and methods and links the theory to practice.

" A lack of evidence

There are plenty of computer science theories that haven't been tested. For instance, functional programming, object-oriented programming, and formal methods are all thought to improve programmer productivity, program quality, or both. It is surprising that none of these obviously important claims have ever been tested systematically, even though they are all 30 years old and a lot of effort has gone into developing programming languages and formal techniques. (Tichy, 1998, p. 33)

"

There is now, therefore, increased attention by some in computing to the empirical assessment and evaluation of computer products and development processes, so that we can have *evidence-based computing*.

This means that when people suggest how to develop systems in better ways, or how to get computers to do new things, we should know that:

- there is proper evidence to support these proposals;
- the ideas are based on more than the opinion of someone in an academic ivory tower, or some well-paid 'consultant'.

We also want to know whether these proposals are practical in the pressurized world of real-life systems development or games production and in situations when they are implemented against a background of office politics. And vice versa: by gathering evidence about what happens in real life, academics (and consultants) can refine their theories about how computer-based systems development should be done or computer products be used.

This book will help computing researchers to do studies that produce the evidence in support of their computer-based products and methods, and to analyse and evaluate the evidence offered by other researchers.

The Internet and Research

The Internet and World Wide Web are becoming increasingly important in our modern world and offer exciting possibilities for both new research topics and new research approaches. Naturally, these are of particular interest to IS or computing researchers. This book therefore includes:

- some possible research topics *about* the Internet or web;
- how the Internet can be used as a tool *within* a research approach (for example, Internet-based surveys, and Internet 'interviewing');
- how Internet-based research is different from other types of research;
- examples of previous research studies that have investigated the Internet or World Wide Web, or used them to support the research process.

What is Research?

So what do we mean by 'research'? Perhaps the word conjures up an image of people in lab coats (and egg-shaped heads?) designing new washing machines or watching liquids boiling in glass cylinders, or trying to insert a gene from a fish into a tomato. All these people are doing research, but research is more than the preserve of an elite group of white-coated individuals. In fact we all do research every day – research is a particular kind of everyday thinking.

Let's use an example. Supposing you come out to your car one day and discover you have a flat tyre. You need to get the punctured tyre repaired, or buy a new one. How will you tackle this problem? Perhaps you will fetch the telephone directory, find tyre suppliers, phone some and find out the price of a new tyre. If the price is affordable you take your car in and have a new tyre fitted. Simple! However, if the price is more than you really can or want to pay, you might take your punctured tyre to one or two repairers and find out whether it can be repaired and how much that will cost. You then consider all your options and

Research task	Everyday thinking
Identify a problem	How can I deal with my punctured tyre?
Gather data	Obtain prices of new tyres
Analyse the data	What is the cheapest?
Interpret the data	That's more than I want to pay. I need more information.
Gather more data	Is it reparable? Obtain prices for tyre repair.
Analyse the data	Can it be repaired? What is the lowest cost? How does the cost compare with a new tyre?
Interpret the data	Repairing it is possible. Repair will cost 20% of a new tyre. Repair rather than replace means I can still afford to go out on Friday night.
Draw conclusion	I will get it repaired at Tyres-U-Like

Figure 1.1   A piece of research – dealing with a puncture

decide: new tyre, repaired tyre or do nothing and hope to get away with it. You have carried out a piece of research. As Figure 1.1 shows, you identified a problem, gathered some data (or evidence) to help you address the problem, analysed the data, interpreted it, decided to gather more data, analysed and interpreted that and drew a conclusion.

So doing research is a type of thinking we do most days. It means *creating some new knowledge*: initially you did not know what to do about your punctured tyre; now you do. However, in everyday thinking we often take shortcuts and use poor or incomplete data. For example, we draw conclusions about what people are like from our first impressions. Doing *good* research means that we do not jump to conclusions but carefully find sufficient and appropriate sources of data, properly record, analyse and interpret that data, draw well-founded conclusions based on the evidence, and present the findings in an acceptable way in a report, thesis, conference presentation or journal article (Figure 1.2).

Returning to our tyre puncture example, you probably would not bother to contact every tyre fitter listed in the telephone directory – life is too short! Nor would you

Everyday thinking is often characterized by:	Good academic research is characterized by:
• Poor data • Incomplete data • Hasty thinking	• Sufficient data sources • Appropriate data sources • Accurately recorded • Properly analysed • No hidden assumptions • Conclusions well-founded • Properly presented As judged by the *users* of the research

Figure 1.2   Everyday thinking versus good research

adopt a very systematic approach, for example by telephoning every third fitter in the directory. You would telephone two or three, and that would do. You might never know that the 29th fitter in a list of 30 has the cheapest tyres of all, but that would not matter, you have gathered enough information to let you deal with the problem *to your own satisfaction*. And that gives us the key to further defining what we mean by research: research is creating new knowledge, *to the satisfaction of the user(s) of the research*.

Systems developers recognize that they could design a perfect computer system, completely bug-free and meeting all of the requirements specification, but the system would still be a failure if it did not satisfy the end-users of the system. Similarly, researchers must satisfy their end-users. This book is concerned with academic research, that is, the 'users' of the research will be members of the academic community – lecturers, other researchers and students. For an undergraduate research project, these academics might just be in your own university, such as your project supervisor. You should ask yourself, 'What can staff and students here learn from my research project report that they would not learn from a standard textbook?' For MPhil and PhD students, and anyone wanting to publish research papers, your users are academics across the world. Academic end-users are usually interested not just in the end product, the research findings, but also in how these were achieved, that is, the *process* of the research should exhibit the characteristics of good research shown in Figure 1.2. Then they will be satisfied that the knowledge you have created can be added to the sum total of knowledge about IS or computing. So now we can define research as shown in the following box.

> Research is the creation of new knowledge, using an appropriate process, to the satisfaction of the users of the research.

DEFINITION: Research

So, as Figure 1.2 indicates, academic researchers want to see *sufficient* data sources, and an *appropriate* process, with the findings *properly* presented. But what do we mean by 'sufficient', 'appropriate' or 'properly'? For some academic disciplines these are well-defined. However, for IS and computing there are several different academic communities, each with different ideas, or philosophies, about the kinds of research questions to ask and the process by which to answer them. These can partly be categorized by the sub-disciplines within IS and computing: for example *computer science* concentrates on technical development and researchers would mostly use design and creation activities, whereas *management information systems* researchers might use a survey carried out by questionnaire to answer research questions about how business executives use IT in their organizations. The different philosophies about research can also vary from country to country. For example, the majority of IS research in the USA is probably based on a '*positivist*' philosophy about how to do research, which believes there is a single reality or truth. IS research in Europe, conversely, often has an '*interpretivist*' philosophy, which believes that there are multiple versions of reality, so multiple truths. The philosophy underlying the choice of a research question and the process of answering it can even depend on an individual: our own views about the nature of the world we live in and therefore about how we might investigate it. This book will therefore explain these different philosophies of research (see especially Chapters 19 and 20). The fact that there is more than one school of thought in IS and computing about what constitutes good research makes research in these disciplines both challenging and interesting.

Let's Have an Argument!

PhD students are expected to produce a thesis. But 'thesis' has two meanings. One refers to the report itself, anything from 100 to 500 or more pages, bound together. The other meaning of thesis is 'an argument to be proposed or maintained'. Such an argument is made in the written report and might also have to be defended at a viva: a face-to-face meeting with the examiners.

In fact, all research consists of assembling and defending an argument. Researchers are essentially making an argument to their users that they have indeed created some new knowledge – see Figure 1.3. They build this argument by a combination of logic (for example, carrying out and reporting the research process in a logical and structured way), drawing upon other people's work (for example, surveying what has previously been argued and citing as evidence what others have written in the literature) and by carrying out their own fieldwork (that is, generating, analysing and interpreting data

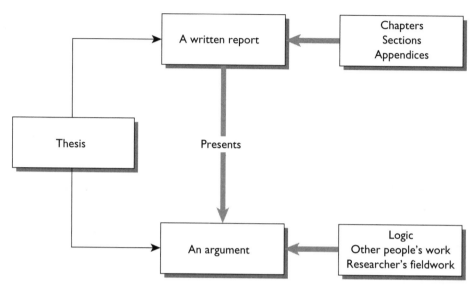

Figure 1.3   A thesis is an argument

and drawing conclusions). This book will help you to build such an argument, to the satisfaction of academic researchers.

Evaluating Research

This book will also show you how to analyse and evaluate the work of other researchers, by providing you with 'Evaluation Guides'. By using these guides you should be able to judge whether the researchers have met the requirements of academic research in your discipline, and whether they have provided the evidence to support their claims. Being able to evaluate the research of others is important because:

- You might want to cite the work of others in your own research – but not if the others' research has been poorly executed.
- Your assessment of the research of others and finding flaws or incompleteness helps you think about and improve your own research.
- Politicians and journalists frequently report research findings as if they must be true because they have been produced by scientists or other academic researchers. As a thoughtful citizen you should be able to assess for yourself whether the findings are based on good research, and not just take someone else's word for it.

'I Just Want to Develop a Computer-based System'

Some readers, perhaps particularly those in the computing disciplines, might by now be asking, 'What's all this got to do with me? I just want to develop a computer system/build a website/create a computer animation [*delete as appropriate*] and write a report about it, not collect and analyse data or make arguments.'

The response is that designing and creating any kind of computer-based product is still a form of research, which requires finding or generating data, analysing it and drawing conclusions. The research question is, 'Is it possible to develop a computer-based product to do X?' In order to define that question fully (for example, What is X? Why is it important to have a computer system to do X?) and then to answer it, you will have to:

- gather data about the computer-based product required (for example, interviewing people, examining company documents, or studying the cultural or genre conventions for a particular kind of animation);
- generate your own data (for example, system models, storyboards, character sketches) to document how and why you designed and implemented the product;
- test the computer-based product and obtain user or viewer feedback, which will involve more data generation and analysis (for example, testing logs, user questionnaires, observation of audience reactions).

Ultimately, you will have to convince the readers of your report (that is, argue) that you went about the design and development tasks in a systematic way, finding, generating and analysing appropriate data, so that you could draw conclusions about whether or not you could indeed develop a computer system to do X.

Of course, some systems development is fairly trivial, for example, using a PC-based software package to build a database to keep track of your music collection. For it to satisfy academics as a valid piece of research, the computer-based product must contribute something new, for example, the system includes some new functions not previously automated using IT, or its design is based on a new theory or algorithm, or the system exhibits some new artistic ideas. Viewing the design and creation of computer systems as research is discussed more fully in Chapter 8.

As explained above, increasingly researchers who build computer-based products are also being encouraged to evaluate their products in use. Effectively, a new research question is being added to design and creation projects: 'What happens when the computer-based product is used in practice/viewed by an audience?' To answer that question, researchers have to use one or more of the other strategies and data generation methods described in this book.

Rigour and Relevance in Research

It is generally believed that IS and computing research should be both 'rigorous' and 'relevant'. However, from time to time IS and computing academics write papers or engage in rather anguished discussions about whether their research is, or can ever be, both rigorous and relevant. Part of the problem is that most researchers do not provide definitions of rigour or relevance, relying instead on supposed common intuition. So what *do* these terms mean?

Rigour encompasses both *systematic conduct* and *validity*. *Systematic conduct* means that the research tasks are undertaken in a rational fashion, with logical relationships between them; they are not random acts or beliefs somehow cobbled together. This book therefore explains how research can be conducted systematically. If a piece of research has *validity*, it means that an appropriate process has been used, the findings do indeed come from the data and they do answer the research question(s). As we noted above, different communities have different ideas about appropriate research questions and processes so, not surprisingly, they also have different ideas about what constitutes 'valid' research in their eyes. This book therefore explains how different research philosophies define 'valid' or 'sound' research.

Relevance is defined as 'being pertinent, having direct bearing'. However, few researchers explain *relevance to whom*. The common assumption is relevance to 'practitioners', but again these are left undefined. 'Practitioners' can be people working in businesses, from chief executives and managing directors, through personnel managers or finance managers to data processing clerks – all use IT themselves or are interested in its use to benefit their organization. 'Practitioners' also includes systems developers, computer artists and digital archivists, that is, those who plan, analyse, design, implement and maintain computer-based products, and who are interested in what kinds of systems to build and appropriate methods for developing and maintaining them. IS and computing research is also potentially relevant to other kinds of practitioners, for example, teachers using IT to aid student learning, or community workers helping disadvantaged communities to use IT to overcome barriers such as geographical or psychological isolation. Since computers and other information and communication technologies are now so pervasive, in the developed world at least, much IS and computing research has the potential to be relevant to *someone*.

Some IS and computing researchers might regard as their users only other academics. Sometimes this is criticized as academics engaging in 'navel-gazing'. But often much research initially seems understandable and relevant only to a few other academics, only later does its relevance to others become apparent – as the following section indicates.

❝ It was said that ...

I think there is a world wide market for maybe five computers. (Thomas Watson, Chairman IBM, 1943)

This telephone has too many shortcomings to be seriously considered as a means of communication. The device is inherently of no value to us. (Western Union internal memo, 1876)

But what is it good for? (Engineer at the Advanced Computing Systems Division of IBM, 1968, commenting on the microchip)

There is no reason why anyone would want a computer in their home. (Ken Olson, president, chairman and founder of Digital Equipment Corporation, 1977)

Computers in the future may weigh no more than 1.5 tons. (*Popular Mechanics*, 1949)

Source: www.ideasmerchant.com/go/useful/facts-quotes.htm **❞**

Other potential users of research are students, like many of the readers of this book. By examining how someone else has carried out a piece of research and the findings that emerged, students can identify their own research questions and plan their research activities, and generally learn about research. Many of the exercises in this book therefore involve you examining actual published research papers.

The 6Ps of Research

The aspects of research covered in this book can be categorized as the 6Ps: *purpose, products, process, participants, paradigm* and *presentation* (see Figure 1.4). All of these aspects need to be considered in any research project.

- **Purpose:** the reason for doing the research, the topic of interest, why it is important or useful to study this, the specific research question(s) asked and the objectives set. Research without a purpose is unlikely to be good research.
- **Products:** the outcomes of research, especially your contribution to knowledge about your subject area. Your contribution can be an answer to your original research question(s) but can also include unexpected findings. For example, you and the academic community might learn something about a particular research strategy as a result of your research. Your thesis, dissertation, conference paper or journal article is also a product of your research. For those research projects that

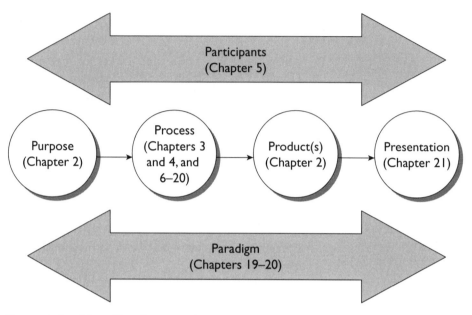

Figure 1.4   The 6Ps of research

involve design and creation, a new computer-based product or new development method could also be a product of your research.

- **Process:** the sequence of activities undertaken in any research project. The process involves identifying one or more research topics, establishing a conceptual framework (the way you choose to think about your research topic), the selection and use of a research strategy and data generation methods, the analysis of data and the drawing of conclusions, including recognizing any limitations in your own research. As explained already, the process should be carried out systematically if the research is to be accepted as rigorous.
- **Participants:** these include those whom you directly involve in your research, for example by interviewing them or observing them, and also those who are indirectly involved, such as the editors to whom you submit a research paper. It is important that you deal with all these people legally and ethically, that is, you do not do anything that might annoy them or cause them harm (physically, mentally or socially). You yourself as a researcher are also a research participant. As we shall see later, for some types of research, researchers are expected to be objective and remain largely unseen in the reporting of their research, whereas in other types of research the researchers are open about their feelings and how their presence influenced the other participants and the research situation.

- **Paradigm:** a pattern or model or shared way of thinking. Managers sometimes talk of the need for a 'paradigm shift' to mean that a new way of thinking is required. In computing, we talk about programming language paradigms, for example, a group of languages that share a set of characteristics, such as the object-oriented paradigm (for example, Smalltalk and C++). Here we are concerned with the philosophical paradigms of *research*. Any piece of research will have an underlying paradigm. We have noted already that different academic communities and individuals have different ideas about the kinds of research questions to ask and the process by which to answer them because they have different views about the nature of the world we live in and therefore about how we might investigate it. These different views stem from different philosophical paradigms. We shall look at three such paradigms: 'positivism', interpretivism' and 'critical research' – each will be explained later.
- **Presentation:** the means by which the research is disseminated and explained to others. For example, it may be written up in a paper or thesis, or a conference paper is presented to an audience of conference delegates, or a computer-based product is demonstrated to clients, users or examiners. It is important that the presentation is carried out professionally – otherwise your audience might assume your whole research project was not undertaken in a professional manner.

Structure of this Book

This book is structured according to the 6Ps (see Figure 1.4). Chapter 2 discusses the *purpose* of research, including generating possible research questions, and some possible *products*, or outcomes, of research. Chapter 3 gives an overview of the research *process* and Chapter 4 discusses the nature of Internet research. Chapter 5 explains the *participants* and ethics of research. The bulk of the book (Chapters 6–18) then covers the research *process* in detail, including a literature review, a chapter on each of six research strategies (surveys, design and creation, experiments, case studies, action research and ethnography), one on each of four data generation methods (interviews, observation, questionnaires and documents) and two on data analysis techniques (quantitative and qualitative). Chapters 19 and 20 discuss the philosophical *paradigms* of research (positivism, interpretivism and critical research). Chapter 21 covers writing up your research and research *presentations*.

At the end of each chapter there are some practical exercises. These will help you both to reflect upon the ideas discussed in the chapter and also to practise reading, analysing and evaluating pieces of research. Each chapter also includes suggestions for further reading that will direct you to other work explaining the ideas discussed in the chapter, and to examples of research in IS and computing where these ideas have been used.

PRACTICAL WORK

1   Find several definitions of 'research' from dictionaries, books on research methods and from friends, family or colleagues, and then compare them to the one given in this chapter. What conclusions can you draw about the concept of 'research'?

2   The section 'Evidence-based Practice' pointed to the lack of evidence for many of the ideas about appropriate methods and products in computing. Study Hirschheim and Newman (1991). This paper is now quite old – consider whether the myths, metaphors and magic rituals the authors identify still exist today. What other myths, metaphors and magic rituals might be observed in your branch of IS or computing? Consider whether they might make suitable research topics.

FURTHER READING

The nature of IS research was discussed in *MIS Quarterly* by Weber (2003) and Benbasat and Zmud (2003). Subsequent issues of *MIS Quarterly* contain papers by other authors agreeing or disagreeing with these views. Debates about rigour and relevance have occurred regularly in the IS literature (Keen, 1991; Kock & Lau, 2001; MISQ, 1999; Robey & Markus, 1998; Senn, 1998) and on ISWorld (www.isworld.org), an online forum for IS researchers and lecturers. 'Relevance to whom?' is discussed in the editor's introduction and in the papers that follow in the special issue of *Informing Science* on bridging the gap between researcher and practitioners (Fitzgerald, 2003).

The nature of computing research, software engineering research in particular, and the need for empirical assessment of computer systems is discussed by Perry, Porter and Votta (2000). This paper would work just as well if the words 'information systems' or 'computing' replaced 'software engineering' throughout. Several papers in O'Brien, Gold and Kontogiannis (2004) review the kinds of empirical evidence that *could* be used in software engineering and lessons that can be learnt from other disciplines. Kling (1993) argues that computer scientists should pay more attention to the application domains of computer products. Tichy, Lukowicz, Prechelt and Heinz (1995) report that 40–50 per cent of computer science and software engineering papers include no empirical validation of proposed designs (of systems, algorithms or models) and argue that this is a serious weakness of computer science research.

References

Benbasat, I., & Zmud, R.W. (2003). The identity crisis within the IS discipline: Defining and communicating the discipline's core properties. *MIS Quarterly, 27*(2).

Fitzgerald, B. (2003). Introduction to the special series of papers on, Informing each other: Bridging the gap between researcher and practitioners. *Informing Science, 6*, 13–19.

Hirschheim, R., & Newman, M. (1991). Symbolism and information systems development: Myth, metaphor and magic. *Information Systems Research, 2*(1), 29–62.

Keen, P.G.W. (1991). Keynote address: Relevance and rigor in information systems research. In H.-E. Nissen, H.-K. Klein, & R.A. Hirschheim (Eds.), *Information systems research: Contemporary approaches & emergent traditions* (pp. 27–49). Amsterdam: North-Holland.

Kling, R. (1993). Organizational analysis in computer science. *The Information Society, 9*(2), 71–87.

Kock, N., & Lau, F. (2001). Information systems action research: Serving two demanding masters. *Information Technology and People, 14*(1), 6–11.

MISQ. (1999). Issues and opinions section on rigour, relevance and research in IS. *MIS Quarterly, 23*(1), 1–33.

O'Brien, L., Gold, N., & Kontogiannis, K. (Eds.). (2004). *Proceedings eleventh international workshop on software technology and engineering practice. STEP 2003.* Los Alamitos, CA: IEEE Computer Society.

Perry, D., Porter, A., & Votta, L. (2000). Empirical studies of software engineering: A roadmap. In A. Finkelstein (Ed.), *The future of software engineering* (pp. 345–355). New York: ACM Press.

Robey, D., & Markus, L. (1998). Beyond rigour and relevance: Producing consumable research about information systems. *Information Resources Management Journal, 11*(1), 7–15.

Senn, J. (1998). The challenge of relating IS research to practice. *Information Resources Management Journal, 11*(1), 23–28.

Tichy, W.F. (1998). Should computer scientists experiment more? *IEEE Computer, 31*(5), 32–40.

Tichy, W.F., Lukowicz, P., Prechelt, L., & Heinz, E.A. (1995). Experimental evaluation in computer science: A quantitative study. *Journal of Systems and Software, 28*(1), 9–18.

Weber, R. (2003). Editor's comments: Still desperately seeking the IT artifact. *MIS Quarterly, 27*(2), iii–xi.

2 The Purpose and Products of Research

In this chapter you will learn about:

- some of the reasons why people do research;
- some possible products, or outcomes, of research;
- how to look for ideas for research topics.

Chapter 1 explained that we could think of research in terms of 6Ps: *purpose, products, process, participants, paradigm* and *presentation* (see Figure 1.4). In this chapter we'll look at two of those 6Ps: the *purpose* and the *products*. The *purpose* of the research incorporates the reason for doing it, the topic of interest, why it is important or useful to study this, the specific research question(s) asked and the objectives set. The *products* of research are the outcomes, especially your contribution to knowledge in your subject area. Let's start with the *purpose*.

Reasons for Doing Research

Why do people do research? You might be embarking upon a piece of research because you have to – you must carry out a piece of research in order to pass your course and get a qualification, or doing research is part of your contract. But doing research because you have to is probably not a sufficient reason to keep you motivated when the going gets difficult. So let's consider some of the other reasons why people do research. You may recognize that at least one of these applies to you. Knowing the reason(s) you choose to do research will help you find a topic that interests you, and also give you a reason to keep going.

To add to the body of knowledge

Some researchers want to add to what is known about their specialist subject, and it does not really matter whether the new knowledge has any practical application. For example, right now someone might be studying patterns of Sunday School attendance in 18th-century England or 19th-century Virginia. Knowing about this is probably not going to affect the current government's educational policy, or suggest new uses for computers. But exploring and finding out the answers to questions is part of what makes us human, so it is natural that some should simply want to explore a subject in depth and find out things we did not know before.

All PhD students are expected to add to the body of knowledge, but for only a few of them is it the *only* reason for doing research. Similarly, undergraduate students try to add to the body of knowledge within their own institution, but that is not normally their only motivation. Usually there are other reasons too, as explained below.

To solve a problem

Many researchers in IS and computing want to solve a problem, for example, 'Is it possible to develop a computer-based product to do X?' If they are developing a computer product to do something in a new way, then it is research. For example:

- Is it possible to develop a website that is based upon the very latest marketing theories to help the ABC company's marketing strategy?
- Is it possible to develop a computer-based tool to support online discussions for teaching purposes?
- Is it possible to effectively render the texture of an animal's hair in a virtual zoo?

Often the computer system developed is of use to someone else (for example, company managers, teachers), but sometimes the problem is seen as just a personal, technical challenge. For example, Linus Torvalds wanted to build a terminal emulation system on his newly acquired 386 computer at home so that he could dial up and use remotely the university's Unix computer (Torvalds & Diamond, 2001). However, for research that is based on addressing a personal, technical challenge it is usually expected that at the end you should be able to discuss how your work could be of relevance to others. (As Torvalds added more features to his terminal emulator, it evolved into the Linux operating system, which is now used by millions worldwide.)

To find out what happens

What happens when a new computer system is put into real-world use? For example, when email systems are provided within an organization, are paper mailing systems abandoned altogether? Is the new email system ignored by some people? What factors might explain what happens? The computing literature is full of papers that describe prototype systems. What happens when these systems are turned into real-life systems and used by non-technical people? Finding out what happens is one of the key areas of interest for IS researchers, who are concerned with the interaction between the social and technical spheres when computer systems are designed and used. As explained in Chapter 1, for computing researchers, the empirical assessment of software systems in use is also becoming increasingly important. Similarly, there is increasing attention, especially in software engineering, to the empirical assessment and evaluation of software *processes*, for example, what happens when a company tries to use a particular development approach such as structured methods or UML? Does the approach live up to the claims made for it by academics or commercial vendors?

To find the evidence to inform practice

How *do* we develop computer systems? How *should* we? Can we come up with better ways? Many methods have been proposed over the years, for example, structured methods, agile methods, formal methods. Similarly, many computer-based tools for developers are marketed: analyst workbenches, project management tools, and so on. Is one approach or tool better than another? In which circumstances should we use each approach or tool? Systems developers are sometimes accused of always seizing upon the latest hyped idea or 'silver bullet'. Good research could provide the evidence that would inform developers about which new ideas are worth taking up and which are not. Similarly, business managers are sometimes accused of blindly following the latest management fad and buying software applications because everyone else is, recent examples being, perhaps, ERP (enterprise resource planning) and CRM (customer relationship management) systems. Good IS research could give managers the evidence about the enablers or barriers to successful adoption of such computer applications.

To develop a greater understanding of people and their world

We might want to find out about people and their world out of simple curiosity (nosiness?). But our findings might also have practical applications. For example, if we know about how people use PCs in the home, that might help companies who want to design software for home PCs. For example:

- Should they make a television more like a computer, or a computer more like a television?
- Do home users feel comfortable with the desktop metaphor currently used to structure the user interface on office PCs, or would they prefer a user interface that looked more like some aspect of their home life?

- What kinds of website advertising are effective for home-based web surfers?
- How does the advent of Internet shopping affect family relationships in the home? Stereotypes suggest women do the weekly grocery shopping, but men are the main technology users, so who does the shopping from an online supermarket? What implications might that have for how supermarkets design their online shopping websites?

" Feminists' joke

If men liked shopping, they'd call it 'research'!

"

To predict, plan and control

Computer-based systems can provide tools to help people predict, plan and control. A lot of work is going on at the moment, for example, to predict the amount and effect of global warming. Evidence is being gathered about the rate of climate change to help us determine what might happen (for example, a rise in sea levels), and how soon, so that we can take action to cope with or even alter the predicted course of events. Computer systems can be built to help with modelling weather patterns and simulating possible scenarios. In the computing world, organizations and politicians are carrying out research to try to predict the number of people that will regularly go online in, say, 5 years' time – so that they can make plans for manufacturing and selling computers and providing the necessary IT infrastructure. Computer-based information systems help many organizations to plan for the future. For example, an accounting and budgeting system helps a company monitor and manage its cashflow, or an admissions-handling system in a university provides information to the people planning timetables and accommodation. Researchers could look at what systems are needed to help with prediction, planning and controlling, develop such systems, or investigate their use.

To contribute to other people's well-being

Some people do research to help make life better for other people. For example, can we research and design better user interfaces so some people, such as older people or disabled people, do not have to struggle when using a computer? Can we design a computer system that makes life easier for people in some way, for example, a system to help people who are frightened of spiders overcome their fear by 'handling' them in a virtual world?

To contribute to personal needs

Some people see doing research, especially studying for a PhD, as a personal challenge. They want to see if they can meet that challenge. Others do it because they think it will help them in their future career. And for women, becoming a 'Doctor' does finally resolve the Mrs/Miss/Ms issue!

To test or disprove a theory

As we shall see later, testing and disproving a theory is the main approach of scientific research. In IS and computing, there are many theories that could be tested. For example, many parents worry that computer games are harmful to the development of their children because of the use of violence, blood and gore, and because they keep children sitting down inside instead of getting exercise by running around outside. Alternatively, others argue that computer games are beneficial because they hone perception and motor skills and reaction times. Can we test these theories?

To come up with a better way

Sometimes a research question appears to have been answered, but another researcher wants to suggest a better answer. For example, a better algorithm, a better explanation, a better method … . Of course, initially a different way may not be accepted by others, as Parnas found – see the box below.

CASE STUDY
Getting a new
idea accepted

In 1972, Parnas proposed a new way of decomposing systems into modules, which eventually became known as 'information hiding', and submitted a paper to the *Communications of the ACM*. A reviewer wrote: 'Obviously Parnas does not know what he is talking about because nobody does it that way.' Parnas responded that an idea claiming to be new should not be rejected just because it was new, and the paper was published (Parnas, 1972, 2003).

To understand another person's point of view

A researcher might join a group of people to find out about their views and ways of see-ing the world. The group might know they are being researched, or they might not even know a researcher is among them. For example, you could work on an IT help-desk and find out about how your co-workers view the end-users who call in with problems. Are they seen as customers, whose needs are paramount, or are they seen as the enemy?

To create more interest in the researcher

Some researchers do research because it makes them look good and they get invited to give keynote speeches at conferences or to appear on television and radio shows to display their authority and knowledge. But let's be honest: if you are embarking on your first piece of research, it is unlikely that it will make you a media star.

There are probably many more reasons for doing research, but those listed here are enough to show that different people have different motives. What motivates you? What all these reasons have in common is that the research they stimulate leads to the creation of some new knowledge.

> **" The rewards of scientists**
>
> The reward of the young scientist is the emotional thrill of being the first person in the history of the world to see something or to understand something. Nothing can compare with that experience … . The reward of the old scientist is the sense of having seen a vague sketch grow into a masterly landscape. Not a finished picture, of course; a picture that is still growing in scope and detail with the application of new techniques and new skills. The old scientist cannot claim that the masterpiece is his own work. He may have roughed out part of the design, laid on a few strokes, but he has learned to accept the discoveries of others with the same delight that he experienced his own when he was young. (Cecilia Payne-Gaposchkin (astronomer). Excerpt from acceptance speech and memorial lecture for the Russell Prize, 1977.) **"**

Possible Products – the Outcomes of Research

So what types of knowledge can be created? There are many types of knowledge. Even given the same research question as a starting point, two different researchers could produce different kinds of knowledge as the outcomes or *products* of their research. Let's consider some of those different types of knowledge outcomes.

A new or improved product

This is the focus of some IS research and much computing research. Indeed, some computing departments expect that a new IT product is always one outcome of a research student's work. It might be a computer application designed to meet a functional specification, or, in a multimedia or computer animation department, it might be an example of digital art. In other cases the 'product' is not necessarily a computer application, it could also be a computing-related process, for example, a new or improved method for developing a particular kind of computer application.

A new theory

Computers and computer-based information systems are still comparatively new in our world and are still evolving. We don't yet always know how to use them efficiently and effectively. Nor do we know much about the interaction between individuals, groups and societies, and computing technology. As new computing technologies are invented, new uses of computers and information systems become possible, raising more questions about efficient and effective use. There is room, therefore for many more theories about how to analyse, build and use computer-based products.

A re-interpretation of an existing theory

Can an existing theory be applied in a new context? This has been a fruitful approach to research in IS and computing. For example, taking theories from psychology or economics or education, and applying them in an IS or computing context, for example, to the development of user interfaces, management information systems or computer-aided learning. The researcher explores whether and how the theory can be incorporated into a new design. Sometimes a theory might need to be re-appraised because it cannot be found to apply in a computing context. For example, retailing theories about consumer behaviour might not apply to e-commerce sites (see the box below).

CASE STUDY Developing a new theory and re-interpreting existing theories	John was researching how online supermarkets could stimulate impulse buying by their customers. However, he was alarmed to find very little about impulse buying in the literature on e-commerce. He told his supervisor that he was worried this would mean a lower mark because his literature review would not be as large as he had hoped. His supervisor, on the other hand, explained to him that this was an excellent opportunity to *improve* his research outcomes. He could use the detailed literature on impulse buying for supermarkets in the physical world and examine how far these theories could be used in the virtual world. He could also carry out field research into existing successful online shopping sites, such as Amazon, and analyse the techniques they used to stimulate impulse buying. Then he could combine the findings from his literature review and his field research to propose a new theory about impulse buying online.

New or improved research tool or technique

In IS research, there has been increasing attention paid to newer research tools and techniques from the social sciences (for example, action research, see Chapter 11, or qualitative data analysis, see Chapter 18), although conventional approaches such as surveys and experiments still predominate, especially in the USA. Very little computing research, conversely, has yet adopted *any* of the newer approaches. There is scope therefore for IS and computing researchers to adopt new research approaches and see if they prove useful. This book discusses some of the newer approaches. However, as a new researcher, you should discuss with your supervisor the acceptability in your department or discipline of your proposed strategy and the risks involved in adopting a non-conventional method. You might decide to leave such a risky course for when you are more established.

A new or improved model or perspective

A research outcome might be to suggest that we look at something in a new way. For example, Chen (1976) proposed that we should view the world in terms of entities and relationships, leading to the entity-relationship diagrams used in database design. Similarly, Morgan (1986) argued that most organizational analysis saw organizations as machines, whereas they could also be viewed as organisms, brains, psychic prisons and so on.

An in-depth study of a particular situation

Since computers and information systems are comparatively new, and since we continue to find new uses for them, there are many opportunities to study them in depth in contexts that have not been studied before. For example, a case study of a particular systems development department that decides to move from its existing method to an approach using UML; or an investigation of a company's website: its original conception, its evolution, its outcomes, and whether what occurred was consistent with the theory found in the literature.

An exploration of a topic, area or field

A literature-based survey of the state of knowledge in a particular area can be one outcome of research. However, a straightforward description is usually not sufficient. The researcher would normally be expected to make a further contribution by ordering the material, picking out themes, comparing and contrasting different views, and identifying areas of controversy or requiring investigation. Such a survey is often one of the first outcomes of an MPhil/PhD student's work.

A critical analysis

An example of a critical analysis might be an examination of a systems development method: its features, its omissions, the claims made for it and whether they are borne out in practice. Another example might be a critical analysis of government policy concerning the development of a national IT infrastructure and its implications for the digital divide still found in most societies.

Sometimes, two or more examples are critically analysed and compared. For example, during the 2001 foot and mouth disease outbreak in the UK, a study analysed and evaluated how different local governments used their websites to inform, communicate and deliberate with those affected (Oates, 2002).

Summary of types of research products

Davis and Parker (1997, p. 64) summarize the different types of contributions to knowledge as:

- new or improved evidence;
- new or improved methodology;
- new or improved analysis;
- new or improved concepts or theories.

To this we can add:

- new or improved computer-based product.

Unanticipated outcomes

Although you may be able to say in advance the kind of outcomes you expect, sometimes there are unexpected outcomes too. For example:

- A research project used an ethnographical approach (see Chapter 12) to investigate the use of IT in a business organization. In addition to anticipated outcomes about the ways IT was incorporated into the organization's culture, new knowledge was also created about the research strategy of ethnography.
- A research project designed and created a software tool to support tutors dealing with large numbers of students. During the evaluation stage, observations about how the class and tutors interacted with the software led to new knowledge about effective user interface design.

When you write up your research, remember to look for new knowledge that you had not anticipated creating.

Remember, too, a thesis, dissertation, conference paper or journal article is also a product of your research – usually these are the means by which your knowledge outcomes are disseminated to the wider academic community.

Finding and Choosing Research Topics

We've now seen that there are many different reasons for doing research, and many different possible outcomes. But how do we get started? That is, how do we find research topics?

Sometimes they emerge out of personal circumstances and opportunities. For example, a disabled person might be frustrated by the poor accessibility of many websites, and then realize that she could turn accessibility into a research topic, asking questions such as:

- What percentage of websites meets the published accessibility guidelines?
- How aware are web developers of accessibility issues?
- What factors in a company support or militate against accessibility being considered from the outset of a web development project?

Most researchers try to be aware of unexpected, serendipitous opportunities for research ideas, such as a conversation at a party, an interesting magazine article or a news event.

However, if an idea for research does not suddenly present itself to you, you will have to follow a more structured approach to look for ideas. You will need to look at what others have done, or suggested, and at what seems to be happening in the world, both in your research community and in the wider world.

Sources of research ideas

Sources for research ideas include:

- Suggestions from staff in your department. In some departments, staff circulate suggested research topics or project ideas.
- Past research students' work. You could ask your supervisor to suggest some recent good examples of student dissertations or theses. Often they discuss a topic in general and a number of research questions, before explaining that they will focus on just one aspect. What they choose *not* to cover could still be available for you to investigate.
- Recent conference and journal papers, especially the sections (often found near the end of a paper) discussing where further research is needed.
- Current events reported in the media. Sometimes a phenomenon is noticed in popular culture before it is taken up by academics. For example, Internet gambling or the use of text messaging by teenagers.

- Needs expressed by potential clients. You might know someone who asks you to use your IT skills to develop an IT product for their organization. Be careful though, to make sure you can identify an academic *research* aspect to such work, and that it does not just call for the use of your technical abilities.
- Calls for conference papers or special issues of journals on a particular theme. These calls can tell you what topics are currently 'hot' in the academic world, and often they list the kinds of research questions that need to be addressed.
- People making assumptions or assertions with little supporting evidence. Could you carry out research to find evidence to support or refute them? For example:

  - 'Organizations that don't go online will perish.'
  - 'Computer-based teaching means the end of universities as we know them.'
  - 'Everyone knows that object-oriented is much better than structured analysis.'
  - 'Open source software is the future.'

Brainstorming and clustering

It is often helpful to discuss ideas with a group of colleagues, perhaps using brainstorming and clustering techniques. Give the group some background information on yourself:

- your interests;
- what subjects you liked or disliked studying;
- your strengths and weaknesses;
- what might motivate you to do research.

Using a whiteboard, blackboard or just a large piece of paper, all the group members write down quickly keywords, ideas and suggestions – as many as they can, in any order, and as quickly as possible. Write down any idea that occurs, regardless of whether it sounds unfeasible or downright silly. When you have run out of suggestions (and only then), examine the ideas more closely. Can some of them be grouped together because they are related in some way? Does that clustering suggest a topic area or research question? Which ideas or clustered sets of ideas could be turned into potential research projects? Which of these possibilities excite you?

Selecting a topic

Having found some potential research topics, you have to choose one. This involves identifying the topic that best meets the two criteria of enjoyability (for you) and feasibility (as a piece of academic research).

Ask yourself, 'Will I enjoy working on that topic?' If the answer is, 'Not really', then find another topic. There are times when many researchers become bored with particular aspects of their research (for example, chasing up reference details, or negotiating access), but if the overall topic does not interest you then it is unlikely that you will do good research.

Try to express each potential topic as a single research question. Now break down what you would need to do to address that question, expressing it as series of objectives you would have to meet. This requires looking at the other chapters in this book to find out, for example, the kind of research strategy and data generation methods you might use and the sort of techniques you would need for data analysis. Examine each of the objectives and ask yourself whether you think doing the work to meet that objective would be both enjoyable and feasible. Only you can really know what you're likely to find enjoyable – although your friends and family might be able to advise you, based on their knowledge of you. To help you think about the feasibility, ask yourself the following questions:

- **Is the research likely to offer something new for your target users?** The previous section discussed the kinds of new knowledge that can be the outcomes of research.
- **Does the topic have 'symmetry of potential outcomes'?** This means, will your results be of value, whatever they are? For example, you might ask a question concerning whether help-desk staff suffer more from stress than other types of IS or computing staff. If they do, this would be interesting and worth further investigation. But if they do not, the result is not particularly interesting. A better research topic, with useful outcomes whatever they are, would be to investigate what factors contribute to feelings of stress in an IS or computing department.
- **Will your research still contribute something to knowledge, even if you do not complete all of the technical product in the time available?** This is an important issue for those doing design and creation research, where a computer-based product is an expected outcome. You need to design your research project to make sure you still have a contribution to knowledge even if the computer-based product is unfinished. For example, your models and design rationale might, on their own, offer something new.
- **Is there a theory (or set of ideas) that will help you structure your approach, at least in the beginning?** Usually there is some theory in the literature that can be used, even if you have to look outside your own discipline. Of course, one of your research outcomes might turn out to be a critique of the theory, or suggestions for how it needs to be modified or extended. If there is no pre-existing theory, then at least you know your research topic is something new, but it could be difficult working out where to start.

- **Is the research and its outcomes likely to be of sufficient scope to meet your course requirements?** The scope expected of a 3–4 week research project carried out as part of a taught course is clearly much less than that expected of a PhD carried out over 3 years or longer.
- **Can the research be carried out in the time available?** Even though PhD students have a long period of time available, they can still be caught out by not allowing enough time for such things as gaining access to a particular research context and writing the thesis. Note that funding bodies are becoming much more prescriptive on the maximum time allowed for PhDs.
- **Does the research topic fit in with your own motivations, strengths and weaknesses, likes and dislikes?** For example, it would be foolish for a student with poor programming skills to take on a highly technical project, just as someone with poor interpersonal skills would be ill-advised to take on research involving a lot of interviewing.
- **Does the research meet your own learning objectives?** That is, do you really want to know the answer to your research question, or will the topic help you to acquire some skills that you want?
- **Do you have the necessary resources?** For example, hardware, software, library resources, money for travel expenses, access to interviewees.
- **Can you approach the topic without too much bias?** Scientific research is expected to be objective, the researcher's own feelings and views should play no part. In other types of research, it is accepted that the researcher's own feelings cannot be ignored, but they must not be allowed to 'force' the research into a particular conclusion. A simple test is to ask yourself, 'Do I know the answer to my research question already?' If you think you do, then you should choose another topic since you are unlikely to be sufficiently open-minded during the research.
- **Will the research be safe and ethical?** You should be able to carry it out without breaking the law, without causing yourself or anyone else discomfort or harm (social, emotional or physical), and within the ethical guidelines agreed by academic researchers (these guidelines are explained in Chapter 5).

Most research students feel uncertain and anxious until they have settled upon a research question and had it approved. However, the good news is that you are not expected to decide in Week 1, and you do not have to do it alone. This book will help you to decide the kind of research you want to do. You should also use your supervisor. A supervisor is there to help you think through possible ideas and decide about their feasibility and whether they would meet your course requirements, so do not wait to see him or her until you know exactly what you want to do!

'I Write Therefore I Think'

As soon as you begin to have ideas about possible research questions and their associated objectives, write them down. Also write down your thoughts about whether you think doing the work to meet each objective would be both enjoyable and feasible, and from that draw your conclusions about whether this is a viable topic for you.

The main reason for writing all this down, rather than just thinking it through in your head, is that most researchers find that the act of writing is not just record-making; it helps them to clarify their ideas, to discover what they really think. It is therefore good practice to write up your thoughts, problems, insights, plans, emerging analysis and interpretations throughout your research project. Additional benefits of writing down as much as possible include:

- You can show your current thoughts to your supervisor, who will find it much easier to understand something written down than something expressed verbally, often hidden within a sequence of 'Erm's' and 'Well, you see, it's sort of ...'.
- You will be able to include some of it in your project proposal, dissertation or thesis.
- The more you acquire the habit of writing up ideas, rationales and arguments, the easier you will find producing your final report, dissertation or thesis.

Evaluating the Purpose and Products of Research

Start to study research papers with a critical eye. Even though you might not yet understand the theory, research approach or findings, you can evaluate the research's purpose and products, and how well the researchers have explained them. Use the 'Evaluation Guide' below to help you.

EVALUATION GUIDE: PURPOSE AND PRODUCTS

1 How do the researchers describe the purpose of their research? Who are the potential users of it?
2 What reasons (if any) do the authors give as their motivation for this research?
3 Which of the reasons listed in this chapter do you think *might* apply?
4 What were the outcomes (*products*) of the research? Classify them by type as in this chapter.
5 How well do you think the authors have explained and justified their purpose and products?

PRACTICAL WORK

1   Practise brainstorming for possible research topics. Imagine you have 4 months to plan, carry out and write up a research project, and you have decided it should be something to do with IT and students. In a group of between two and six, do the following:

   a   On paper or a white board, write 'IT' and 'Students'. Brainstorm and write down concepts related to IT, students, or 'IT and students': single words, short phrases or questions. (Remember students have home and social lives, as well as their university-based lives, you could take 'students' to be at school or university, or 'life-long learners', and IT could cover digital communications, such as mobile phones, as well as computers.) Every suggestion should be written down, however silly it sounds. Continue until you have filled the page/board or have no more ideas (15 minutes to 1 hour).

   b   Look through the list, cluster related ideas together, remove those that do not seem to lead anywhere, and identify two or three potential research topics concerning IT and students.

   c   Turn each of these research topics into a research question and a series of objectives. Try to come up with questions that will always have an interesting and fulsome answer, for example avoid: Question: 'Do most university students have their own PC at home?' Answer: 'No'.

   d   Decide what knowledge outcomes might emerge from each research topic, and who might be interested in the research findings (for example, politicians, salespeople, historians, parents, lecturers or …).

   e   Assess the feasibility of each topic, using the suggestions given in this chapter.

2   Start to practise analysing and evaluating research. Study two research papers – look in academic IS or computing journals or ask your supervisor to suggest some. Answer the questions in the 'Evaluation Guide' above, using the material in this chapter to help you.

FURTHER READING

The knowledge outcomes were based on suggestions in Cryer (1996), an excellent guide for researchers in any discipline. Other general research guides include Davis and Parker (1997), which concentrates on the US model of a PhD, and Phillips and Pugh (1994), which mostly relates to the UK model.

Calls for conference papers and special issues of journal papers can be found in online bulletin boards and newsletters serving academics. For example, see the archives of ISWorld (www.isworld.org) and of Design Research News, a digital newsletter of the Design Research Society (www.designresearchsociety.org).

Alter and Dennis (2002), two researchers in the IS field, propose a framework for selecting research topics, and reflect on how they chose their own topics. Broy and Denert (2002) provide the proceedings of a fascinating conference in 2001, where many of the 'software pioneers' gathered together. These pioneers are some of the key contributors to computer science and software engineering, for example, Boehm, Chen and Parnas. Using book and DVD format, the proceedings contain both the original seminal works and a discussion by the authors on how they developed their groundbreaking ideas, how they were received, what has happened since, and how they now view those ideas. Browsing these proceedings will provide illustrations of how ideas for research emerge in a variety of ways and how often the significant contribution to knowledge is not realized until some time later.

References

Alter, S., & Dennis, A.R. (2002). Selecting research topics: Personal experiences and speculations for the future. *Communications of the AIS, 8*(Article 21), 314–329.

Broy, M., & Denert, E. (Eds.). (2002). *Software pioneers. Contributions to software engineering*. Berlin: Springer.

Chen, P. (1976). The entity relationship model – Toward a unified view of data. *ACM Transactions on Database Systems, 1*(1), 1–36.

Cryer, P. (1996). *The research student's guide to success*. Buckingham: Open University Press.

Davis, G.B., & Parker, C.A. (1997). *Writing the doctoral dissertation* (2nd ed.). New York: Barron's.

Morgan, G. (1986). *Images of organization*. Beverly Hills, CA: Sage.

Oates, B.J. (2002). Foot and mouth disease: Lessons from local government websites. In D. Remenyi (Ed.), *2nd European conference on e-government, Oxford, 1–2 October* (pp. 341–352). Reading: MCIL.

Parnas, D.L. (1972). On the criteria to be used in decomposing systems into modules. *Communications of the ACM, 15*(12), 1053–1058.

Parnas, D.L. (2003). The secret history of information hiding. In M. Broy & E. Denert (Eds.), *Software pioneers. Contributions to software engineering* (pp. 399–409). Berlin: Springer.

Phillips, E.M., & Pugh, D.S. (1994). *How to get a PhD*. Buckingham: Open University Press.

Torvalds, L., & Diamond, D. (2001). *Just for fun. The story of an accidental revolutionary*. New York: Texere.

3 Overview of the Research Process

In this chapter you will learn about:

- the process of doing research;
- the components that make up the research process;
- some models of the research process.

So far we've looked at the *purpose* of research (the reasons people do research) and the *products* of research (outcomes from research projects). In this chapter we'll start to look at another of the 6Ps of research – the *process*. The majority of chapters in this book are concerned with the research process. This chapter gives an overview of it, and later chapters go into greater detail.

- **Question:** You've got a research question that interests you, you're keen to get started, so what should you do next?
- **Answer:** You start to plan the sequence of activities you need to perform that will:

    - take you from your initial research question to an answer, or set of answers;
    - enable you to present your evidence and conclusions to an academic audience and argue convincingly that you have created some new knowledge.

Remember that it's not enough just to come up with an answer to your research question – gratifying as that might be for you. For academic research, you have to put your findings and the process you followed to the scrutiny of other academics – only if they accept your evidence, process and argument will they be satisfied that you have created something that can be added to the sum total of knowledge in IS or computing.

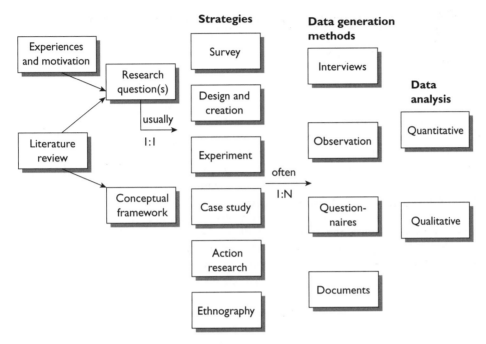

Figure 3.1   Model of the research process

A Model of the Research Process

Figure 3.1 gives an overview of the research process and its components: personal experiences and motivation, literature review, research question, conceptual framework, strategies, data generation methods and quantitative and/or qualitative data analysis. As Figure 1.4 showed, these are all shaped by the participants and underpinned by a philosophical paradigm. At the end of the research process you should have some outcomes, as explained in Chapter 2: knowledge outcomes and, possibly, a new artefact such as a computer-based product or a new development method.

Personal experiences and motivation

As we saw in Chapter 2, people do research for a variety of reasons. You need to think about why *you* are doing research. Thinking about your motivation, as well as your personal experiences, likes, dislikes, strengths, weaknesses and so on will help you think about possible research questions that you could address. Reminding yourself of why you are doing the research can also help keep you going through the difficult, boring or frustrating times – there will be some, guaranteed!

Literature review

The literature review is covered in detail in Chapter 6. All academic researchers have to review the literature in their chosen area of study: the books, journal articles and conference papers that have already been written on the topic and, for digital designers and creators, any related computer artefacts that have previously been produced. By studying the literature you can find out what has been done before, and what topics remain to be addressed. This helps you to decide upon a viable research question that has not already been fully addressed.

You also have to critically evaluate previous work, and look for themes that link different authors' work together. You will be assessed on the thoroughness of the review, your analysis of the literature and your ability to synthesize it into a coherent account that justifies your own research and places it in context. The literature review should help provide the *conceptual framework* for your research (see below).

Research question

To get going on research you need a research question or set of questions. As we saw in the previous chapter, you can find a question by thinking about:

- **Yourself**: what motivates you, the kind of research you would like to do and the kind of knowledge outcome you would like to achieve.
- **What others propose**: suggestions in the literature of where more research is needed, and calls for papers for conferences and journals on a particular topic.

Conceptual framework

A conceptual framework makes explicit how you structure your thinking about your research topic and the process undertaken. It therefore makes clear such things as:

- the different factors that comprise your topic;
- your way of thinking about the topic (for example, via a particular theory such as actor network theory or semiotics, or via a particular technology such as web services);
- your way of tackling your research question(s) (that is, the combination of strategies and methods you adopt – often called your *research methodology*);
- your approach to analysing any generated data (for example, quantitative analysis, which uses mathematics and statistics, or qualitative analysis, which uses thematic approaches);

- your approach to designing and creating any new IT product (for example, the systems development methodology you follow, or the genre you want to use);
- your approach to evaluating your research (for example, whether you will focus on technical accuracy, greater understanding, increased efficiency or aesthetic criteria).

Much of the conceptual framework is derived from, and justified by, a study of the literature.

Strategies

A strategy is your overall approach to answering your research question. In this book we look at six strategies: survey, design and creation, experiment, case study, action research and ethnography.

- **Survey**: focuses on obtaining the same kinds of data from a large group of people (or events), in a standardized and systematic way. You then look for patterns in the data using statistics so that you can generalize to a larger population than the group you targeted. (See Chapter 7.)
- **Design and creation**: focuses on developing new IT products, or *artefacts*. Often the new IT product is a computer-based system, but it can also be some element of the development process such as a new construct, model or method. (See Chapter 8.)
- **Experiment**: focuses on investigating cause and effect relationships, testing hypotheses and seeking to prove or disprove a causal link between a factor and an observed outcome. There is 'before' and 'after' measurement, and all factors that might affect the results are carefully excluded from the study, other than the one factor that is thought will cause the 'after' result. (See Chapter 9.)
- **Case study**: focuses on one instance of the 'thing' that is to be investigated: an organization, a department, an information system, a discussion forum, a systems developer, a development project, a decision and so on. The aim is to obtain a rich, detailed insight into the 'life' of that case and its complex relationships and processes. (See Chapter 10.)
- **Action research**: focuses on research into *action*. The researchers plan to do something in a real-world situation, do it, and then reflect on what happened or was learnt, and then begin another cycle of plan–act–reflect. (See Chapter 11.)
- **Ethnography**: focuses on understanding the culture and ways of seeing of a particular group of people. The researcher spends time in the field, taking part in the life of the people there, rather than being a detached observer. (See Chapter 12.)

Typically one research question has one research strategy. If you think you need more than one strategy, you probably have more than one research question embodied in your plan. This is acceptable (assuming you have the time to use two strategies within your research project), but you should spend time thinking about the different research question that each strategy will address (see the case study below). Often one journal or conference paper will report the use of just one of the research strategies, because of the word number restrictions imposed by journal publishers and conference organizers.

CASE STUDY
Example of
two research
strategies within
one project

Michael wanted to investigate the use of Intranets by people working in Personnel Departments (sometimes called 'Human Resource' Departments). He planned to use two research strategies: a case study followed by a survey. He realized each strategy would help him address a different research question associated with his main topic:

- Case study: What issues in Company X affect the use of Intranets by those working in the Personnel Department?
- Survey: Are the issues found in Company X unique to that company, or found in many other similar companies?

Data generation methods

A data generation method is the means by which you produce empirical (field) data or evidence. Data can be either quantitative or qualitative. *Quantitative data* is numeric data, for example, number of website hits, number of employees, annual turnover, last year's profit. *Qualitative data* is all other types of data: words, images, sounds and so on.

In this book we look at four data generation methods: interviews, observations, questionnaires and documents.

- **Interview**: a particular kind of conversation between people where, at least at the beginning of the interview if not all the way through, the researcher controls both the agenda and the proceedings and will ask most of the questions. One-to-one and group interviews are possible. (See Chapter 13.)
- **Observations**: watching and paying attention to what people actually do, rather than what they report they do. Often involves looking, but it can involve the other senses too: hearing, smelling, touching and tasting. (See Chapter 14.)
- **Questionnaire**: a pre-defined set of questions assembled in a pre-determined order. Respondents are asked to answer the questions, often via multiple choice options, thus providing the researcher with data that can be analysed and interpreted. (See Chapter 15.)
- **Documents**: documents that already exist prior to the research (for example, policy documents, minutes of meetings and job descriptions) and documents that

are made solely for the purposes of the research task (for example, a researcher's logbook or design models). Also includes 'multimedia documents': visual data sources (for example, photographs, diagrams, videos and animations), aural sources (for example, sounds and music) and electronic sources (for example, websites, computer games and electronic bulletin boards). (See Chapter 16.)

Some data generation methods are commonly associated with particular research strategies: an experiment usually uses observations, and a survey often uses questionnaires. However, one research strategy can use more than one data generation method. For example, a researcher using an action research strategy in an organization might interview people, observe what occurs, ask some people to complete a questionnaire and collect documents produced during the action research project.

Using more than one data generation method enables us to look at the phenomenon of interest in different ways. For example, if you are carrying out a case study of how people interact with a web-based system, you could observe people using it, collect documentary data electronically about their movements around the website, interview them about their attitudes and perceptions concerning it, and ask them to complete an evaluation questionnaire. By using more than one method you are likely to produce more data, which could improve the quality of your research, but this may take longer and cost more.

Using more than one data method also allows the findings from one method to be corroborated or questioned by comparing with the data from another method. For example, the people you interview might tell you they found the website easy to use, but your documentary data shows that they frequently had to access the website's help system. If your data shows some consistency across methods, then it can increase confidence in your findings, showing that they are not too closely linked to the particular method you used to generate the data.

The use of more than one data generation method to corroborate findings and enhance their validity is called *method triangulation*. Many types of triangulation are possible in a research project:

- **Method triangulation**: the study uses two or more data generation methods.
- **Strategy triangulation**: the study uses two or more research strategies.
- **Time triangulation**: the study takes place at two or more different points in time.
- **Space triangulation**: the study takes place in two or more different countries or cultures to overcome the parochialism of a study based in just one country or culture.
- **Investigator triangulation**: the study is carried out by two or more researchers who then compare their accounts.
- **Theoretical triangulation**: the study draws on two or more theories rather than one theoretical perspective only.

Triangulation gives researchers multiple modes of 'attack' on their research question. However, researchers differ over whether they should expect triangulation of method or time or space, and so on, to lead to consistency of findings. It depends on their underlying research philosophy (see Chapters 19 and 20 for a detailed explanation). 'Positivists' subscribe to the idea of a single 'truth' or 'reality' and would expect the multiple lines of attack to lead to a consistent set of findings. 'Interpretivists', on the other hand, do not subscribe to the idea of a single reality, believing any notion of 'reality' to be constructed by individuals and groups, so there are multiple realities for people in our world, and different research approaches are likely to lead to different findings. Interview data about recollections of a meeting and company minutes of the same meeting, for example, are two different 'stories', created by different people for different audiences. Interpretivists would not always expect to see convergence in the data they generate using triangulation.

Data analysis

After you have generated some data, by using your chosen research strategy and one or more data generation methods, you need to analyse the data, looking for relationships or themes. *Quantitative data analysis* uses mathematical approaches such as statistics to examine and interpret the data. *Qualitative data analysis* looks for themes and categories within the words people use or the images they create. Both approaches are discussed in Chapters 17 and 18. Note that it *is* possible to apply quantitative data analysis to qualitative data: you could, for example, analyse some interview transcripts (words, qualitative data) and count the number of times a particular phrase is used (quantitative analysis).

You can draw upon your conceptual framework to help you analyse the data. The theory (or theories) in your conceptual framework can get you started by suggesting relationships or themes to look for. However, you should not be too wedded to your conceptual framework so that it blinds you to seeing interesting things in your data. You might discover that the theory in your conceptual framework needs amending, or you might find you have data that does not map onto any existing theory. Some researchers who use qualitative data even argue that you should not analyse it with *any* pre-conceived ideas or theories in mind, you should just analyse the data you have in front of you in its own terms. This approach is known as *grounded theory* and is explained further in Chapter 18.

Figures 1.4 and 3.1 imply an ordered progression from initial thoughts about areas of interest through to a literature review, selection and use of a strategy and data generation methods, through data analysis to final outcomes and presentation. Of course, in real life it's never as straightforward as that. Your plans are likely to change as your research progresses, your research questions evolve over time and you will still be discovering new things in the literature and your data when you are putting together the final presentation of your work. In real life, the process is therefore iterative and you move backwards and forwards between the different components of the model.

Alternative Models of the Research Process

Figure 3.1 gave a model of the research process, but there are other ways of characterizing it. Let's briefly consider two of them.

Conceptualize, operationalize, generalize

This model has three stages. You start off by *conceptualizing* the research topic – you make explicit what the question or problem is and how you propose to address it. This includes the theories from the literature you will use, and the research approach you will adopt (strategies, methods, legal aspects, ethical issues and underlying research paradigm). In the case of design and creation projects, you can also often express your conceptualization via models and diagrams such as storyboards or use-case scenarios.

You then *operationalize* – you put your plans into effect, by following your strategy, generating and analysing the data or developing and testing a computer-based system or other IT artefact.

Finally you *generalize* – you assess what can be learnt from your work (that is, your knowledge outcomes) that has wider applicability than just your single project.

The SDLC analogy

We can also characterize the research process by drawing an analogy with the conventional systems development life cycle (SDLC) used in developing computer-based systems (often called the 'waterfall model' of systems development). Both systems development and research are concerned with creating something new:

- Systems development creates new software.
- Research creates new knowledge.

The SDLC has four main stages: analysis, design, implementation and testing. Each of these stages in the SDLC has an analogy in stages of the research process.

Analysis

- *SDLC: Analyse the current system, if one exists, analyse the proposed system and produce a requirements specification or client brief, which normally includes a number of system objectives.*
- **Research:** Analyse the current state of knowledge (the literature review), decide what still needs to be done and develop a research proposal, which normally includes one or more research questions and objectives.

Design

- **SDLC:** *Design the planned system, initially at a high level (for example, centralized versus distributed system, relational versus object-oriented database), then at a more detailed level (for example, produce storyboards, design a database, write program algorithms).*
- **Research:** Design the planned research approach, initially at a high level (strategy to be used), then at a more detailed level (data generation methods within the chosen strategy).

Implementation

- **SDLC:** *Follow the design to develop the software (for example, write the program code or produce the webpages).*
- **Research:** Follow the design to do the research (for example, issue a questionnaire and analyse the responses).

Testing

- **SDLC:** *Evaluate the system to see if it functions as intended and meets the requirements specification or client's brief and is accepted by the users.*
- **Research:** Evaluate the research to see if it has answered the research question and is accepted as valid by the academic research community.

Evaluating the Research Process

Now that you know something of the research process, you can start to analyse and evaluate how well other researchers have described their process. Use the 'Evaluation Guide' below to help you.

EVALUATION GUIDE: RESEARCH PROCESS

1. Do the researchers make clear their research question(s)?
2. Do the researchers explain the theory(ies) they use to conceptualize the research topic?
3. Do the researchers make clear both their strategy and the data generation method(s) within that strategy?
4. Do the researchers indicate their criteria for judging the success or usefulness of their work?
5. Is there a clear process summarized, from the original motivation and literature review through to final outcome(s)? If not, how does that affect your confidence in the research and its reporting?

PRACTICAL WORK

1   Ask your colleagues or supervisor to suggest a journal in your area of interest that is widely read. Analyse one complete volume of it (that is, a year's worth of articles) to see which research strategies and data generation methods are used, and how often. Does one type predominate? Decide whether you would prefer to:

a   follow the strategy and method(s) used by the majority of researchers in your area;
b   follow a less-used research methodology.

What are the advantages and disadvantages of each approach?

2   This chapter suggested an analogy can be drawn between the conventional systems development life cycle (SDLC) and the research process. Read Parnas and Clements' (1986) paper, entitled 'The rational design process. How and why to fake it.' Consider whether their notion of faking the rational design process destroys the analogy drawn in this chapter between the SDLC and research, or suggests further similarities between them.

3   Gain practise in analysing and evaluating research undertaken by others. Study a piece of research and answer the questions in the 'Evaluation Guide' above, using the material in this chapter to help you.

FURTHER READING

Palvia, Mao, Midha, Pinjani and Salam (2004), and Palvia, Mao, Salam and Soliman (2003) examine papers published between 1993 and 2003 in seven key IS journals (including *Communications of the ACM*, which is also widely read by computing researchers). They look at the relative popularity of different research strategies and data generation methods, and of different research topics. Glass, Ramesh and Vessey (2004) report a similar survey of articles published between 1995 and 1999 in journals for the computer science, software engineering and IS research communities.

Myers and Avison (2002) provide a useful resource for those thinking of researching with qualitative data via case studies, action research or ethnography: they have collected together some of the key texts on such research in IS and reprinted them in one volume. Mingers and Willcocks (2004) and Avgerou, Ciborra and Land (2004) are two edited collections which both provide overviews of a range of social theories and philosophies that have been used as conceptual frameworks in IS research, including actor network theory, structuration theory, phenomenology and hermeneutics.

References

Avgerou, C., Ciborra, C., & Land, F. (Eds.). (2004). *The social study of information and communication technology – Innovation, actors, and contexts.* Oxford: Oxford University Press.

Glass, R.L., Ramesh, V., & Vessey, I. (2004). An analysis of research in computing disciplines. *Communications of the ACM, 47*(6), 89–94.

Mingers, J., & Willcocks, L.P. (2004). *Social theory and philosophy for information systems*. Chichester: Wiley.

Myers, M.D., & Avison, D.E. (Eds.). (2002). *Qualitative research in information systems. A reader*. London: Sage.

Palvia, P., Mao, E., Midha, V., Pinjani, P., & Salam, A.F. (2004). Research methodologies in MIS: An update. *Communications of AIS, 14,* 526–542.

Palvia, P., Mao, E., Salam, A.F., & Soliman, K.S. (2003). Management information systems research: What's there in a methodology? *Communications of AIS, 11,* 289–309.

Parnas, D., & Clements, P.C. (1986). The rational design process. How and why to fake it. *IEEE Transactions on Software Engineering, 12*(2), 251–257.

4 Internet Research

In this chapter you will learn about:

- the rise of the Internet and World Wide Web;
- some possible research topics on the Internet and web;
- using the Internet within a literature review;
- using the Internet to support research strategies and data generation methods;
- legal and ethical aspects of Internet research.

The last chapter gave an overview of the research process and the components within it. Before we look in more detail at each of the components, let's focus on one type of information system that is of particular interest to many IS and computing researchers: the Internet. The Internet offers both new research topics and new ways of doing research. Many readers of this book are likely to do research into, or supported by, the Internet, so this chapter pulls together some of the themes and issues of Internet research. Greater detail will be found in the chapters that follow.

Background to the Internet and World Wide Web

The Internet is a worldwide computer network (or network of networks) based on a suite of software protocols that enable all the computers linked to the network to communicate with each other. These communication protocols enable us to view websites using web browsers, send and receive emails, listen to Internet radio, download text files, music and videos, participate in discussions with others across the globe, play games, watch webcams and so on.

The idea of the Internet probably originated with Vannevar Bush's 1945 vision of an automated information management system (Bush, 1945). This vision began to be realized in the 1960s with the development of the theory of packet switching, which forms the basis of Internet connections. The Internet, then known as Arpanet, came online in 1969 and provided a means for researchers and academics to share computer-based information. It was also designed as a military defence communications network that would work even if some of the computer sites were destroyed by nuclear attack. If the most direct route was not available, routers would direct traffic around the network via alternative routes.

Through the 1970s and 1980s, various communication protocols were developed and agreed, and increasing numbers of educational and research institutions made use of the Internet. In 1989, Tim Berners-Lee at the European Laboratory for Particle Physics (CERN), proposed a new protocol for information distribution which became the basis of the World Wide Web (Berners-Lee, 1989). The World Wide Web Consortium was established in 1994 to promote and develop common standards for the web. It is based on hypertext, which enables users to jump from one page to another by clicking on text or graphical hot spots on a webpage. In the 1990s, easy-to-use web browsers were developed (e.g., Mosaic®, Netscape® and Internet Explorer®). These further boosted the World Wide Web and now also form the basis of the user interface for many non-web applications.

Commercial uses of the Internet and web were allowed from the early 1990s and many businesses rushed to establish an Internet presence. There was a 'dot.com boom', where any business organization proffering an Internet-based proposition seemed to be able to find willing investors, followed by the 'dot.com crash', when realism returned to the stock market and many Internet-based businesses went bust. Now in the early 21st-century, most businesses have a website and use the Internet for some of their operations and functions, and some businesses are Internet only. Many businesses are still looking for Internet models that work financially – that is, a model that enables them to make money from the Internet and not just offer free information.

Today people use the Internet for such things as:

- buying and selling goods and participating in online auctions;
- sending email messages electronically to recipients around the world;
- sharing views on a topic with others around the globe via discussion lists;
- using Internet Relay Chat (IRC) to talk to other people in online, real-time sessions in virtual rooms;
- playing adventure games with multiple players (known as MUDs);
- listening to radio broadcasts from around the world via Internet radio.

As satellite, cable and telephone technology develops, multimedia documents and applications, which use sound and video, are increasingly available over the Internet. The Internet can also be accessed from devices other than a standard desktop computer, including mobile phones and personal handsets, leading to the notion of 'ubiquitous computing' or 'anytime, anywhere computing'.

However, the rise of the Internet and web has also led to some undesirable outcomes. Parents worry about what their children might find on the web, and what undesirable people might be taking part in chat rooms intended for youngsters. New opportunities for fraud have been realized by criminals. Businesses can find their operations are brought to a halt by denial of service attacks on their websites or viruses and worms delivered via the Internet into their computer systems.

As the Internet touches upon more and more aspects of our lives, it offers a huge number of research possibilities, as the next section briefly describes.

Internet Research Topics

The technological advances that produced the Internet as we know it today, and that will help to shape its future, are all the work of computing researchers. Current areas of technological research include mobile or ubiquitous computing, the semantic web, grid computing, search engines, web services and web engineering.

Many IS researchers are interested in how business organizations can make use of the Internet and web. Organizations are developing applications that enable business to consumer transactions (B2C) or support transactions between themselves and other businesses such as suppliers (B2B). There are therefore research opportunities in developing Internet-based systems for businesses, and evaluating the use of such systems. However, as the previous section mentioned, many companies are still struggling to find ways of making money from the Internet. So there are also research opportunities in looking for new business models which *can* make money via the Internet.

Many people have found that their working lives have been changed by the introduction of email systems. Some find that they spend most of their working day dealing with their email, with little time left for anything else. There are also suspicions of email addiction, where people feel compelled to check their emails regularly, even during their leisure or holiday time. Some have found ways of using email to manipulate or even bully other organization members. Yet it has been noted that there has been surprisingly little investigation of email by IS and computing researchers (Weber, 2004). There are research opportunities to examine email behaviour and develop better systems that help users to handle and organize the huge number of emails dispatched and received.

Of course, the development of the Internet and web has not just affected business organizations and their customers. Although some IS researchers think that the discipline of information systems equates to 'management information systems', the reach of the Internet and web into so many parts of our lives reminds us that many people other than managers make use of information systems. There are many research opportunities in investigating how individuals, families, groups, communities, governments and societies use such information systems – which are often based upon the Internet and web.

For example, the field of community informatics examines how information and communication technologies can be used to foster and strengthen social cohesion, overcome cultural or geographic isolation and combat social exclusion or deprivation. This field offers many research opportunities for working with communities and non-profit making organizations to utilize the power of the Internet to improve people's quality of life.

Governments have also noticed the spread of the Internet and web and are interested in how the technology can be used to improve the service they provide to their citizens (e-government). There is also interest in the possibility of the Internet and web increasing democracy and improving people's participation in the political process (e-democracy), through such things as online voting and citizen's forums. Again, many research opportunities are available.

As websites have developed from the simple initial 'cyber-brochures' to today's sophisticated web-based information systems, web developers have had to devise new methods and processes for creating web systems, leading to the comparatively new discipline of 'web engineering'. The principles of software engineering that have been developed for conventional non-web systems should still apply, but web development has some unique characteristics. For example, the time available for the creation and implementation of a web-based system is usually much less than that for a conventional system, even though the functionality and complexity may be similar. There are research possibilities in investigating how and why this perception of the need for rapid deployment of web systems has emerged and is maintained. Web developers also require new skills, such as graphic design and the ability to organize unstructured data. So research is needed into the best methods for designing web systems.

Artists are also exploring the possibilities of Internet art – often called *net art*. This includes email art, websites and interactive artworks. Some artists are employed to enhance the aesthetic quality of commercial websites. Others have no financial objective and seek only to investigate the possibilities of Internet and web technologies, such as the scope for audience participation in a piece and the conflation of art with political activism. As well as design and creation research aimed at adding to the body of Internet art, research is also needed into the history and ongoing development of such art, the criteria for evaluating it, the particular problems of archiving and curating it and the socio-technical practices of artists collaborating with digital technology and audiences to produce artworks.

The Internet does not just support the gathering or dissemination of information. Its information and communication technologies also enable new types of play, such as online games, new ways of communication, such as blogging (online diary-writing), and new means of teaching, such as distance learning. All of these can be studied by researchers. The Internet can even trigger new ways of philosophizing about ourselves and our existence: what does it mean 'to be' in cyberspace? Who am I, when I can be one person in the offline world and another in an online world?

As this section has indicated, there are many, many possible research topics if you are interested in the Internet. But the Internet is also useful to IS and computing researchers in other ways – it can support the methods we use when doing research, as the sections that follow indicate.

The Internet and a Literature Review

When it comes to doing a literature review, the Internet and web can be a boon for researchers. From the comfort of your own home or office you can access previously published or presented work. For example:

- many journals, conferences and authors put their articles and papers online;
- an online catalogue tells you about the holdings (books and journals) of a particular library;
- online databases developed for academic researchers allow you to enter key words related to your area of interest and find previously published academic research on that topic;
- web gateways or portals developed by academics provide links to other useful websites on particular subjects.

However, the web contains a lot of poor-quality material as well as highly respectable academic research. You must therefore pay particular attention to the authorship, credibility and authenticity of anything you find on the web.

Chapter 6 discusses the literature review in more detail, including the use of the Internet to help with a literature review.

The Internet and Research Strategies and Methods

This book looks at six research strategies: survey, design and creation, experiment, case study, action research and ethnography. Each of these can be Internet-based. Table 4.1 summarizes some of the possibilities and limitations of basing each of these strategies on the Internet, and Chapters 7–12 discuss the topic in more detail.

The book also looks at four data generation methods: interviews, observations, questionnaires and documents. Each of these can be Internet-based. Table 4.2 summarizes some of the possibilities and limitations of using each of these methods via the Internet, and Chapters 13–16 discuss the topic in more detail.

Table 4.1 Research strategies and the Internet

Research strategy	Possibilities	Limitations
Survey (Chapter 7)	Obtain data from many people across the world, cheaply and quickly. Could email a list of questions to people and ask them to answer them and return their responses by email. Visitors to a website could be asked to complete an online questionnaire.	People might view your emailed questionnaire as spam. Not everyone has Internet or web access, so your respondents may not be typical of the whole target population.
Design and creation (Chapter 8)	Led to the development of the Internet and the web in the first place. Still many opportunities to design and create new ways of using Internet technology, for example: • mobile computing; • tools for distance learners; • methods for developing web-based systems; • new user interfaces; • new search tools; • new forms of digital art.	Your university's security mechanisms for protecting its networks from intruders and viruses may make it difficult for you to develop a working version of a system. You will not be allowed to do anything that breaches the system's firewall. You might have to develop your Internet application on a home PC or on your supervisor's PC system if it is isolated from the university's network.
Experiment (Chapter 9)	Could design experiments to test for such things as: • the effectiveness of a web-based user interface, • the results from using a particular Internet-based program, • the effect of intervening in an online community.	Most of the Internet is beyond the control of the researcher, so it is difficult to design an experiment that controls for everything that might bias the results, and that can be repeated to see if the same results occur again. People have an offline existence that can influence their online actions and that cannot be monitored or controlled by the researcher.

(Continued)

Table 4.1 (Continued)

Research strategy	Possibilities	Limitations
Case study (Chapter 10)	Study in depth a single instance of some aspect of the Internet e.g.: • an online community, • the use of the web by a particular company, • the evolution of a website over time.	Members of an online community also have an offline existence, and a company website is subject to decisions, culture and office politics that occur in the offline world. If you study only the online aspects of your chosen case, your analysis may be incomplete.
Action research (Chapter 11)	Develop and refine the methods people use for developing web- or Internet-based systems. Explore new ways of using Internet technology.	People you work with online have an offline existence too, which might influence their online practices. If you study only the online aspects of your action research, your analysis may be incomplete.
Ethnography (Chapter 12)	Examine what people do in cyberspace. By participating in an online group, you could study the group's culture – the interactions, how some people acquire more authority or power in the group than others, the conventions and norms that develop.	People you interact with online have an offline existence too, which might influence their online behaviour. If you study only the online aspects of your chosen social group, your analysis may be incomplete.

Table 4.2 Data generation methods and the Internet

Data generation method	Possibilities	Limitations
Interviews (Chapter 13)	Can question people wherever they are in the world without the expense and time of travelling to meet them. 'Interview' is not spoken, but a set of written questions and answers bounced back and forth between you and the interviewee.	Because written rather than spoken, answers tend to be less detailed. No social cues such as facial expression and body language, so uncertainties and misunderstandings can arise.
Observations (Chapter 14)	Observe what occurs online, e.g. the contributions people make to an online discussion. Can participate as a member of an online group, or just lurk, i.e. watch without people knowing.	Often not ethically acceptable to observe others without them knowing. Online group likely to be angry if they discover you have infiltrated the group.
Questionniare (Chapter 15)	Can be placed within an email message, as an email attachment, or as a web form. Much cheaper form of distribution than postal questionnaires.	Cannot just replicate a paper-based questionnaire in an electronic format. Need to focus on the needs of respondents who are typing or mouse-clicking their answers.
Documents (Chapter 16)	Essential part of Internet-based research since much of what we can know about the Internet is only discoverable by studying (electronic) documents: websites, emails, discussion list archives, bulletin boards, online auctions, cookies, web server logs, etc.	Transitory nature of many Internet-based documents: webpages change, archives go offline, websites disappear. Need to keep copies of all online documents, and monitor whether they change over time.

Internet Research, the Law and Ethics

All research must, of course, be legal and ethical. However, research into or about the Internet can raise both legal and ethical problems.

The Internet causes problems for legislators, the police and researchers because it spans the world, so that no single country's code of law applies. What may be legal Internet behaviour in one country may be illegal in another – for example, what kinds of data companies are allowed to keep on customers visiting their website, and how they are allowed to use and sell that data. Downloading images without permission from a website might be considered acceptable in your country, but illegal in the country where a reviewer of your research, or the owner of the image, lives. You might want to look at a certain website as part of your research, but to do so would mean breaking your country's laws. For example, in the UK visiting a site aimed at paedophiliacs and downloading material from it would be illegal – and saying you were doing it for research purposes would not be a satisfactory defence. In some countries just accessing the Internet is illegal.

In every country, the law about the Internet lags behind people finding new uses for it. When someone believes that some aspect of Internet behaviour is unlawful, prosecutors and defence lawyers have to find analogies from the offline world, where legal precedent has been established, and argue that this analogy holds true for the online world. For example, when someone posted messages to a financial bulletin board criticizing a company as a bad investment, the company sued. The legal arguments compared electronic bulletin boards to books, bookshops, newspapers, telephones, billboards, radio talk shows and a town crier (Holyoak & Thagard, 1996, p. 155). Some of these analogies benefited the complainants, some the defendants. If you want to use the Internet in a new way in your research, don't assume it will be viewed as legal because you see it as analogous to something in the real world. Ask yourself whether another person might draw an analogy with something else in the offline world and argue it is therefore illegal.

Just as the law about the Internet is still being developed, codes of conduct for doing ethical Internet research are still under discussion. Ethics committees normally want to see that researchers have obtained informed consent from any human participants, and ensured anonymity and confidentiality for the participants. However, each of these requirements is difficult to meet in Internet research. For example, does a researcher need to obtain permission before quoting from someone's contribution to an online discussion? Different researchers have different views. And if it is decided you should get permission, who should give it – the contributor, the person who manages the discussion forum or the organization that provides the technical infrastructure to host it? Again, different researchers have given different answers. More on the ethics of Internet research is given in Chapter 5.

PRACTICAL WORK

1   This chapter suggested Vannevar Bush and Tim Berners-Lee were two of the founders of today's Internet and web. Research into the history of the Internet – easily done on the web – and suggest some more key figures in its development, with reasons.

2   Many academic journals are being launched that cover some aspect of the Internet and web. Do an online search to see how many such journal titles you can find. (Hint: as well as including 'Internet' or 'web' in your online search, use the prefix 'e-', for example, e-marketing, e-government, e-democracy, e-play, e-art, and so on) How many of these journals are *only* available online, that is, they are not printed on paper? Could any of the journals be useful to your own research?

FURTHER READING

Tim Berners-Lee (2000) gives his own account of the origins of the Internet and the development of the World Wide Web. Two other members of CERN, where Berners-Lee worked, also discuss the Internet's history and development (Gillies & Cailliau, 2000). A more scholarly review of the Internet and its implications, from a social rather than a technical perspective, is provided by Castells (2003). The dot.com boom and bust is reviewed, for a popular rather than academic audience, by Cellan-Jones (2003), who adopts a UK perspective, and by Lowenstein (2004), who adopts a US perspective. An overview of community informatics and e-democracy can be found in Keeble and Loader (2001). A review of Internet art is given by Greene (2004). Rheingold (2003) looks at the next wave of Internet technology – including mobile communications technology, wireless-paging and Internet-access devices – and what it could mean for us. Finally, as a relief from much of the Internet excitement and hype, Standage (1999) describes the spread of the telegraph in the Victorian age, and reviews how it invoked the same worries, exaggeration and social panic that now surround the Internet.

References

Berners-Lee, T. (1989, March). *Information management: a proposal*: CERN. Retrieved 7 July 2005 from www.w3.org/History/1989/proposal.html.

Berners-Lee, T. (2000). *Weaving the web: Origins and future of the World Wide Web*. Mason: Texere Publishing.

Bush, V. (1945). As we may think. *Atlantic Monthly* (July), 101–108.

Castells, M. (2003). *The Internet galaxy: Reflections on the Internet, business and society* (paperback ed.). Oxford: Oxford University Press.

Cellan-Jones, R. (2003). *Dot.bomb: The strange death of dot.com Britain* (paperback ed.). London: Aurum Press.

Gillies, J., & Cailliau, R. (2000). *How the web was born: The story of the World Wide Web*. Oxford: Oxford Paperbacks.

Greene, R. (2004). *Internet art*. London: Thames & Hudson.

Holyoak, K.J., & Thagard, P. (1996). *Mental leaps: Analogy in creative thought* (paperback ed.). Cambridge, MA: MIT Press.

Keeble, L., & Loader, B.D. (Eds.). (2001). *Community informatics. Shaping computer-mediated social relations*. London: Routledge.

Lowenstein, R. (2004). *Origins of the crash: The great bubble and its undoing* (paperback ed.). London: Penguin.

Rheingold, H. (2003). *Smart mobs: The next social revolution*. New York: Basic Books.

Standage, T. (1999). *The Victorian Internet* (paperback ed.). London: Phoenix Mass Market.

Weber, R. (2004). Editor's comments. The grim reaper: The curse of e-mail. *MIS Quarterly, 28*(3), iii–xiii.

5 Participants and Research Ethics

In this chapter you will learn about:

- the rights of your research participants;
- your ethical responsibilities towards those who are involved in your research, whether directly or indirectly;
- the Internet and ethical research;
- the difficulties of being an ethical researcher;
- how to analyse and evaluate the ethics of research.

Before we look in detail at the research process, it is important that we look at another of the 6Ps of research – the *participants* – and consider how they should act or be treated during research. These participants include:

- the people directly involved in your research – the people you interview or observe, or ask to complete a questionnaire or supply you with documents;
- you as the researcher, along with your colleagues if you are in a research team;
- the members of the academic community who read, review and learn from your research;
- people who may use or be affected by any computer-based product you design and create.

You should treat everyone involved in your research, whether directly or indirectly, fairly and with honesty – that is, you should be an *ethical* researcher. Increasing attention is being paid to the rights and responsibilities of those involved in research; what might have been considered acceptable practice in the past might now be considered unethical.

Most institutions now require that you consider the ethical aspects of your research project when you design it, and that you obtain ethical clearance before you start. The procedures for such clearance vary from institution to institution, but normally involve the researcher explaining the purpose of the project, its funding, whether and how other people will be involved in it, and what ethical issues have been considered. This description is scrutinized by people outside the project, often by members of an experienced research ethics committee. They will want to satisfy themselves that people affected by the research in any way will not be harmed and will be treated fairly and with dignity. If they are happy that the research is ethical, the project is approved and the research can start. If they are unhappy with the ethics of any part, the researcher will be asked to think again and redesign the project.

The Law and Research

Of course, your research and behaviour throughout the project, from an initial litera-ture review and thinking about possible research topics through to the final outcomes, must be *legal*. It is impossible for this book to cover the relevant national legislation for each reader. You must therefore find out about the law in your country concern-ing such things as:

- the specified data protection rights of individuals, and the duties of organizations and researchers who hold personal data on individuals;
- whether it is permissible to offer a prize draw to encourage people to participate in your research;
- intellectual property rights, for example, who owns the right to an image you want to use in your research, and who has the copyright of your own thesis or other pub-lications or any software you produce;
- restrictions on the kinds of technology you are allowed to use and investigate, for example, whether your country allows unrestricted access to the Internet, if you are permitted to use encryption software, or whether you may share your technologi-cal innovations with colleagues based in other countries.
- the legal liability of software developers for the systems they design and create.

We shall focus in this chapter on the *ethical* aspects of research. Remember that it is possible to do research that is legal but not ethical.

Rights of People Directly Involved

Let's start by thinking about the rights of the people most obviously affected by your research: the people you interview or observe, or ask to complete a questionnaire or supply you with documents. The literature on the different strategies might refer to these people in different ways:

- for experiments, they are often called the research *subjects*;
- for surveys, they are often called the research *respondents*;
- for case studies and ethnography, they are often called research *informants, members* or *participants*;
- for action research, they are often called the research *participants* or, especially in the more emancipatory forms of action research, *co-researchers*.

There seems to be a hierarchy of involvement, reflected in the terminology used, from the experimental 'subjects' who have little say in the design of an experiment and may not even know its purpose, to 'co-researchers' in an action research project who work alongside the academic researcher as equal partners. However, whatever their degree of involvement and whether they are described as subjects or co-researchers or something in-between, all these participants are *humans*. They have a right to be treated with dignity and, whenever possible, to gain some benefit from the research. They should not be 'used' simply for the researcher's own ends or for the advantage of whoever is paying the researcher. You should consider carefully whether your work is both ethical and legal, and ensure that your participants suffer no adverse consequences – physiological, psychological, social, political or economic.

As well as individuals, collectives of individuals are also affected by your research: the business organizations, hospitals, schools, charities, families or communities that you might want to study. These collectives have the same rights as individuals to be treated fairly and with dignity and suffer no ill-effects. These rights are summarized in the box below.

The rights of participants

- Right not to participate
- Right to withdraw
- Right to give informed consent
- Right to anonymity
- Right to confidentiality

These rights are explained below.

Right not to participate

If someone doesn't want to participate in your research, whether an individual or a company, they don't have to. You should accept their decision, and not try to force them by wheedling or threats. Their non-participation may affect your ability to complete your research, but that's your problem, not theirs. This right is sometimes overlooked when researchers are normally in a position of power over the people they want to involve in their research. For example, a manager in an organization asks their subordinate employees to take part in some research, or a teacher or lecturer requires that their students do something that will form part of their research. These people are normally accustomed to doing as their boss or instructor asks. It is important to remember that, in a research context, the researcher doesn't have the right to order others to do *anything*.

Right to withdraw

Even if someone initially agrees to take part, they can change their minds at any time. Again, if this messes up your research, possibly even ruins it, that's your problem, not theirs. People also have the right to opt out of parts of your research – for example, by declining to answer certain questions, or by refusing to participate in some activities.

Right to give informed consent

Individuals, and collections of individuals, have the right to give *informed* consent. This means that if they agree to participate, their consent is given only when they have first been made fully aware of the nature of the research and their involvement. They should be informed about:

- the purpose of the research, why it is being undertaken and what benefits are expected from it;
- who is undertaking the research (name, address, contact details) and which organization is sponsoring it – either by funding it or overseeing and authorizing it;
- what will be involved (for example, interviews, completing a questionnaire and so on) and how long this is likely to take;
- whether they will receive any expenses, payment or incentive (for example, individual feedback on performance in a test, or a copy of the final research report);
- how their data will be used (for example, whether their details will be anonymized so no one can recognize them in the research report) and how the research findings will be disseminated.

They must also be informed that they have the right not to participate and the right to withdraw from the research at any time.

It is considered good practice to provide these details in writing to each potential participant. However, this should be a concise description, not pages and pages for people to plough through, and written in language that is easy for the participants to understand. It is also often recommended that the participants' consent be given in writing. However, such written consent should not be interpreted as a formal, binding contract – a participant can withdraw at any time.

There are some cases where it is not feasible to obtain informed consent – such cases will be scrutinized particularly carefully by an ethics committee. For example, your research might require that the participants do not know the purpose of your research, because otherwise they would alter their behaviour. Sometimes in an experiment, for example, the results could be distorted if the participants knew what you were testing them for. In such a case you would have to convince your ethics committee that it was acceptable not to obtain informed consent, and that the participants would not come to any harm (physical or emotional) through participating without knowing the purpose. You should always try to give as much information as possible to participants in such circumstances, even if you can't give the full picture. It is also considered good ethical practice that afterwards you *do* give the participants a proper explanation and debrief them on what you found out through their participation. At this debrief you should also give them the option of withholding the data you obtained from them, that is, you ask them afterwards to give their informed consent to the use of data about them.

You might want to use covert observation – where you watch people without them knowing it (see Chapter 14). In such cases, the people observed do not even know they are participating in your research, let alone give informed consent. Such research *can* be ethically acceptable if your observations take place in a public setting, where people are aware that their actions can be seen by others. Covert observation in a private setting – for example, observing the rituals and use of jargon in a managers' meeting via a concealed camera – is less ethically acceptable. Wherever possible, use overt observation, that is, let the people know you want to observe them and obtain their informed consent. Even in private settings permission is often given, and the people usually soon forget the observer's presence and behave as they normally do.

Sometimes informed consent cannot be obtained because the research participants are too young to understand, or too ill. For children, it might be possible to get the permission of a parent (or guardian), although increasing attention to the rights of children means that it is important to involve the children too and not just accept their parents' permission. Similarly, for someone who is too ill to give informed consent (for example, to the use of a new computer-operated device that might help their recovery), informed consent might be obtained from the patient's relatives.

It is important to remember that obtaining informed consent is not just a one-off event at the start of your research project. For research projects that take place over time, such as case studies, ethnographies and action research, you will often have to renegotiate with your research participants about what you would like to do, and renew their informed consent. If the nature of your research and the involvement of people changes substantially, you will also have to go back to your ethics committee for further clearance.

Right to anonymity

Participants in your research have the right that their identity and location will be protected – by disguise where necessary. If you want use names for your participants in your research report, normally you would give them pseudonyms. Sometimes you might also have to change their gender during your writing-up, or disguise them in other ways. For example, if you are writing about the views of a company's IT department, where only one woman and many men work, it would be easy for readers to know which comments were attributable to the woman, unless you changed her gender in your report. In a small department or company, it might also be easy for readers of your report to deduce who said what – again you would need to find a way of disguising participants, so that there are no harmful or embarrassing repercussions for them.

Organizations' identities too should be disguised in your report, unless they specifically permit you to use their name. Before granting this permission they will probably want to read your report and discuss where you intend to disseminate your findings.

Right to confidentiality

Participants in your research have a right that the data you obtain from them is kept confidential. This means, for example, that you should not leave your data lying around on your desk where anyone can look at it; you should keep it safe and secure.

Sometimes a participant may tell you something, 'in confidence'. This means they do not want you to write about it in your research report, however tempting that might be. If you feel this is something significant for your research, you must ask them to release you from that request for confidentiality, which can sometimes be achieved if you guarantee their anonymity. Similarly, an organization might allow you to carry out some research on it, but want you to keep your findings confidential, so that its competitors cannot gain from the findings. If you cannot publish your findings in journal articles or a thesis, the research is not much use to you, so you should discuss the issue of confidentiality before you start. The organization might allow you to publish your research if you explain how you will disguise its identity so others do not know which organization was involved. Alternatively, it might agree that the research can be published after a suitable delay – perhaps after one or two years – and you will have to decide whether such a delay is compatible with your research goals.

The right to confidentiality also means that participants can trust that you will not pass on what you have learnt about them to others in authority. This is particularly difficult for researchers where they discover wrongdoing by their participants – some researchers have been imprisoned for refusing to hand over data from their studies to the police.

Responsibilities of an Ethical Researcher

Now let's consider the responsibilities of an ethical researcher. Some of these responsibilities can be inferred from the previous section about the rights of the people directly involved in your research. For example:

- researchers should respect participants' expectations of anonymity and confidentiality;
- they should not try to coerce people into participating in the research, by dint of their persuasive abilities or position of power;
- they should obtain informed consent and not deceive people about the research unless there really is no alternative *and* no harm can ensue.

There are also additional duties of an ethical researcher: both to the people directly involved and to the members of the academic community to which a researcher belongs, who are indirectly involved in the research. These duties are summarized in the box below.

The responsibilities of an ethical researcher

- No unnecessary intrusion
- Behave with integrity
- Follow appropriate professional codes of conduct
- No plagiarism
- Be an ethical reviewer

No unnecessary intrusion

Researchers should not intrude unnecessarily into the participants' activities. Before undertaking a piece of research, you must be satisfied that the knowledge you're looking for is not already available. Nor should you ask questions for which you don't really need the answers. For example, in designing questionnaires, researchers sometimes automatically insert questions asking about the participants' age, which respondents may find intrusive. You should ask yourself whether it is really necessary to know someone's exact age – would an indication of age range (which is less intrusive) suffice? Or can you omit the age question altogether?

Behave with integrity

An ethical researcher will record data accurately and fully. This means not keeping quiet about data that does not support your case, or not manipulating data to present the picture you want. You should be open and honest about how you conducted your research and the results you obtained, without any falsification or fabrication.

You should also keep the data secure and make sure no one else can access it. If paper-based, it should not be left on your desk. If on a computer you should think about how lack of password security, insecure networks, power failures, poor backup procedures, hackers and viruses might compromise your data.

As explained in the previous section, you should try to provide a debriefing and feedback to your participants, so that they too learn something from the research. If you think this might be upsetting for them in any way, you might need to involve a counsellor, to help them deal with what they are told.

An ethical researcher also thinks about how the research findings will be used and tries to make sure they can do no harm. Scientists often argue that science is morally neutral, it is society, politicians or army generals who might put the fruits of their research to use in harmful ways. However, this argument is rejected by many people – we all, including researchers, have a duty of care to fellow members of the human race. If our research outcomes can be put to a use that might harm people, maybe ethical researchers should not be doing it.

You should also make it clear who has sponsored your research, so that readers can be aware of possible influences on the way it was conducted and presented. Sometimes, for example, medical research has been questioned when it has emerged later that a large pharmaceutical company paid for it.

Follow appropriate professional codes of conduct

Most professional bodies have produced codes of conduct. These codes capture the profession's commitments and responsibilities, to help members make ethical decisions. Even if you are not a paid-up member of any professional body, you can be guided by their codes. It's therefore worth looking up such codes on the Internet. Professional bodies relevant to IS and computing research include the ACM, AIS, BCS, IEEE and the Association of Internet Researchers (see the box on p. 62). The social science disciplines, such as psychology and sociology, make great use of research with the direct involvement of people, so their professional bodies' codes of conduct can also be helpful to IS and computing research.

No plagiarism

You should not pass off someone else's work as if it were your own. This is seen as akin to stealing. It also deceives anyone who reads your report and deprives the original author of recognition. You should give full credit to the original author, with enough information in the reference so that any subsequent reader can find the same material (see Chapter 6).

Examples of professional codes of conduct relevant to IS and computing research

ACM   Association for Computing Machinery
       www.acm.org

AoIR   Association of Internet Researchers
       www.aoir.org

AIS   Association for Information Systems
       www.aisnet.org

APA   American Psychological Association
       www.apa.org

ASA   American Sociological Association
       www.asanet.org

BCS   British Computer Society
       www.bcs.org.uk

BPS   British Psychological Society
       www.bps.org.uk

BSA   British Sociological Association
       www.britsoc.co.uk

IEEE   Institute of Electrical and Electronics Engineers
       www.ieee.org

You should also avoid 'self-plagiarism' – where you submit a paper for publication that is very similar to one you have already published. It is, however, often acceptable to present a conference paper for discussion, revise the paper in line with any comments received at the conference and then submit it for journal publication. But it is still good practice to:

- inform the editor of the journal at the time of paper submission that an earlier version was presented at a conference;
- show by a footnote in the published journal article the conference where the earlier version was presented.

It is also poor ethical practice if you submit a manuscript for review to two places at the same time. This is not fair to the editors and reviewers who spend time evaluating your work, when you know that one set of reviewers is wasting its time because you will withdraw the manuscript if the other journal accepts it.

Be an ethical reviewer

As you become established as a researcher you might be asked to review manuscripts submitted for conference presentation or journal publication. To do this in an ethical manner, you should:

- Carry out reviews as promptly as possible. Many academic researchers complain about the long review process of journal publication and the delay from manuscript submission to decision. Much of this delay is down to fellow academics who take a long time to get round to doing a review.
- Maintain the confidentiality of the content of the paper you are reviewing – both the ideas and the data. You are put in a position of trust by the author, and should not abuse that trust by making use of the content before it has been published.
- Write the review in a professional way – not, for example, as almost illegible handwritten comments scrawled on a hard copy of the manuscript. You should try to find at least one positive thing to say about the paper, even if your overall recommendation is to reject the manuscript. You can also often help the authors by suggesting one or two citations that they might find useful.

Design and Creation Projects and Ethics

So far this chapter has covered issues in research ethics that all researchers, regardless of discipline, have to consider and abide by. There are, however, some additional issues to consider for those IS and computing researchers using the design and creation research strategy (see Chapter 8). This is because the output of such research is often an IT system or a model for one, which brings with it its own ethical problems. In such research, as well as thinking about the ethical issues of data collection, analysis and reporting, researchers also have to try to ensure that their systems are only *used* in ethical ways.

IT systems offer various temptations for unethical or even unlawful acts, whether committed by researchers or the clients or sponsors of research. These temptations include:

- **Ease of access and copying**: digital data can be accessed or copied without wiping out or altering the original in any way. Data about people that was collected for one reason can therefore easily be used for another reason, which the people who supplied the personal data are unaware of and have not given permission for. Similarly, digital works over which someone has copyright or patent rights can easily be copied and reused without the owner's permission.

- **Privacy and anonymity**: the increasing availability of computers in private homes and public places such as libraries and Internet cafés, combined with software that can guarantee the anonymity of the perpetrator of an unethical or unlawful act, make it less likely that a wrongdoer will be caught.
- **New means of data gathering**: new information and communication technologies offer a variety of ways of covertly observing people, including tiny digital cameras, keystroke monitors, website cookies and RFID (radio frequency identity) tags. If the people about whom data is collected have not given informed consent, such surveillance could be seen as unethical.

If researchers who design and implement IT systems follow the guidance of this chapter about the rights of participants and duties of a researcher, they should be able to act ethically. But they do need to be aware of the particular temptations offered by IT systems. They also need to ensure their clients or sponsors do not put the system they design to unethical use. Ethical researchers cannot argue that it's solely up to the client or sponsor how a system is used.

Internet Research and Ethics

The Internet poses more problems for ethical researchers. It offers a range of new virtual venues in which, and about which, research can occur: email, chatrooms, websites, weblogs, forms of instant messaging, multi-user environments (MUDs and MOOs), newsgroups, bulletin boards, and so on. But legislation and codes of ethical conduct have not yet caught up with these new research possibilities. Requirements that may be reasonable for ethical research in the offline world cannot always be easily met in the online one.

The requirement for informed consent by participants may be difficult to define, justify or achieve for Internet research (see the box on the facing page). Sometimes, for example, it is not clear who should give consent. In an online discussion list, who owns the comments posted: the people who submit them, the list-owner, the service provider? If an email, or contribution to a discussion, is forwarded by one person onto someone else or another discussion, who now owns it and should give permission for its use? Is it even necessary at all to obtain consent if you want to study the comments posted to online discussions? Some argue that it is not necessary, because the contributors know they are posting messages to a public forum which anyone with an Internet connection can access. Others argue that, to the participants on bulletin boards, they *perceive* their messages as private to the group, and therefore should have the right to authorize or refuse permission for their postings to be used by a researcher. However, Internet researchers have reported a hostility to academic researchers, so that a request for consent is often refused, meaning research into important aspects of modern life may not be possible if we adhere to informed consent as a necessary pre-requisite.

Subjects or authors?

Some of the ethical difficulties in Internet research arise from not being clear about whether people in the online world are the *subjects* of research, as in, for example, medical research in the offline world, or *authors* of works (emails, websites, and so on) which they have knowingly put into the public domain for information and comment.

The Internet also makes it difficult to ensure confidentiality for research participants. Researchers can promise confidentiality in the way that they use and handle data, but they cannot guarantee that electronic communications between participants and the researchers will be kept fully confidential. Insecure networks and unscrupulous systems administrators mean that unauthorized people *could* read the correspondence. Communications *can* be kept confidential if encryption software is used, but this is illegal in some countries and makes technical demands of both the researchers and their participants.

It is also difficult in Internet research to ensure anonymity for research participants, and to know how far that anonymity should stretch. Should you use a person's online pseudonym, or give them a pseudonym for their pseudonym? Should you also use a pseudonym for the name of an online discussion group? If you don't, someone could visit the online forum and do a search on the archive to find out who made a particular comment. Even if you do use a pseudonym for an online discussion, someone could type a quote you give from it into a search engine and quickly locate the true name and contributor. So maybe you should not provide any direct quotes at all? But then you will not be able to provide enough raw, qualitative data to satisfy reviewers of your research report.

There are no easy answers to ethical issues in Internet research. If you plan to do Internet-based research, I suggest that:

- as far as possible, you should treat people and your data in the same way as you would in offline research;
- if you want to use data from websites, discussion forums, and so on, look carefully for any published policy from the owners or contributors about what usage they will and will not allow, and what procedures you should follow.
- be guided by the emerging codes of conduct for Internet research and discussions of how other Internet researchers have tackled ethical issues (see, for example, the Further Reading section in this chapter).

'It's Not that Simple!'

In the earlier sections of this chapter, the ethical requirements of researchers were presented as a series of dos and don'ts. The previous section then showed how ethical behaviour in Internet research was not easy to define and adopt. In fact, ethical research, whether online or offline, is often not simple to achieve. If it merely required the adherence to a set of rules, there would be no need for ethics committees.

Sometimes ethical difficulties occur because some of the guidelines conflict with the aims and requirements of the research. For example, ethnographers (Chapter 12) and other interpretive researchers (Chapter 20) often cannot specify in advance the topics they will cover during interactions with their informants. Themes will emerge only during prolonged engagement in the field. It is hard, therefore, for their participants to be fully informed before giving their consent. Similarly some data (for example, from observations) may only be obtained without bias if the researcher deceives the participants in some way.

An ethical dilemma

Experimental research (see Chapter 9) often involves the use of a group that is treated in some way, and a control group, to which no treatment is given. If researchers believe the treatment they give the other group is beneficial, is it ethical to withhold that treatment from the control group?

Further difficulties can occur because the guidelines assume that a researcher is free to act ethically. In practice, however, the researcher's low position in a hierarchy of power may mean that they are constrained in what they can and cannot do. For example, supposing a client asks for a new kind of computer system to be developed that will enable covert surveillance of an organization's employees (that is, to secretly spy on them). In some countries that would be illegal, and it would certainly be seen by many as unethical because the employees had not given informed consent to data being collected about them in this way. However, if the researcher refuses to develop the system because it would be unethical, the client may terminate the whole research project – threatening the researcher's academic progress and career. In such a circumstance, the researcher is not an equal partner with the client so it is hard, if not impossible, for them to dissuade the client from doing something unethical.

There are also different assumptions about reasonable and ethical behaviour in different cultures, causing difficulties for a researcher who wants to research within a different culture from their own. This chapter has a UK/USA view of ethical behaviour, and some of its recommendations would not be acceptable in other cultures. For example, written informed consent can be seen in some developing countries and western sub-cultures as:

... a token of the bureaucratization of Western societies, with its institutionalisation of trust into formal bodies of organisation, written documentation and well-organised filing systems. In oral societies an invitation to sign formal documents may work as an unintended device to accentuate existing differences rather than building relations in cross-cultural settings. (Ryen, 2004: 232)

Different research philosophy paradigms also have different assumptions about ethical behaviour. For example, in the more emancipatory forms of action research (see Chapter 11) and the critical research paradigm (see Chapter 20), participants are seen as co-researchers. It is therefore demeaning to them, and belittles their contribution, if they are rendered anonymous in the reporting of the research. Critical researchers would also question the ethics of research if it complied with all the guidelines listed in this chapter but did not have the potential to create a more just world.

Where there is conflict about what is the 'right' thing to do, we need an ethical decision-making framework. Unfortunately, there is more than one such framework. For example:

- In the USA, a *utilitarian* approach to decision-making about ethics tends to be used. The cost or harm to an individual is weighed against the potential benefits to the many.
- In Europe, in contrast, an approach the philosophers call *deontological*, tends to be used. An individual has rights, such as data privacy, which cannot be overridden, no matter the benefit to the wider community.
- Other decision-making frameworks classified by ethics philosophers include consequentialism, virtue ethics and feminist ethics.

Discussion of each of these frameworks is beyond the scope of this book. If you find yourself in an ethical dilemma, be guided by your supervisor and ethics committee. They may not be able to name the ethical decision-making framework that they use, but they will be able to guide you in what your culture and research community sees as acceptable ethical behaviour.

Evaluating Research Ethics

When analysing any piece of research, you should think about the ethics of it. Use the Evaluation Guide to help you. If there is insufficient information for you to answer the questions, you should not completely reject the research report, but you should treat it with some caution, since it would be unethical for you to base your work on a study that might itself be unethical.

EVALUATION GUIDE: ETHICS

1　Do the researchers discuss the ethics of their research and whether they were guided by any code of ethical conduct? If not, how does that affect your confidence in the research?

2　Do the researchers tell us of any ethical dilemmas they faced and how they resolved them?

3　Are there additional ethical issues you think the researchers would have needed to address?

4　Overall, how ethically do you think the researchers behaved?

5　How effectively do you think the ethics of the research has been reported?

PRACTICAL WORK

1　The following questions have been posed to researchers in the nursing discipline, but they are equally relevant to IS and computing researchers. Straight 'yes' or 'no' answers are not sufficient. For each question you should be able to argue both 'yes' and 'no'. (Abbott & Sapsford, 1998, p. 20.)

　a　Is it ever justifiable to withhold from participants the aims of the research?

　b　Is it ever justifiable to carry out research when the subjects of the research cannot give informed consent?

　c　Is it justifiable to use people as the objects of research?

　d　Is it justifiable to carry out research that will solely or mainly benefit the researcher by, for example, leading to a PhD?

　e　Is it justifiable to carry out research when those funding the project retain the right to censor the findings?

　f　Is it justifiable to accept funding for health research from the tobacco industry?

　g　Is it justifiable to carry out research when the findings might be used to reduce staffing levels or withdraw treatment from certain categories of patients?

2　Study the scenarios in Weiss, Parker, Swope and Baker (1990) (in Part III of the article). Decide in each case whether you think the behaviour was ethical, unethical or not an ethical issue. Now read the remainder of the article. Reflect on how your understanding of ethics has been affected by this exercise.

3　There has been debate, particularly in the USA, less so in Europe, about whether cookies on websites are acceptable and ethical. Investigate the main arguments used and decide your own position.

4　Many authors, journals and conferences place copies of their papers and articles on the web. This makes them more easily accessible for other researchers. However, often the research participants have not given permission for this form of dissemination. If asked, they might even have refused consent, reasoning that web publication is a more public form of dissemination than presentation of a paper at an obscure academic conference or publication of an article in a low-circulation journal. Find out whether researchers in your department think it necessary to obtain specific consent for publication on the web. What is the majority view? Do you agree? Can you argue the opposite view?

5   Practise analysing and evaluating research ethics. Study a piece of research and answer the questions in the Evaluation Guide given above using the material in this chapter to help you.

FURTHER READING

Books on computer ethics include Baird, Ramsower and Rosenbaum (2000), Johnson (2001) and Tavani (2003). Journals that focus on ethics and computing include *Ethics and Information Technology*, and the *Journal of Information, Communication and Ethics in Society*. ISWorld (www.isworld.org) also has a useful resources section on ethics.

Bell and Adam (2004) argue that IS has developed as a separate discipline from computer ethics, survey some of the key texts on ethics and IT, and discuss how computer ethics might be taught to IS undergraduates. Oliver (2003) addresses many of the ethical issues and questions that can occur in academic research. Lee (1995) offers advice on how to do a good academic review of a paper. Of course, if you are asked to do a review, you could also use the Evaluation Guides given throughout this book. Ryen (2004) discusses the ethical dilemmas she has faced in her own fieldwork, and shows how different cultures have different values, so that any guide to ethical conduct may not be universally applicable.

Internet research and ethics is discussed well by Mann and Stewart (2000). The Association of Internet Researchers also gives recommendations on ethical Internet research, as well as a discussion of the differences between the utilitarian and deontological approaches to ethical decision making, and a valuable annotated bibliography of resources on computer and Internet ethics (Ess & committee, 2002).

Ethics for researchers using qualitative data in interpretive and critical research (see Chapter 20), especially feminist researchers, is explored by Mauthner, Birch, Jessop and Miller (2002). Finally, Stahl (2004) argues that critical research (see Chapter 20) is by its very nature based on ethics, but critical researchers need to analyse better their work's ethical foundations.

References

Abbott, P., & Sapsford, R. (1998). *Research methods for nursing and the caring professions*. Buckingham: Open University Press.

Baird, R.M., Ramsower, R., & Rosenbaum, S.E. (Eds.). (2000). *Cyberethics: Social and moral issues in the computer age*. Amherst, NY: Prometheus Books.

Bell, F., & Adam, A. (2004). Information systems ethics. In B. Kaplan, D. Truex, D. Wastell, T. Wood-Harper, & J. DeGross (Eds.), *Information systems research. Relevant theory and informed practice* (pp. 159–174). Boston, MA: Kluwer.

Ess, C., & the AoIR ethics working committee (2002). *Ethical decision-making and Internet research: Recommendations from the AoIR ethics working committee.* Approved by AoIR, 27 November 2002. Retrieved 7 July 2005 from www.aoir. org/reports/ethics.pdf.

Johnson, D. (2001). *Computer ethics* (3rd ed.). Upper Saddle River, NJ: Prentice Hall.

Lee, A.S. (1995). Reviewing a manuscript for publication. *Journal of Operations Management, 13*(1), 87–92.

Mann, C., & Stewart, F. (2000). *Internet communication and qualitative research. A handbook for researching online.* London: Sage.

Mauthner, M., Birch, M., Jessop, J., & Miller, T. (Eds.). (2002). *Ethics in qualitative research.* London: Sage.

Oliver, P. (2003). *The student's guide to research ethics.* Maidenhead: Open University Press.

Ryen, A. (2004). Ethical issues. In C. Seale, G. Gobo, J.F. Gubrium, & D. Silverman (Eds.), *Qualititive research practice* (pp. 230–247). London: Sage.

Stahl, B. (2004). The ethics of critical IS research. In A. Adam, A. Basden, H. Richardson, & B. Robinson (Eds.), *Critical reflections on critical research in information systems. Proceedings of the 2nd International CRIS Workshop.* Salford: University of Salford.

Tavani, H.T. (2003). *Ethics in an age of information and communication technology.* Chichester: Wiley.

Weiss, E.A., Parker, D.B., Swope, S., & Baker, B.N. (1990). Self-assessment XXII. The ethics of computing. *Communications of the ACM, 33*(11), 110–132.

6   Reviewing the Literature

In this chapter you will learn about:

- the purpose of a literature review;
- the range of available literature resources;
- how the Internet can be used during a literature review;
- how to do a literature review.

Early in their research, most students are advised by their supervisors to 'study the literature'. But when students are just beginning, it is often hard to know what this means, and where to start. This chapter therefore explains why we use the literature, and how to conduct a literature review.

Purpose of a Literature Review

A literature review normally falls into two parts. Initially, research students explore the literature to look for a suitable research idea and discover relevant material about any possible research topics, for example, journals that regularly publish articles on the chosen subject area, authors who are frequently cited in articles about the problem and survey articles that review the previous work on a particular topic and identify where more research is needed. This helps students to get a feel for the area and define a research problem.

The second part of the literature review begins once a topic is chosen. It carries on throughout the remainder of the research time, up to and including writing the thesis or dissertation and preparing for a viva or presentation – in case a paper relevant to your research is published at the last minute. The aim is to gather and present evidence to support your claim that you have created some new knowledge. Remember in Chapter 1 we said that one meaning of 'thesis' was an argument to be proposed or maintained? Well, one of the ways in which we propose and maintain an argument is by presenting evidence from the literature. A useful analogy is a barrister or attorney, who assembles evidence to support a legal case by referring to previous cases that have been heard in the courts, and explaining why this case is the same as, or different from, previous cases. Similarly, researchers assemble evidence to support their claims that:

- the topic is worthwhile;
- the research does not merely repeat the work of others (or if it does, there is a deliberate reason for this);
- the researcher has created some new knowledge that was not known before.

A successful literature review will meet most of the objectives shown in the box below:

Objectives of a literature review

- Show that the researcher is aware of existing work in the chosen topic area.
- Place the researcher's work in the context of what has already been published.
- Point to strengths, weaknesses, omissions or bias in the previous work.
- Identify key issues or crucial questions that are troubling the research community.
- Point to gaps that have not previously been identified or addressed by researchers.
- Identify theories that the researcher will test or explore by gathering data from the field.
- Suggest theories that might explain data the researcher has gathered from the field.
- Identify theories, genres, methods or algorithms that will be incorporated in the development of a computer application.
- Identify research methods or strategies that the researcher will use in the research.
- Enable subsequent researchers to understand the field and the researcher's work within that field.

The literature review therefore provides the foundation for your research. It is hard to conceive of a research paper or thesis that does not contain any references to the literature – there is no escape. Therefore a further, often unspoken, purpose of a literature review is simply for research students to demonstrate that they are capable of doing one. Many examiners turn first to the list of references in a thesis, dissertation or report, to get a feel for the work. If the list is too short, contains out of date references or misses out important authors in the chosen topic area, then the examiner will mark the work down, or possibly even fail it. But it is not enough to cite relevant work. You will be assessed on your ability to discover, analyse and evaluate what has been done before, and also to synthesize this into a coherent account that justifies your own research and places it in context. As explained in Chapter 3, your literature review should help provide the *conceptual framework* for your research.

Literature Resources

There is a wide range of sources you can use in a literature review, for example, books, journal articles, conference papers and catalogues. Some of them are considered to be more worthy than others in academic research. Let's briefly consider these different sources.

Books

Textbooks can be useful as introductory sources. They explain a field and the main approaches or theories used within it, and they give guidance on particular methods or techniques. However, these books are aimed at students on taught courses, not at academic researchers, which is what you should be aspiring to be, so they are only rarely cited in a literature review. Instead, you should look at the list of references the textbook author has used, and follow up and cite those that are relevant to your chosen area. Some books, sometimes called 'monographs' *are* aimed at an academic audience and can be cited in a literature review. They have a theoretical rather than practical slant, do not contain exercises for the student to complete, and make more frequent use than textbooks of references and footnotes. They are often useful because the authors are able to survey a field in depth and develop ideas and discuss them in detail – in a journal article or conference paper (see below) word length restrictions often mean authors cannot supply as much information as they might wish. However, all books, whether textbooks or monographs, may be outdated even by the time of their first publication, and so might contain theories or views that are out of line with current thinking.

Manuals

Manuals can be a valuable source of information, particularly for design and creation projects where you will often need to use the relevant technical manuals to use particular software packages or computer systems. However, useful as they are, they are *not* refereed academic works giving insight into current thinking in the field. They are not often cited in a literature review.

Journals

Academic journal articles are where you should find information on the current thinking and research in your area of interest. Your final literature review will probably contain mostly journal articles. They can be difficult to read at first, so you might find it best to gain an understanding of the area through books before exploring journal articles for the latest developments. Also useful when you first start are journal articles that are themselves a survey of the literature on a particular topic. The publications *MISQ Review* and *ACM Computing Surveys* specialize in such surveys.

Those journals containing refereed articles are rated more highly than those with non-refereed articles. 'Refereed' means that articles have been 'peer reviewed': academics unknown to an article's authors assess its suitability and quality before a decision is taken on whether to publish it in the journal. (Look at a journal's website under 'Instructions for Authors' to find out whether articles are normally submitted for peer review before acceptance or rejection.)

Some highly rated journals in IS and computing

- *ACM Computing Surveys*
- *Communications of the ACM*
- *Digital Creativity*
- *IEEE Transactions*
- *Information Systems Research*
- *MIS Quarterly*

It is not uncommon for it to take two years or more from submitting an article to an academic journal to it appearing in print. This means that academic journal articles, like books, may be out of date by the time they are published.

You might also use publications aimed at practitioners rather than academics, for example, computing magazines aimed at systems developers, newsletters for artists or journals published for members of professional organizations such as the American Institute of Certified Public Accountants, the Chartered Institute of Personnel and

Development or the British Computer Society. These often contain articles about current issues and problems in a profession. However, such articles are often not peer reviewed, and they can be biased towards the author's views or those of the organization concerned. When reporting research, they often do not provide sufficient detail on the research methodology to satisfy an academic audience. You should therefore be wary of basing your literature review primarily on such publications.

Conference and workshop proceedings

Often researchers will present their work initially via a paper at a conference or workshop, before writing and submitting a more detailed journal article. Conference and workshop proceedings are therefore where you are likely to find the most up-to-date theories, as well as suggestions for further research, which you, of course, could follow up. However, conference and workshop proceedings do have their disadvantages.

First, it can be difficult for a research student to know the standard of a conference. Some conferences receive a high number of submitted papers and therefore reject many, so that you can be reasonably confident that the papers that *are* accepted are of high value. Such conferences send all their papers for peer review by two or more academics before making a decision about acceptance. Other conferences and workshops do not use peer review, or do but have a high acceptance rate, so you can be less certain of the quality of their papers.

Second, it can be hard to obtain copies of conference and workshop papers. Some proceedings are published as books, and can be obtained through an inter-library loan service. Some conference and workshops make available the complete papers on the web, others provide just the paper titles and abstracts online and others only the titles. Unfortunately, many conferences and workshops do not put the papers online and only provide copies of the papers for the delegates who attended. If you are having trouble obtaining a copy of a particular paper, you might find the best approach is to contact the authors directly and ask them for a copy.

Reports

These include market research reports, reports produced by consultancy groups and think-tanks, and government reports. These reports are often difficult to obtain and not available via an inter-library loan service, so you would have to buy them. They can be expensive. Although often produced to a high professional standard, such reports have not normally been reviewed by objective outsiders, and must therefore be treated with caution. Organizations such as consultancy groups might have published a report in order to advertise their expertise and obtain new business. Their reports are therefore unlikely to conclude that there is not a problem in their specialist area. For example, reports about the costs to businesses of computer viruses and hackers might have been produced by an organization specializing in computer security products.

Governments produce a wide range of reports and official statistics. You might think that you can trust government publications to be credible, factual and accurate. However, this is not always the case – governments, too, often have a point they wish to make. Even where they seem objective, their statistics may be misleading. For example, some things can be readily measured and reported, such as statistics on births, deaths, marriages and divorces. Others are less easy to define and therefore measure. For example, the number of people with Internet access: does it include those with a PC at home, and also those who access the Internet from school or from their place of employment? What about those who use a friend's PC, or an Internet café?

For all these types of reports you should therefore consider whether the event or thing being measured is clear-cut and easily defined, and whether there are vested interests in how the statistics or findings are produced and reported. This does not mean that you should avoid using such resources. You can use them, but be cautious, and make it clear to your readers where you think there might be problems with accuracy or bias.

Newspapers, magazines, radio and television

Newspapers, magazines and broadcast programmes can be a valuable resource for up-to-date information. Some carry authoritative articles by expert journalists, for example the *Financial Times* or *Wall Street Journal*, the *Economist* or *Time* magazines, and the BBC or CNN. They are often available on CD-ROM or microfiche, and online. However, many press and broadcasting organizations are biased politically or geographically, and the articles and programmes are not subject to peer review. They can therefore be useful for finding a way into a subject, but you should not normally use them much in your literature review.

Art exhibition catalogues

Those researching into computers and art find art exhibition catalogues useful. Here artists often offer personal statements or essays on their aims and their artistic process. Such catalogues often also contain critical reviews by art critics, who analyse the work and place it in a broader historical context. Remember, however, that such essays are not peer reviewed as in most academic research – they reflect the personal, subjective views of the artist or art critic.

Multimedia 'literature'

The meaning of 'literature review' is now being stretched to go beyond textual material to include such things as images, films, photographs and animations, sound clips and software. These are multimedia 'documents'. For those researchers using a design and creation strategy, in particular, it is often important to review such multimedia sources. For example, someone working as a computer artist would examine other artists' work, both digital artists and those working in conventional media, to find themes, or see how they tackled the problem the artist-researcher is interested in. Similarly, a systems developer creating a new computer application would look at any existing software programs in the same domain. (See Chapters 16 and 18 for further discussion of the use and analysis of multimedia documents.)

Resource catalogues and online databases

A catalogue is a resource that tells you about the holdings of a library – the journals it subscribes to and the books it contains. It is often put online. If there's a particular book you want, you can find out its shelf location, and whether any copy is currently available or whether all copies are out on loan. Your library probably also offers the facility to look at the online catalogues of other libraries, such as those of other universities, the British Library or the US Library of Congress. This is useful if something you need is not held at your own library.

Online databases help you find your way through the millions of academic books, articles and papers that have been published or presented at conferences. Your library will probably subscribe to a number of them. You enter your search parameters, such as keywords associated with your topic and whether you want to find all relevant entries or just those that have been published in, say, the last two years. The results should provide you with a list of authors and titles of relevant entries. Some databases also provide the abstract for an article, which can help you decide its relevance before ordering a copy of the whole article. If the abstract does suggest that the article would be useful, make sure that you do order and read the whole text. Do not cite an article in the review if you have only read the abstract – sometimes an article turns out to be very different from what the abstract implies. Some databases also provide access to the full article. Examples of online databases are listed in the box below.

Examples of online databases relevant to IS and computing

- **ACM Digital Library**: Bibliographic information and text of articles from Association for Computing Machinery's many journals and conference proceedings.
- **Business Source Premier**: Database providing access to over 3000 business journals.

(Continued)

(Continued)

- **INSPEC**: Database produced by the Institution of Electrical Engineers, including articles on computing, IT, engineering and physics.
- **ISI Web of Knowledge/ISI Web of Science**: Contains three databases – Science Citation Index, Social Sciences Citation Index and Arts & Humanities Citation Index – which can be searched separately or together.
- **Design and Applied Arts Index**: Indexes articles from more than 500 design and craft journals.

You might also find that an academic community has assembled lists of references on particular topics and made them available on the web. For example, at the time of writing, the ISWorld website (www.isworld.org) offers lists of references on topics such as e-commerce, knowledge management, IS assessment and IT in developing countries.

Gateways

Academic gateways (also called portals) are websites that provide links to other websites on particular subjects. Since the links provided have been chosen by academics in the relevant subject area, they are useful places to look for better quality information than much that is on the web. Some information gateways relevant to information systems and computing are shown in Table 6.1. Ask your librarian for an up-to-date list of such gateways. At the time of writing, one list can be found at the Pinakes-Subject launchpad (www.hw.ac.uk/libWWW/irn/).

People

The number of publications is increasing rapidly, so it is difficult to be confident that you are aware of all the main themes and trends in the literature. No matter how

Table 6.1   Information gateways relevant to IS and computing

Name	Subject areas covered	URL
Artifact	Arts, design, architecture, media	www.artifact.ac.uk/
Biz/ed	Business and economics	www.bized.ac.uk
EEVL	Engineering, maths and computing	www.eevl.ac.uk
GEM	Education	www.thegateway.org
MCS	Media and communication studies	www.aber.ac.uk/media/index.html
SOSIG	Social sciences	www.sosig.ac.uk

proficient you become at using catalogues and databases and tracking down relevant literature resources, there is always the worry that you have missed out an important publication. By enlisting the help of other people you can increase your confidence that you have not overlooked something vital.

You should enlist the help of the information librarian in your university who specializes in your subject area. They know about suitable sources and databases, and can help you plan effective searches. Your supervisor will also be able to point you towards relevant sources, particularly when you first start. If you are having trouble finding relevant articles, you can also ask for help and suggestions from Internet-based mailing lists and newsgroups for academics who are interested in your area. Be careful, though, not to irritate these academics by making such a request before you have looked properly yourself. You can also put something back into the academic community by collating the responses you receive and posting them back to the mailing list.

You should also make sure other research students and staff know about your research topic. As they do their own research they might come across an article relevant to you, and pass on the details, so never miss an opportunity to tell others about your research interests.

The Internet and Literature Reviews

The Internet is a very useful resource to researchers. As noted above, gateways and online databases and catalogues are an important tool in searching for relevant publications. They have speeded up the whole business of literature searching and made it more convenient – often you can access them from home, at a time suitable for you rather than within your library's normal opening hours.

Search engines such as Google (www.google.com) or Alta Vista (www.altavista.com) can also help you find web-based material. There are also meta-search engines – they use a number of other search engines and sort the combined results, for example, MetaCrawler (www.metacrawler.com). Many search engines are all-purpose – they index everything they find on the web. Others undertake more restricted searches. For example, Google Scholar (scholar.google.com) searches only for online academic publications.

Journal publishers and conference organizers are increasingly putting copies of articles and papers online; the abstracts if not the whole text. There are also some online public repositories of scientific papers, such as CEUR (ceur-ws.org) and CiteSeer (citeseer. ist.psu.edu/). Many journals now also offer an email service that automatically informs you when a new issue of a journal is about to be published, and describes its content. Some journal publishers also let you submit keywords related to your research and will email you when any article is published containing your keywords. Newspapers, television and radio programmes often provide extracts of their reports online, as well as links to other relevant web-based resources. Governments and other public bodies put many of their reports on the web. Researchers also often put copies of their papers on their home or university website, sometimes including further data or illustrations (such as screenshots) for which there was not room in the 'official' publication. You may also find that lecturers have put their teaching notes on the web. Although lecture material has not been peer reviewed and should not be cited in the literature review, often the course reading list gives you a guide on where to start looking in the literature.

However, there are some problems with the Internet as a literature resource. First, there are few restrictions on what is placed on the web – anyone can put material there. This means you have to look carefully at the authorship, credibility and authenticity of anything you find on the web, particularly if you found it via an all-purpose search engine such as Google, rather than one aimed specifically at academic researchers, such as Google Scholar or the ISI Web of Knowledge.

Another problem is the volume of material on the web. It is easy to search and download potentially relevant material, but downloading is *not* reading – and you may become overwhelmed by the pile of material you then have to work through.

When using websites, it is easy to follow links to other sites and end up becoming, if not lost, then certainly side-tracked from your original purpose. Try to be disciplined: don't follow up every link unthinkingly, bookmark sites that look relevant and come back to them later. It is also a good idea to restrict yourself to, say, an hour of web surfing before coming offline and working on what you have gathered so far. Remember also that webpages can move or disappear without warning. Be careful to make a copy of anything vital to your research – but copying must be for your individual research purposes only and not break any copyrights.

Conducting a Literature Review

We can break a literature review down into seven different activities, each of which is discussed in this section: searching, obtaining, assessing, reading, critically evaluating and writing a critical review. Finally, when conducting a literature review you must never plagiarize, as explained below.

Searching

Initially, you can simply walk along the shelves in your university library and browse the books. You can also scan the journals in your subject to which your library subscribes. But soon you will need to do a search of all the literature, not just that to be found in your own university library. You therefore need to use a catalogue, an online database or a search engine. To search one of these resources you first have to define some key words or search terms and then use them methodically to produce a list of potentially useful references.

Start by thinking about your topic or area of interest and trying to clarify your ideas. For example, if you are interested in the use of IT in sales and marketing, are

Concept 1	Concept 2	Concept 3	Concept 4
Attitudes	Advertising	Mobile phones	Text messaging

Figure 6.1   Splitting a research topic into separate concepts

Concept 1	Concept 2	Concept 3	Concept 4
Attitudes	Advertising	Mobile phones	Text messaging
Beliefs	Marketing	Cell phones	SMS
Prejudices	Selling	Telephones	

Figure 6.2   Alternative terms for research concepts

you interested in all kinds of IT, or specific types, for example, websites, mobile phones, interactive digital television? And are you interested in this topic from a particular perspective, for example, historical, psychological, sociological, technical, economic? Each perspective is feasible. Knowing which one interests you will help you decide which source(s) to search, for example an online database for psychology references or one for business and management.

Now define your topic in one phrase, for example, 'attitudes to advertising via mobile phone text messaging'. This phrase can now be split into separate concepts (see Figure 6.1).

For each concept you should now make a list of alternative terms that could also be used to express that concept (Figure 6.2). You might need to use a dictionary or thesaurus and get the help of others to do this.

Think about different forms of the same concept and include them all in your list, for example, 'selling' and 'sales'. Remember also that there might be differences in spelling for different nationalities, for example, UK English and US English (for instance, 'organisations' and 'organizations').

Now choose an appropriate resource, for example, a book index, an all-purpose search engine, a catalogue or an online database. Carry out an initial search of this resource, using at most two of your search concepts.

Review the results from your initial search. Did it produce the desired information? Did it produce too many results, many of which are not appropriate, so you need to narrow down your search? Or did it produce too few, so you need to try again, using an alternative form?

Keep on searching, using different words for the concepts, and different combinations. For electronic searches you can also use the features supplied in your resource, such as

Example	Outcome
attitud*	Results contain words such as attitude, attitudes, attitudinal
mobile AND phones	Results contain both terms, but they do not necessarily occur together
mobile OR phones	Results contain at least one of these terms
'mobile phones'	Results contain the phrase 'mobile phones'

Figure 6.3   Using symbols and Boolean operators in a search

symbols or Boolean operators (for example, AND, OR and NOT) – see Figure 6.3. (Be aware, though, that different systems use different symbols and use Boolean operators differently, so always check the help text for the particular resource you are using.)

Remember to record your search terms as you work. This helps you to be methodical, prevents you repeating searches you have already done, and can help you spot combinations or terms you have not yet used.

As well as searching for material specifically on your chosen research topic, you might also want to search on other topics for contrast, information on your chosen research method, and material that can provide you with an underlying theory or analytic categories for use in your research (see the case study below).

CASE STUDY
Use of a
literature
review

Gail was interested in the use of e-learning in primary schools. In addition to looking for previously published work on this topic, she also looked at material on e-learning in secondary schools and higher education, for contrast. She thought she wanted to use a case-study approach, so looked at the use of case studies in a variety of different domains. She also looked at material on educational theory (such as 'constructivism') and social theory (such as 'structuration theory') to help her refine her research question, find suitable analytic categories and select a theory to help her structure her critical literature review and gather and interpret her data.

Once you have found some useful references, the search becomes easier. You can see if the authors have suggested keywords that define their research and so might be useful in your next searches. You can also look at the references they cite and follow them up, which in turn leads to more references to follow up, and so on. You can also use a citation index facility, often provided with online databases, to discover other authors who have cited the reference in which you are interested in their own work.

If they have cited it, it might be that their article is also relevant to you. Soon the problem is not so much finding suitable references but obtaining and dealing with the many references you have found.

Obtaining

Having developed a list of potentially useful references, you now need to obtain them. Some of them will be held in your library – check the catalogue to find out. If they are, you need only make a note of the shelf number and then find their location.

For books and journals not held by your library, you can use the inter-library loan service. Since this service is not free, there may be restrictions on your inter-library loan requests, such as a limit on the number you can place, or a charge per item. You might also need to obtain your supervisor's signature as authorization. Be aware that the time for requests to arrive can vary from less than a week to over 6 months. To access articles more quickly it's often worth trying the web, since many authors put a copy of their journal articles and conference papers on their university's staff web-pages. If you know the university where they work, these can usually be found quickly using a search engine such as Google.

Assessing

It is important that you assess the credibility of any text that you find and do not just take it at face value. Questions that you could ask yourself about a book include:

- Is the author someone eminent in the field?
- Have you heard of the publisher before?
- Is the publisher a university press (for example, Oxford University Press)? This might reassure you about the academic quality of the work.
- Is the book in a second or subsequent edition, or has it been reprinted? You can find this out from the page that gives the publishing date, usually between the title and contents pages. If there has been more than one edition or reprint, this suggests that there has been a high demand for the book, implying others think it has something worthwhile to say.

For a journal article, you need to assess the journal itself. For example:

- Is it aimed at academics or practitioners? You should concentrate on those aimed at academics.
- How long has the journal existed? You can tell this by looking at the volume number: the higher it is, the longer the journal has existed. One that has existed for a long time is likely to have established itself as a respectable journal. However, the converse is

not true. IS and computing are rapidly evolving fields, so new journals appear regularly. It is not valid to infer that a journal that has not existed for long cannot be a respectable source.

- Does the journal provide a list of its editorial board and advisors, and do these people seem to be of high standing? If they are, then the journal is probably an acceptable resource.
- Does the journal state clearly its policy for reviewing articles? Are all articles peer reviewed, some, or none at all? You should concentrate on those articles that are peer reviewed.

For conferences and workshops, you need to ask:

- Is it an academic conference or one aimed solely at practitioners?
- Is the conference/workshop well established? As with journals, conferences that have been held annually for many years are likely to be respected, but the converse is not necessarily true.
- Does the conference/workshop give details of its programme committee? Do they appear to be scholars of high standing?
- Does it make clear its reviewing policy, or were all papers accepted for presentation?

For Internet sources, you have to be especially careful, since, as we know, anyone can publish almost anything on the web. Some material is simply an electronic version of what appears elsewhere in another format, for example, electronic versions of papers that also appear in printed journals or conference proceedings. For these you can ask the questions suggested above for journal or conference papers. In your literature review, you should cite the *printed* version, if one exists, rather than the web version. Other material might be articles in electronic journals, that is, those that have no print equivalent. Again, you can ask yourself the questions given above about journals. For any other webpages you have to ask yourself the following questions:

- Does the site make clear who owns it and provide contact details if you want to query something?
- Does it seem to be authoritative, for example, one owned by a university or government rather than a private individual?
- Does it make clear its purpose, including any disclaimers?
- Does it show when it was last updated? Is it up-to-date?

Reading

Having obtained and assessed a literature source, you need to read it. Reading for academic purposes is different from reading as a leisure activity. There is often no need to read a text from beginning to end, as you would read a novel. Instead you have to 'gut' a text quickly, finding the information you need before moving swiftly on to the next item. For a journal article or conference paper, concentrate first on the abstract, which should give an overview of the whole, and then look at the introduction section and conclusions. Further detail about the content can be gleaned by looking at the section headings. If you want more information, the first and last sentences of each paragraph are usually those containing that paragraph's key ideas. For a book, there is usually no abstract, but scanning the index can serve instead to give you an idea of the topics covered and in how much detail. Once you have gained an overview of a text's content, you can decide if it is necessary to read the whole thing.

Critically evaluating

When reading a text, you should also critically evaluate it and its relevance to your own research. This means that you think about what the text offers you. Is it useful to you? Why? Look again at the list of objectives of a literature review given earlier in this chapter, to remind you why you might be reading each paper. You also have to consider whether there are flaws in the paper or omissions. Are there parts you disagree with? Why? Do you feel its conclusions are justified on the basis of the evidence presented, or is there some false logic or unwarranted assumptions? It can be difficult at first to have the confidence to criticize a paper or disagree with its content. Surely if the work has been accepted for publication or presentation at a conference, it must be of high value? Well, no, not necessarily. And even high-quality papers can have omissions. As your knowledge of the literature increases, you will be able to see, for example, where authors have not cited other relevant work, or not fully explained their research process. The checklists for the evaluation of research papers that are provided throughout this book will help you assess each paper you read.

Recording

All researchers eventually realize they must devise a system to keep track of the material they are reading and evaluating. The sooner you can devise such a system that suits you, the better. You should keep note of:

- a brief summary of the content – to act as an aid to your memory;
- a brief summary of your evaluation – again to aid your memory;
- bibliographic details of the literature source, so that you, your examiners and anyone else who reads your paper or thesis can find the text again (see the box on the facing page).

Bibliographic details

- For a *book* you should record: author(s) (surname, initials), year of publication, title of book, edition (if not the first edition), place of publication, publisher.
- For a *chapter* in an edited book you should record: author(s) (surname, initials), year of publication, title of chapter, editor(s) of book (surname, initials), title of book, edition (if not the first edition), place of publication, publisher, page numbers of chapter.
- For a *journal article* you should record: author(s) (surname, initials), year of publication, title of article, title of journal, volume number of journal, issue number of journal, page numbers of article.
- For a *conference paper* you should record: author(s) (surname, initials), year of presentation, title of paper, title of conference, location of conference, date of conference, page numbers of paper in conference proceedings.
- For a *web resource* you should record: author(s) (surname, initials), date (that is, date when last updated), title of website/webpage, URL, date you accessed it.

Many researchers use 8 × 5-inch index cards (one per source) to record summaries and bibliographic information. However, software packages are now also available. Bibliographic software such as EndNote (Adept scientific, www.endnote.com), or ProCite® (Thomson Research Soft, www.procite.com) allow you to maintain an electronic record of both the bibliographic information and your notes. The records can easily be searched by author, date of publication or using keywords. Such software packages often provide a link to commonly used word-processing packages, so that when writing your report you can automatically insert the bibliographic details of each source without having to type them out again. However, you might find that it is not always possible to be seated at your computer when reading and evaluating literature sources, so you might still need to note the details manually and transfer to your electronic database later. Of course, be sure to keep backup copies of your electronic database.

Writing a critical review

Finally, you have to write a critical literature review. This can be one chapter in a thesis, or one section in a paper, or it can be spread across your whole thesis/paper as you tackle different issues. Critical reviews can also be written up as journal articles.

The critical literature review is not, though, a summary of everything you have read, much as you might like to boast about the scope of your literature search. Let's remind ourselves of the purpose of a literature review, as explained earlier in this chapter: gathering and presenting evidence to support your claim that you have created some new knowledge, specifically that:

- the topic is worthwhile;
- the research does not merely repeat the work of others (or if it does, there is a deliberate reason for this);
- You have created some new knowledge that was not known before.

You therefore need to focus on your research topic and its objectives, and relate your critical review directly to them. The review is a discussion of *only* the material you have read that is directly relevant to your research.

You need to link together the different ideas you have read in the literature into a coherent and persuasive argument for the value and necessity of your research. One way of approaching this is to think of your critical review as a funnel, which starts at a general level by explaining key ideas in the domain before narrowing down to explain your specific research questions and objectives, and to highlight where your research will provide fresh insights.

A common mistake is to make a critical literature review 'author-centric', that is, structured around the authors. For example:

Jones (1995) found A, Smith (1996) found B, Atkins (1996) found both A and B and Bell (2000) proposed C, though she offered no empirical evidence for C.

Instead, the critical review should normally be structured around concepts, for example:

Evidence for A has been found (Atkins, 1995; Jones, 1996), and for B (Atkins, 1996; Smith, 1996), and more recently C has been proposed, but without any empirical evidence for C (Bell, 2000).

In order to structure your report around concepts, you might find it useful to produce a matrix that maps which papers cover which different concepts (see Figure 6.4).

You should check the details of the referencing system you are expected to use. They fall into two main types. The IS literature mainly uses the Harvard system, where author(s) and publication date appear in the text, and full bibliographic details are then given alphabetically by author in a list of references at the end of the text. The computing literature, on the other hand, often uses a system of numbers in the text that refer to a list of references at the end of the text, that are sorted by number (see the boxes on pages 88 and 89). The specific ordering of the bibliographic details within each reference is decided by your institution or the journal publisher or conference organizers.

	Concepts			
Articles	A	B	C	...
Atkins (1996)	*	*		
Bell (2000)			*	
Jones (1995)	*			
Smith (1996)		*		
...				

Figure 6.4   Using a matrix to map papers to concepts

Example of the Harvard referencing system (author, date)

Conventional ISD methodologies are criticized for paying insuffi-cient attention to the organizational context of computer systems. It is argued that the lack of consideration of the social and behav-ioural dimensions is the cause of failure of many information systems (Checkland & Holwell, 1998; Kling, 1992; 1993; Walsham, 1993). This failure might be experienced as rigid inflexible systems which cannot adapt to changing circumstances, the neglect of human needs and aspirations, or users' poor productivity, lack of motivation or resistance to change (Walsham, 1993, p. 30).

Checkland, P., & Holwell, S. (1998). *Information, systems, and informa-tion systems: Making sense of the field.* Chichester: Wiley.
Kling, R. (1992). Beyond the terminal: The critical role of computing infrastructure in effective information systems development and use. In W.W. Cotterman & J.A. Senn (Eds.), *Challenges and strategies for research in systems development* (pp. 365–413). Chichester: Wiley.
Kling, R. (1993). Organizational analysis in computer science. *The Information Society*, 9(2), 71–87.
Walsham, G. (1993). *Interpreting information systems in organizations.* Chichester: Wiley.

Source: Oates, 2000

Example of referencing convention using numbers

Conventional ISD methodologies are criticized for paying insufficient attention to the organizational context of computer systems.
It is argued that the lack of consideration of the social and behavioural dimensions is the cause of failure of many information systems
[1–4]. This failure might be experienced as rigid inflexible systems
which cannot adapt to changing circumstances, the neglect of
human needs and aspirations, or users' poor productivity, lack of
motivation or resistance to change [4, p. 30].

1. Checkland, P. and S. Holwell, *Information, Systems, and Information
    Systems: Making Sense of the Field*. 1998, Wiley: Chichester,
    Sussex,
2. Kling, R., 'Beyond the terminal: the critical role of computing
    infrastructure in effective information systems development
    and use', in *Challenges and Strategies for Research in Systems
    Development*, W.W. Cotterman and J.A. Senn, Editors. 1992,
    Wiley: Chichester. pp. 365–413.
3. Kling, R., 'Organizational analysis in computer science'. *The
    Information Society*, 1993. 9(2): pp. 71–87.
4. Walsham, G., *Interpreting Information Systems in Organizations*.
    1993, Wiley: Chichester.

Source: Oates, 2000

Plagiarism

Finally you must know what is meant by plagiarism, and make sure you are not guilty
of it. In brief, plagiarism means that you have used someone else's words or ideas
without giving them credit. It is a serious misdemeanour, and if found guilty of it
research students will probably be failed. A good test for whether you are in danger
of plagiarizing another author's words is whether you are able to write your discussion of a paper without having to refer frequently to the author's original. The more
you find your eyes going back and forth from the keyboard or screen to the original
paper, the more likely it is that you might plagiarize. Cutting and pasting from electronic sources is also plagiarism. If you want to use someone's words because they

express an idea perfectly, then you should put those words into quotation marks, and cite the original author. If you summarize the original author's words, or rewrite the author's ideas in your own words, you should still cite the original author. By being careful to cite other authors, you win twice over: you cannot be accused of plagiarizing and you demonstrate how aware you are of other published work.

Evaluating Literature Reviews

As you study research papers, you should assess how the authors use the literature. Use the 'Evaluation Guide' below to help you.

EVALUATION GUIDE: CRITICAL LITERATURE REVIEW

1   Does the paper review any previous literature?
2   What types of literature sources does it draw upon (for example, books, journal articles, conference papers) and in what proportion?
3   Are all the sources of a suitable type for use in academic research?
4   What referencing system is used?
5   Are complete bibliographic details provided for each reference?
6   Does the literature review appear primarily in one section, or is it spread throughout the paper?
7   What objectives does the literature review meet in this paper? (Use the list of possible review objectives given in this chapter to help you.)
8   Is the review primarily 'author-centric' or structured around concepts?
9   Given your current state of knowledge, can you identify flaws or omissions in the paper's use of the literature?
10 Overall, how effectively do you think the literature has been used in this paper?

PRACTICAL WORK

1   It is important that you become familiar with your university library and its resources. Many libraries offer short training courses for new researchers, to introduce the facilities, explain the databases and catalogues available and give guidance on effective literature searches. If your library offers such a course, you should attend it. If you are not able to attend such a course, visit the library yourself – its bricks-and-mortar site and its website if it has one. Find where books and journals in your subject area are situated, browse the factsheets for users that it probably offers and collect copies of any that seem relevant. You should also try to introduce yourself to the relevant subject librarian, explain your area of interest and ask about possible sources for research on topics in that area.

2   The following reference details should be in the style and order used in *MIS Quarterly*. Find out about this style (see *MIS Quarterly's* website), and identify the mistakes in each of the references. Either write each reference out correctly or explain what is wrong with it.

   a   Dahlbom, B., and Mathiassen, L. *Computers in Context: The Philosophy and Practice of Systems Design* NCC Blackwell, Oxford.

   b   Checkland, P., and Holwell, S. Information, Systems, and Information Systems: Making Sense of the Field Wiley, Chichester, Sussex; 1998.

   c   Adam, A., Howcroft, D., Richardson, and Robinson. (eds.) *(Re-) Defining Critical Research in Information Systems. Proceedings of the Workshop 9–10 July 2001*. University of Salford, Salford, UK, 2001.

   d   Baskerville, R., and Wood-Harper, A.T., '*Diversity in information systems action research methods*,' *European Journal of Information Systems* (7) 1998, pp. 90–107.

   e   Schmidtke, O. 'Berlin in the Net: Prospects for cyberdemocracy from above and below,' in: *Cyberdemocracy. Technology, Cities and Civic Networks,* Tsagarousianou, Tambini and Bryan (eds.), Routledge, London, 1998, pp. 60–83.

   f   Fitzgerald, B., and Howcroft, D. 'Towards dissolution of the IS research debate: From polarisation to polarity,' *Journal of Information Technology* (13:4) 1998.

   g   Markus, M.L. 'Power, politics and MIS implementation,' *Communications of the ACM* 1983, pp. 430–445.

   h   Nielsen. *Designing Web Usability* New Riders, Indianapolis, 2000.

   i   Orlikowski, W.J., and Baroudi, J.J. *Information Systems Research* (2:1) 1991, pp. 1–28.

   j   Giddens, A. *Central Problems in Social Theory*, London, 1979.

   k   Vidgen, R., Avison, D.E., Wood, B., and Wood-Harper, T. *Developing Web Information Systems* Butterworth-Heinemann, 2002.

   l   Yourdon, E. *Modern Structured Analysis* Yourdon Press/Prentice-Hall, Englewood Cliffs, N.J., 1989, pp. x, 672.

3   Practise analysing and evaluating how other researchers use the literature. Find a research paper relevant to your own area of interest and answer the questions in the 'Evaluation Guide' above, using the material in this chapter to help you.

FURTHER READING

Useful books that concentrate on literature sources and how to carry out a literature review include Fink (2005) and Hart (2001).

   Work-Learning Research (2003) discuss some statistics that are commonly quoted by educationalists ('People generally remember 10 per cent of what they read, 20 per cent of what they hear, 30 per cent of what they see ...', and so on). The authors argue that these statistics are bogus, and yet they have been quoted widely by other authors who appear not to have read the original publications from which they came. The website provides a good discussion of the mistake of citing work just because it has been cited by others, without looking at the original work yourself, and of how such a mistake can be ▶

▶ propagated through subsequent literature. (Of course, you will need to evaluate whether this website is itself a credible source.)

You can learn about literature reviews by looking at examples, particularly those in journals that specialize in review articles such as *MISQ Review* (part or *MIS Quarterly*) and *ACM Computing Surveys*. Webster and Watson (2002) offer guidelines on how to structure and write such review articles. Although their advice is aimed at authors wishing to submit papers to *MISQ Review*, it is useful for anyone writing a critical review, whether as a journal paper or as part of a report or thesis.

Ned Kock (1999) discusses what happened and the difficulties he faced when he published some research in a journal and later discovered a plagiarized copy of the article had been submitted under another author's name to another journal. Kock and Davison (2003) discuss this experience again, explore the factors that can drive plagiarism, and suggest potential measures to prevent it.

References

Fink, A. (2005). *Conducting research literature reviews. From the Internet to paper* (2nd ed.). London: Sage.

Hart, C. (2001). *Doing a literature research. A comprehensive guide for the social sciences*. London: Sage.

Kock, N. (1999). A case of academic plagiarism: The perils of Internet publication. *Communications of the ACM, 42*(7), 96–104.

Kock, N., & Davison, R. (2003). Dealing with plagiarism in the information systems research community: A look at factors that drive plagiarism and ways to address them. *MIS Quarterly, 27*(4), 511–532.

Oates, B.J. (2000). Metaphors for organizations during information systems development. PhD thesis, University of Teesside.

Webster, J., & Watson, R.T. (2002). Analyzing the past to prepare for the future: Writing a literature review. *MIS Quarterly, 26*(2), xiii–xxiii.

Work-Learning Research (2003). *Bogus research uncovered*. Retrieved 1 February 2005 from www.work-learning.com/chigraph.htm

7 Surveys

In this chapter you will learn about:

- what is meant by a survey research strategy;
- issues to address in planning and designing survey research;
- how survey research might be carried out via the Internet;
- how surveys have been used in IS and computing;
- the advantages and disadvantages of survey research;
- analysing and evaluating survey research.

Defining Surveys

The idea of a survey is that you will obtain the same kinds of data from a large group of people (or events), in a standardized and systematic way. You then look for patterns in the data that you can generalize to a larger population than the group you targeted. For example, opinion pollsters might survey the views of around 1000 people and analyse the results to draw conclusions about the voting intentions of a whole country's population. Many people automatically assume that a survey will use a questionnaire for its data generation method. However, surveys are also possible using other data generation methods such as interviews, observations and documents. An obvious example is the literature survey, which examines printed and online published documents. The survey strategy is mostly associated with the philosophical paradigm of positivism (see Chapter 19), since it is looking for patterns and generalizations, but it can also be used with interpretive and critical research (see Chapter 20).

Surveys are widely accepted and used in the IS field. It is quite likely that you will find an issue of an IS journal where all the articles that report on empirical research (that is, research involving the generation of data from the field) used a survey. In computing, a common use of a survey is in the user evaluation of a software system, although it must be said that many such surveys appear to have been 'tagged on' at the end of systems development since they are poorly designed and executed. Read on to find out how to avoid that criticism yourself.

Planning and Designing Surveys

The planning and conducting of surveys can be broken down into six different activities under the following headings: data requirements, data generation method, sampling frame, sampling technique, response rate and non-responses, sample size. Each of these is discussed in this section.

Data requirements

You need to decide what data you wish to generate (see the case study below). The data could be on topics directly associated with your research question(s), or it could be only indirectly related, such as demographic data about your respondents (the people who provide you with data), for example, their age and gender. As you normally only get one opportunity with your respondents in a questionnaire- or interview-based survey, it's important to think carefully beforehand about all the data you wish to generate – you probably will not get a second chance to go back and ask about things you forgot the first time. This means thinking ahead about how you might analyse your data, patterns you might look for, and interpretations that might arise for which you will need additional data.

CASE STUDY
Establishing
data
requirements

Simon wanted to investigate the use of email by employees in business organizations. Data he decided to generate included:

- **Directly topic related:** whether the respondents had regular access to email facilities at work, how often they sent emails, how many in a day, whether they received emails, how many in a day, an estimate of daily time spent reading emails, and so on.
- **Indirectly topic related:** age of respondents, gender, size of employing organization, existence of written company policy on email usage, and so on.

When he analysed his data, as well as generating statistics about how much time was being spent on email work, he looked for whether there was a relationship between email usage and the age of an employee or the size of an organization. He also looked for such things as whether his respondents all fell within a particular age group, which would suggest that there might be a bias in his data and results.

Data generation method

As we have already noted, although the survey research strategy is often assumed to be based on questionnaires, it can also use other data generation methods such as interviews, documents and observations (see the case study below). You therefore have to decide which data generation method you will use. For one survey usually just one method is chosen.

> Simon, Stephen and Sally were all interested in the use of email by employees in business organizations, and each proposed to use a survey.
>
> Simon decided to generate his data via a *questionnaire*. He rejected sending an email questionnaire because he realized he would only be able to get it to people who *did* use email, and chose a postal questionnaire instead, although that was more costly.
>
> Stephen considered using *observations* of his colleagues, but realized it would be difficult and possibly unethical to look over people's shoulders constantly to see if they were dealing with email. He therefore decided to base his survey on *interviews* about email usage with a large number of people in his own organization.
>
> Sally decided to use *documents*. Having obtained the necessary permission, she analysed the logs of some organizations' mail-servers to find out about the numbers of emails sent and received. She also wrote a program that some respondents agreed to have installed on their office PC, which was able to capture the time spent on email work.

Whichever method you choose, you will then have to decide exactly how it will generate the data. If you choose a survey via questionnaire, you must design the questionnaire (see Chapter 15), for interviews you need to plan the interview format (see Chapter 13), and for observation you need to design observation schedules (see Chapter 14). If you choose a document survey, the relevant documents might already exist, or you might need to create them yourself (see Chapter 16), and you need to decide exactly what you are looking for in the documents.

Sampling frame

A sampling frame is some kind of list or collection of the whole population of people (or events or documents) that *could* be included in your survey, from which you will choose a sample. If your research question is concerned with how an IT help-desk handles queries from users, for example, your sampling frame might be the help-desk's log of all requests for help. You might decide that the telephone directory for a town constitutes your sampling frame, and your sampling technique might be to choose a number of names from it at random. Of course, your sampling frame must be up-to-date, accurate and contain the whole population of people in which you are interested. Choosing the telephone directory would not be appropriate if you wanted to contact homeless people, for example. Nor would the telephone directory for just one town be suitable if you wanted to find out about people living in the whole country. Remember, also, that some people choose not to have their name listed in the telephone directory, which might bias your data. Examples of sampling frames that are fairly readily available include telephone directories, attendance registers, the electoral roll (register of voters) and lists of members published by professional organisations. There are also companies that will sell you mailing lists (for example, 'all schools in the Edinburgh area').

Sampling technique

Having obtained a sampling frame, you have to decide a sampling technique, that is, how you will select actual people or events from your sampling frame. There are two kinds of sampling: *probability* and *non-probability sampling* (Table 7.1). Probability sampling, as its name suggests, means that the sample has been chosen because the researcher believes that there is a high probability that the sample of respondents (or events) chosen are representative of the overall population being studied. That is, they form a representative cross-section of the overall population. Non-probability sampling means that the researcher does not know whether the sample of people (or events) is representative – each member might have unique characteristics not shared with others in the overall population. Non-probability sampling provides at best only a weak basis for generalizations to the wider population.

Let's look first at some *probability sampling* techniques.

• **Random sampling:** people or events are selected literally 'at random'. At its simplest, you put the names of all the people in your population into a hat and draw out the required number of names. For larger sampling frames such as a telephone directory, you could first obtain a list of random numbers – such lists are published in

Table 7.1   Sampling techniques

Probabilistic	Non-probabilistic
Random	Purposive
Systematic	Snowball
Stratified	Self-selection
Cluster	Convenience

books of mathematical tables and in statistics textbooks, or you can generate one using a spreadsheet package. You then work through the list, using each number to identify the directory page and line on the page to select a person for inclusion in your sample.

- **Systematic sampling**: this builds on random sampling by adding a system of choosing people at regular intervals in the sampling frame. For example, if using the telephone directory, you might decide to choose every 100th person. Note that researchers using this technique would not start with the first person in the directory but would choose the first name at random and then carry on from there.

- **Stratified sampling**: here the idea is to build up a sample where the types of members in it are in the same proportion as they are in the overall population in which you are interested. Suppose, for example, you want to carry out a survey on employees' perceptions of stress in an IT organization where 70 per cent of the employees are male and 30 per cent female. You would first divide your sampling frame into males and females, and then choose 70 per cent of your sample at random from the male list and 30 per cent at random from the female list. In this way, your sample would match the gender balance in the organization's workforce.

- **Cluster sampling**: this uses the fact that instances of the types of people (or events) in which you are interested might naturally occur together in clusters. By working with all the members of a cluster (or a sample from it), the researcher can cut down on travel costs. Suppose, for example, you wanted a national sample of people in order to interview them about their use of computers in the home. Any of the techniques outlined so far would have you criss-crossing the country interviewing perhaps just one person in a town before moving on. Instead, you could identify the clusters naturally occurring in your population (here, towns), choose several towns at random and then identify a sample from those towns using one of the techniques outlined already. Other examples of clusters include schools (collections of young people), bars (people who like to drink and socialize) and business organizations (people of working age). Of course, restricting your sample to one or a few geographical clusters may reduce the representativeness of your sample. You have to trade off costs against the representativeness of a sample drawn from a larger frame.

Let's turn now to *non-probabilistic sampling*. This is used when the researcher believes it is not feasible or necessary to have a representative sample. Perhaps the time and costs of obtaining one are too great. Sometimes researchers do not know enough about the population – who, how many – to be able to do probability sampling. Sometimes it might not be possible to contact a sample derived from probability sampling techniques. For example, even if you were able to obtain a list of people successfully prosecuted for software piracy, it is unlikely you could choose some of them at random and simply send them a questionnaire in the post and expect them to complete and return it. Sometimes researchers are not interested in generalizations that apply to a larger population than the sample. Rather they want to explore a topic in depth, deliberately including instances that are extreme, unusual or somehow atypical (as in interpretive and critical research – see Chapter 20), so that a wide number of issues can be raised and examined. Non-probability sampling techniques include:

- **Purposive sampling:** here, the researcher deliberately hand-picks the sample, choosing instances that are likely to produce valuable data to meet the purpose of the research. Instead of choosing a cross-section of people to represent the wider population, the researcher would choose instances offering a wide variety, possibly even extreme cases. In a non-probabilistic survey of attitudes to online purchasing, for example, you might deliberately choose people you know who regularly buy online and people who have never shopped online.
- **Snowball sampling:** the researcher finds one person who comes from the target population. Having gathered data from this person, the researcher asks for suggestions about other people relevant to the research topic. These are now approached, with the advantage that the researcher has in effect been introduced or sponsored by the original respondent. After gathering data from these people, the researcher asks for further names, so that the sample soon snowballs in size. This approach can be used in conjunction with purposive sampling: when asking for nominations, the researcher can explain, for example, the gender of respondents needed, or type of employment or any other necessary criteria. This technique is useful when the researcher does not know how to gain access to the target group. Having found just one respondent – still often difficult, of course – the researcher is put on to the track of others. This could be used, for example, if you wanted to find out about computer hackers, their beliefs and motivations. A group of hackers is hardly likely to make itself widely known. If you could find one active hacker willing to talk, you might be put in touch with others.
- **Self-selection sampling:** researchers advertise their interest in a particular topic and their need for respondents, and collect data from anyone who responds. Again, this is a useful technique when a researcher does not know how to contact potential respondents. People who select themselves for research often do so, however, because they have strong feelings on the subject, so clearly may not be typical of the wider population. Others volunteer because they think it will bring them personal benefit or approval, for example, students might volunteer to take part in their tutor's survey if they think it might influence their tutor to give them higher marks.
- **Convenience sampling:** here, the researchers simply select respondents who are convenient for them, because they are easy to reach or willing to help (see the case study on the facing page). Clearly there can be an element of convenience in many sampling techniques – if there are two possibilities for inclusion in a sample, for example, and the researchers need just one of them, the one that is more convenient will be chosen. However, choosing respondents on the basis of convenience *only* would not be considered good research. You should especially bear this in mind if using students as part of your study. If your research is concerned with students'

views or experiences, students will, of course, make up your survey respondents. But if you were really interested in some aspect of information systems or computing in the world beyond a university, using students as surrogates for practitioners because they were more convenient for you would probably be criticised.

Maria was completing an undergraduate research project where she had concentrated on the design and creation of a computer-based system in a new domain. When it came to testing and evaluation, she was running out of time. She designed a questionnaire for user evaluation, but was only able to get five of her friends to use her system and complete the questionnaire. However, in her report she explained that her user evaluation was only based on convenience sampling, discussed the limitations and possible bias arising from such a sampling technique, and explained, with reasons, which sampling strategy she would have used if she had had more time. She obtained a high mark for her project and the examiners commented favourably on her critical evaluation of her work.

Maria's boyfriend, Mark, was completing his PhD, which also involved the design and creation of a computer system. He proposed using the same approach as Maria for user testing and evaluation. However, his supervisor informed him that for work at PhD level a higher standard of research was required. Mark realized that it would be better to delay completing and submitting his thesis until he had taken the time to do a well-designed user evaluation survey.

Response rate and non-responses

If you posted a questionnaire to 100 people, you would be doing well if you received 30 replies. Response rates of just 10 per cent are not uncommon. You therefore need a strategy to try to increase the number of responses. If you suspect that certain types of people in your sample will be less willing to respond, you could deliberately include more of that type in your sample, so that you receive the number of responses you need. If you give a good explanation of the purpose of your survey and what you hope to learn from it, you might persuade more people to participate. If feasible, hand-delivering a questionnaire and explaining its purpose face-to-face can also influence people to help you. You can also include stamped addressed envelopes with a postal survey, to make it easy for people to reply to you. If you monitor who has received a survey questionnaire and who has not yet returned it, you can issue a follow-up notice, reminding people and (politely) asking them again to participate. Whenever possible, you should devise a way of finding out at least some characteristics of the people who have not responded, so that you can analyse whether their non-response is meaningful in its own right, or whether their lack of response has resulted in a bias in your final sample.

Sample size

You need to decide how big you want your final sample to be, taking into account your best estimate of the likely non-response rate of participants. For small-scale research projects, as in many first-time researchers' projects, a good rule-of-thumb is to have a final sample of at least 30. If you have less than 30, statistical analysis (such as calculating the average or mean, see Chapter 17) is not reliable. It can sound significant to say that 10 per cent of your sample believed X, but that seems less impressive once the reader realizes that that means just three people out of 30 believed X. For this reason, if you have a sample of less than 30 and want to use percentages, you should always give the actual numbers involved too.

If you want to generalize your findings from the sample to the whole population in which you are interested, the sample must be of an adequate size (see the box below). The greater the accuracy required in your claim that your sample represents fully the whole population, the larger your sample size needs to be. Statisticians have produced tables that correlate population size against the sample size needed for a required level of confidence and accuracy. Researchers normally work to 95 per cent confidence level and an accuracy range of +/−3 per cent.

Accuracy range and confidence level

The *accuracy range* (also called 'margin of error' and 'confidence interval') tells us how close to the true population value we are. If it is reported that 70 per cent of the population think the prime minister (or president) is doing a good job, with an accuracy range of +/− 3 per cent, then the true value of people who think that is somewhere in the range 67 per cent to 73 per cent of the population. If you wanted perfect accuracy (that is, a range of +/−0 percentage points), you would have to survey the whole population.

A *confidence level* of 95 per cent means that we are 95 per cent sure that the true population value falls within the range of values obtained from the sample. Another way of expressing this is to say that if we took an infinite number of samples from the target population, 95 per cent of the time the true population value would fall within the range of values obtained from the sample.

Table 7.2 shows some target population sizes and the number required in a sample for a confidence level of 95 per cent and an accuracy range of −/+ 3 per cent. For example, for 95 per cent confidence, a target population of 50 people and accuracy range of +/−3 per cent, you would need to have 47 in your sample, but if your target population had 5000 people, you would need 760 in your sample.

Table 7.2   Target population sizes and sample sizes

Target population size	Required sample size for 95 per cent confidence level and +/- 3 per cent accuracy range
50	47
5000	760
100,000	888
900,000	895

Source: www.geneseesurvey.com/web/webcalc.asp

Note that the sample size does not need to increase at the same rate as the target population size (Table 7.2). For a target population of 100,000 you would need a sample size of 888, but for 900,000 you would need a sample of 895, that is, only seven more people. For a target population of 1 million or more, as in the opinion polls beloved of politicians and journalists, just over 1000 people in a stratified sample are normally required. You don't need to worry about how these sample sizes are calculated, since it is easy to find tools with target population sizes and sample size calculators on the web (for example, www.surveysystem.com/sscalc.htm).

Accuracy ranges matter!

The next time you read a newspaper article reporting the results of an opinion poll, look at the sample size and see whether it is large enough according to the statisticians' calculators. Look also at the accuracy range, which should be somewhere in the small print. If the headline value(s) were changed to a range of values (for example, 70 per cent might become 67–73 per cent), would that require a rewrite of the article?

Having designed your survey, you need to carry it out. Before you do, however, you should read Chapter 5, 'Participants and Research Ethics', to ensure that you work ethically. Then you can send out questionnaires, or conduct interviews, or make observations, or collect documents (see Chapters 13–16). You will then need to analyse your data and make interpretations (see Chapters 17–20) and present your findings (see Chapter 21).

Grounded Theory and Surveys

The previous section explained a structured way of planning and designing surveys: deciding data requirements and data generation methods, choosing a sampling strategy, and so on. Such a sequence of tasks is carried out for most surveys, but there is one exception. Researchers following a 'grounded theory' approach follow a path of discovery, letting the emerging data and interpretations of that data dictate what research steps to take next. The researchers might not have known at the outset that a survey would be useful. They might interview one or two people, for example, decide to interview more, because a useful clue has been thrown up, then decide more data was needed on just a few issues, which could be gathered via a questionnaire. As additional data is collected from more and more people, the researchers might find that a survey has been carried out almost by default. Here, the data generation method, units in the sample and the sample size are not decided in advance – instead the emphasis is on sequential discovery. Researchers using grounded theory will also often use non-probability sampling to focus on special instances or extreme examples in order to get maximum variety in the collected data. More on grounded theory can be found in Chapter 18.

The Internet and Surveys

The Internet offers researchers the possibility of accessing many people across the world cheaply and quickly. Surveys via questionnaire can be carried out by emailing questionnaires to people to be completed and returned by email, or by asking people to visit a website and complete an online questionnaire. Target respondents could be found in company employee email lists, or newsgroup members, or bulletin board subscribers. Remember that you may need to get the permission of the list owner or moderator first. (For the design of Internet-based questionnaires see Chapter 15.)

There is not yet agreement on whether Internet surveys using questionnaires produce a higher response rate than postal surveys. It is known that unsolicited questionnaires are regarded as junk mail by many people. In the offline world they might just throw such a questionnaire away. Online they can also simply delete an email questionnaire, but they are more likely also to send *you* an angry email. It is a good idea to send a short introductory message prior to the actual questionnaire – people can then decline to receive it, or delete it as soon as it arrives – though even this introduction will anger some people. Remember also that spam filters prevent bulk emails being delivered to people's inboxes, so your email-based questionnaire might not even reach its intended recipients.

Alternatively, visitors to a website could be asked to complete an online questionnaire – as in user feedback surveys. If you ask every 100th visitor to a website to complete a questionnaire, for example, this is a form of probabilistic, systematic sampling.

If a questionnaire is returned electronically, the researcher gains the further advantage that the data is already in electronic form, removing the danger of errors creeping in if you type the responses yourself into a software program. Indeed, if designed carefully, it may be possible to input reply forms straight into a data analysis program, again removing the possibility of human error.

Surveys using other data generation methods are also possible via the Internet:

- a series of *interviews* can be conducted over the Internet, via email, bulletin boards, chatrooms or messaging services (see Chapter 13);
- a set of *observations* can be made of online communities, looking for, for example, types of comments made or frequencies of postings (see Chapter 14);
- a collection of electronic *documents* such as the archives of bulletin boards or a sample of websites, can be surveyed and analysed (see Chapter 16).

However, not everyone has online access. Currently people from poorer homes or in developing countries may have no Internet access. Typically, the Internet user population is thought to be predominately male, American, in an educational, computer or professional occupation and earning an above-average salary (Hewson, Yule, Laurent, & Vogel, 2003). Be aware, then, that the findings of your study might be distorted if only those who are online are surveyed. It is thought that over time the Internet population is becoming more representative of the general population. Unfortunately, surveys that attempt to find out the characteristics of the Internet population have themselves been criticized for biased sampling techniques (Hewson et al., 2003).

Examples of Surveys in IS and Computing Research

Surveys are often used in IS and computing research. As mentioned already, a common use of them is in the user evaluation of systems. They are also commonly used to investigate managers' practices or views concerning some aspect of IS or computing. Newsted, Huff, Munro, and Schwarz (1998) have a databank of over 600 surveys in IS research alone. Indeed, back in 1996, a conference panel discussed whether surveys have outlived their usefulness in IS research (Newsted, Chin, Ngwenyama, & Lee, 1996). Some examples of survey research include:

- Cegielski, Rebman and Reithel (2003) investigate the common assumption that IS network managers who possess network certification (Novell or Microsoft) are better network managers than those who do not have such certification. Using Davis's (1989) technology acceptance model, which theorizes that a user's acceptance of an information system is based on the system's perceived ease of use and perceived usefulness, Cegielski et al. (2003) examined the perceptions of end-users of a LAN about ease of use and usefulness of their LAN. This was done via a survey of 299 respondents from 11 firms drawn from the financial services sector. The article argues that end-users of LANs administered by certified network professionals do not have better perceptions of the network than end-users of LANs administered by people without network certification.

- Davis's (1989) technology acceptance model is also used by Heijden (2004) in his study of user acceptance of 'hedonic information systems'. Such a system is one that is used for fun (for example, computer games and some websites), whereas a 'utilitarian' information system is used for work and productivity. Hejden bases his work on a movie website – one that contains movie news and cinema listings. He emailed users of this website an invitation to participate in a web-based survey. He uses the data obtained to argue that perceived enjoyment and perceived ease of use are stronger determinants of intention to use a hedonic information system than perceived usefulness. He goes on to suggest that introducing hedonic features into utilitarian systems could enhance their acceptability to users.
- Yetton, Martin, Sharma and Johnston (2000) use two postal surveys to investigate critical success factors for systems projects under development (that is, before implementation). They analyse the data obtained to argue that successful project management depends on a project team being stable, experienced and cohesive, and having effective management of risk, senior management support and active user involvement.

Evaluating Survey-based Research

Advantages of surveys include:

- They provide a wide and inclusive coverage of people or events, so that the results are likely to be representative of the wider population. This means that generalized conclusions can be drawn.
- Relative to some other strategies (for example, ethnography), they can produce a lot of data in a short time at a reasonably low cost. Costs and time can also be reasonably predicted in advance, which helps the planning and managing of a research project.
- They lend themselves to quantitative data analysis. Many readers of research are impressed by numbers. *Some* researchers and readers think (falsely) that quantitative data is the only 'proper' kind of data.
- They can be replicated, that is, the same data can be collected again from another sample (for example, in another organization or another country) or at a later time with the same people (providing they are willing to answer the same questions all over again). This means that a survey can be subjected to further testing leading to confirmation or refutation of its findings. Replication of studies is an essential part of the scientific method (see Chapter 19).
- Surveys via postal or web questionnaire, observations or documents are suited to people who do not have good inter-personal and communication skills.

Disadvantages of surveys include:

- They lack depth. They do not provide much detail on research topics; instead the focus is on breadth of coverage.
- They tend to focus on what can be counted and measured, and subject to statistical analysis. Aspects of the research topic that cannot be reduced to numbers may therefore be overlooked.
- They provide snapshots of particular points in time, rather than examining ongoing processes and change.
- They do not establish cause and effect (as experiments do – see Chapter 9). They can only show associations, for example, analysis of survey results might show that older managers prefer paper to email, but that does not mean that age *causes* such a preference.
- With postal, telephone or Internet surveys, researchers cannot judge the accuracy or honesty of people's responses by observing their body language.

Use the 'Evaluation Guide' below to help you analyse and evaluate survey-based research. If there is insufficient information for you to answer some questions, you should not completely reject the research report, but you should treat the findings with caution and be wary about treating the report as evidence.

EVALUATION GUIDE: SURVEYS

1   Was the research aimed at a wide and inclusive coverage of people/events?
2   What data generation method was used? Was it used via the Internet? Was an Internet survey appropriate or feasible for this research topic?
3   What information is given about the sampling frame and sampling technique used? What additional information would you like to have?
4   What sample size was used? Do you think this was enough?
5   What information is given about the response rate and dealing with non-respondents? What additional information would you like to have?
6   Did the researchers make efforts to see if there were significant differences between respondents and non-respondents?
7   Do the researchers use the survey results to make generalizations about a larger population? Is this appropriate?
8   What limitations in their survey strategy do the researchers recognize?
9   Can you identify other flaws or omissions in the researchers' reporting of their survey strategy?
10 Overall, how effectively do you think the survey strategy has been reported and used?

PRACTICAL WORK

1 Suggest a suitable sampling frame and sampling technique for each of the following research questions:

   a How much money do managers of companies employing more than 1000 people anticipate spending on IT over the next 2 years?

   b What research topics do managers think IS and computing academics should be addressing?

   c What research topics do IS and computing academics think they should be addressing?

   d How much money do companies lose because of computer-based fraud?

   e How do employers' opinions vary concerning the effect of proposed new data protection legislation?

2 Brainstorm: what kinds of reasons might people have for using the web and/or online communication with others? Now brainstorm: what factors might affect whether or not people *do* use the web and/or communicate with others online? Are some groups more likely than others to find it difficult or impossible? How could you research whether your lists (of reasons and factors) are true or complete? Who might be interested in the results of your research, and why? Finally, suggest two research topics, one where you think it would be appropriate to use an online survey, and one where it would not be appropriate.

3 Practise analysing and evaluating survey-based research. Study a piece of research that used a survey (concentrate on how the survey was designed and conducted, rather than on any statistical analysis in the paper). Answer the questions in the 'Evaluation Guide' above, using the material in this chapter to help you.

FURTHER READING

Fink (2003) is a comprehensive ten-volume kit on survey-based research. Individual volumes from the kit can also be bought separately. Detailed guidance is also provided by De Vaus (2002) in a four-volume set. Shorter and easier-to-read guidance is provided by Punch (2003) and Fowler (2001).

Kraemer (1991) is a collection of papers on survey use in IS. Unfortunately, it is currently out of print, but your library may have a copy. Newsted et al. (1998) is an online 'living' document (that is, regularly updated) intended to help IS researchers with surveys. The authors provide introductory information on the survey process, plus a list of references on surveys, both general and IS-specific. They also provide a search engine where you enter a concept you wish to include in a survey, for example, 'user satisfaction', and it provides you with IS references that have included that concept in a survey, sometimes including the text of the relevant questionnaire items. Finally Hewson, Yule, Laurent and Vogel (2003) is a book-length treatment of Internet research methods, with particular emphasis on online surveys via questionnaire. The authors offer plenty of practical guidance, including sample program code for web-based questionnaires. They also review in detail the research methodologies for some surveys carried out via the Internet. One involved a simple email-based questionnaire, and another a documentary study of email communications. They discuss what was learnt about the benefits and pitfalls of the research methodology in each case.

References

Cegielski, C.G., Rebman, C.M., & Reithel, B.J. (2003). The value of certification: An empirical assessment of the perceptions of end-users of local area networks. *Information Systems Journal, 13*(1), 97–107.

Davis, F.D. (1989). Perceived usefulness, perceived ease of use, and user acceptance of information technology. *MIS Quarterly, 13*(3), 319–340.

De Vaus, D. (2002). *Social surveys*. London: Sage.

Fink, A. (2003). *The survey kit*. London: Sage.

Fowler, F.J. (2001). *Survey research methods* (3rd ed.). London: Sage.

Heijden, H. van der (2004). User acceptance of hedonic information systems. *MIS Quarterly, 28*(4), 695–704.

Hewson, C., Yule, P., Laurent, D., & Vogel, C. (2003). *Internet research methods. A practical guide for the social and behavioural sciences*. London: Sage.

Kraemer, K. (Ed.). (1991). *The information systems research challenge: Survey research methods*. Boston, MA: Harvard Business School.

Newsted, P., Chin, W., Ngwenyama, O., & Lee, A. (1996). Resolved: Surveys have outlived their usefulness in IS research (panel). In *International Conference on Information Systems*, Cleveland, OH, 16–18 December. Retrieved 3 February 2005 from www.ucalgary.ca/~newsted/ppt/icis96.htm

Newsted, P., Huff, S., Munro, M., & Schwarz, A. (1998). Survey instruments in information systems. *MISQ Discovery*, 22(4), 553–554. Retrieved 3 February 2005 from www.isworld.org/surveyinstruments/surveyinstruments.htm

Punch, K.F. (2003). *Survey research. The basics*. London: Sage.

Yetton, P., Martin, A., Sharma, R., & Johnston, K. (2000). A model of information systems development project performance. *Information Systems Journal, 10*(4), 263–289.

8 Design and Creation

In this chapter you will learn about:

- what is meant by a design and creation research strategy;
- issues to address in undertaking design and creation research;
- design and creation research and the Internet;
- how design and creation research has been used in IS and computing;
- the advantages and disadvantages of design and creation research;
- analysing and evaluating design and creation research.

Defining Design and Creation

The design and creation research strategy focuses on developing new IT products, also called *artefacts*. Types of IT artefacts include (March & Smith, 1995):

- **Constructs:** the concepts or vocabulary used in a particular IT-related domain. For example, the notions of entities, objects or data flows.
- **Models:** combinations of constructs that represent a situation and are used to aid problem understanding and solution development. For example, a data flow diagram, a use case scenario or a storyboard.
- **Methods** (also called 'methodologies'): guidance on the models to be produced and process stages to be followed to solve problems using IT. They include formal, mathematical algorithms, commercialized and published methodologies such as Soft Systems Methodology (Checkland & Scholes, 1990) or Information Engineering (Martin, 1989), organizations' in-house procedure manuals and informal descriptions of practice derived from experience.
- **Instantiations:** a working system that demonstrates that constructs, models, methods, ideas, genres or theories can be implemented in a computer-based system.

A researcher following the design and creation research strategy could offer a construct, model, method or instantiation as a contribution to knowledge. Often the research outputs are a combination of these.

> ## " The ultimate goal of computer science and programming
>
> The art of designing artefacts to solve intricate problems. Some call it the art of constructive thinking. (Niklaus Wirth, Opening Keynote address, Proc. 7th annual SIGCSE Conference on Innovation & Technology in Computer Science Education, 24–28 June, Aarhus, Denmark, 2002.)   "

For many research projects, especially in computing, the research involves analysing, designing and developing a computer-based product such as a website, group support system or computer animation. These projects explore and exhibit the possibilities of digital technology. For such projects to be considered as research, rather than only an illustration of technical prowess, they should demonstrate not just technical skills but also academic qualities such as analysis, explanation, argument, justification and critical evaluation. They must also contribute to knowledge in some way. How such projects might contribute to knowledge depends on the role that the IT system plays. It can have one of three roles: the main focus of the research, a vehicle for something else, or a tangible end-product of a project where the focus is on the development *process*.

Examples of research projects where the IT application is the main focus and thus is itself a contribution to knowledge include:

- An IT application that uses IT in a new domain, which has not previously been automated. The researcher argues for using IT in this new domain and the IT system developed demonstrates the technical viability of the argument.
- An IT application that incorporates a new theory. Often such a theory is new to computing, but is drawn from another discipline where it is an established theory. For example:

  - a theory on the psychology of colour in different cultures applied to a user interface design;
  - an educational theory incorporated into a computer-aided learning package;
  - an economic theory on consumer behaviour applied to an e-commerce site.

The researcher argues for the relevance or utility of this theory and demonstrates that it can be incorporated into a computer-based system.

- An IT application that expresses or explores novel artistic ideas, for example, how feelings of fear or wonder might be induced via computer art. The researcher examines how this has been tried in previous artistic works (conventional and digital) and then explores the artistic and technical viability of their alternative ideas using computer technology.

Examples of research projects where the IT application is a vehicle for something else include:

- A project where the contribution to knowledge is based on a literature review and/or field research, but the conclusions drawn from this work are illustrated via a prototype IT application. For example, a literature review to derive a set of principles for using IT to enhance democracy, an analysis of whether some political parties' websites currently conform to these principles, followed by a prototype application for a mythical political party that does demonstrate application of the principles.
- An IT application is developed, but the contribution to knowledge is based on what happens next, that is, the research examines what happens when the computer application is used in a real-life context. For example, a computer-aided learning package could be developed, but the primary focus of the research is on how the students and teachers then use and adapt it in the classroom.
- An IT application is developed using two different software programs, so that the researcher can compare and evaluate the different programs. The comparison and evaluation is the contribution to knowledge.
- An IT application presents and explains the results of a literature and/or field research. For example, a project's contribution to knowledge is based on a literature survey that examines what has been published about the use of IT in human resources departments: the applications used, critical success factors, views of individual managers, and so on. The literature review is then presented via a multimedia CD-ROM for a defined target audience. This way of using an IT product is sometimes used by students who do not want to concentrate on technical development, but whose institution requires that there be a technical implementation element to their research project.

Examples of research projects where an IT application is a tangible end-product, but the focus is on the development *process* include:

- An IT application is developed in order to examine the use of a particular development method. For example, in order fully to understand and illustrate an object-oriented approach to the development of web-based systems, a prototype system is analysed, designed and implemented using object-oriented techniques. Here, the contribution to knowledge is what is learnt about the use of the object-oriented approach that wasn't known before.

- A research project analyses existing development approaches and then argues for, develops and illustrates the use of a new, better approach for developing IT applications. For example, the contribution to knowledge might be a new construct, technique, model, algorithm, process model, diagramming notation or development method, demonstrated via the analysis and development of an IT system.
- A research project investigates, compares and evaluates two or more development methods (or constructs, or models) by following these methods to analyse, design and implement an IT application. The contribution to knowledge is the critical comparison and evaluation.

The design and creation strategy might be the only research strategy employed, where the IT artefact is itself the main contribution to knowledge – as in much computer science research. Alternatively, design and creation may be just one strategy within the overall research methodology, used alongside, for example, a case study (see Chapter 10) or experiments (see Chapter 9). IS researchers, in particular, are usually keen to investigate what happens when a new IT artefact is used in a real-life context by real people, and software engineering researchers are also becoming increasingly interested in empirical research into the real-world use of their IT artefacts. Both these groups of researchers might therefore use a design and creation strategy followed by another strategy to understand and evaluate the IT artefact in use.

Planning and Conducting Design and Creation Research

Whatever IT artefact is being produced, for whatever purpose, and whether the design and creation research strategy is the only strategy or one of several, the design and creation activities must be based on the established principles of systems development. In this section, we look at some of the issues you must address when conducting design and creation as a research strategy.

The design and creation process: Learning via making

Typically design and creation is a problem-solving approach. It uses an iterative process involving five steps (Vaishnavi & Kuechler, 2004): awareness, suggestion, development, evaluation and conclusion.

- **Awareness** is the recognition and articulation of a problem, which can come from studying the literature where authors identify areas for further research, or reading about new findings in another discipline, or from practitioners or clients expressing the need for something, or from field research or from new developments in technology.

- **Suggestion** involves a creative leap from curiosity about the problem to offering a very tentative idea of how the problem might be addressed.
- **Development** is where the tentative design idea is implemented. How this is done depends on the kind of IT artefact being proposed. For example, an algorithm might need the construction of a formal proof. A new user interface embodying novel theories about human cognition will require software development. A systems development method will need to be captured in a manual that can then be followed in a systems development project. A new approach in digital art might require the development of an art portfolio tracing the development of the artist's creative ideas.
- **Evaluation** examines the developed artefact and looks for an assessment of its worth and deviations from expectations.
- **Conclusion** is where the results from the design process are consolidated and written up, and the knowledge gained is identified, together with any loose ends – unexpected or anomalous results that cannot yet be explained and could be the subject of further research.

These steps are not followed in a rigid, step-wise fashion. Instead they form a more fluid, iterative cycle. Thinking about a suggested tentative solution leads to greater awareness of the nature of the problem; development of a design idea leads to increased understanding of the problem and new, alternative tentative solutions; discovering that a design doesn't work according to the researcher's expectations leads to new insights and theories about the nature of the problem, and so on. In this way, the researcher using a design and creation strategy learns through *making*.

Systems development methodology

As discussed already, many computing research projects involve the development of a computer-based product. In your research report, you must explain and document how you worked through the stages of analysis, design, implementation and testing, that is, your *systems development method* or *methodology* (both terms are used). This is not to be confused with your *research methodology* – the combination of research strategies and data generation methods that you use in your research project (see Figure 8.1).

You can choose to use a published systems development methodology such as WISDM (Web Information Systems Development Methodology) (Vidgen, Avison, Wood, & Wood-Harper, 2002), December's web development methodology (December, 2005), Information Engineering (Martin, 1989) or SSM (Soft Systems Methodology) (Checkland & Scholes, 1990). Or you can use your own systems development

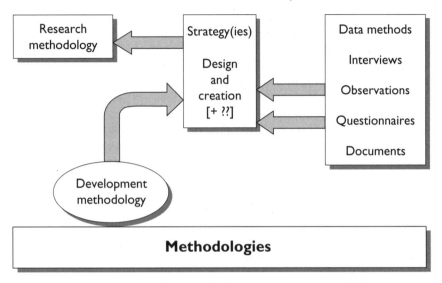

Figure 8.1   Research methodology and development methodology

methodology, possibly unique to this one project, drawing upon modelling techniques and process stages with which you are already familiar, such as UML (Rumbaugh, Jacobson, & Booch, 1999) or structured methods (Yourdon, 1989). What is important is that you use an appropriate combination of text, diagrams, models, mathematics and code segments so that the readers can see how you moved from your initial awareness of a problem to increasing understanding, to possible design solutions, to a bug-free implemented computer-based product. Equally, your final system and report should show *traceability*: readers should be able to look at your final implemented product and trace back to see how this implementation is related to the design and analysis stages. For example, if an implemented system includes a relational database with 25 tables, it should be possible to see how all 25 tables are related to an earlier entity-relationship diagram.

Some systems development methodologies involve what is called a *waterfall model* of development. That is, all analysis is completed before moving onto design, and all design is completed before moving onto implementation. The argument for such an approach is that each stage is carried out thoroughly so it is more likely to be correct, before moving onto the next stage. However, for complex systems development it may not be possible to do a full analysis first. As already explained, often it is only through designing and implementing a possible solution that increased understanding of the original problem is obtained.

An alternative approach is therefore to use *prototyping*. A first version, or prototype system, is analysed, designed and implemented. The understanding from this is used to modify the analysis and design models and create a revised system prototype. Again the understanding gained is used to revisit the analysis, design and implementation stages, and so on. The prototype is gradually modified until a satisfactory implementation is produced. An advantage of this approach is that it is not necessary to fully understand a problem before exploring tentative solutions. It can also be reassuring to the researcher to have a tangible implemented system fairly early on, even if it needs some modifications. With the waterfall model approach, on the other hand, the implementation stage may only be reached as the researcher's time is running out. Many researchers therefore prefer the prototyping approach. However, if you choose this approach, your report must still make clear how the implemented solution emerged from repeated cycles of analysis, design and implementation and that there is a thought-through design rationale, otherwise you will be accused of just hacking together an implementation and sloppy development work.

'Normal' design and creation versus design and creation research

If your research has the development of a computer-based product as its main focus, you must be able to refute the criticism that your work is only 'normal' design and creation work as practised in industry, and not 'research'.

As explained earlier, a research project based on design and creation should demonstrate not just technical skills, but also academic qualities such as analysis, explanation, argument, justification and critical evaluation, and it must also create some new knowledge. Often in a typical industry-based design and creation project, the less that is learned, the more successful the project is considered to be. If all goes according to plan, using existing knowledge and avoiding backtracking and changes of design, then the project is seen as successful. For a research project, on the other hand, the need for backtracking and revising ideas, leading to interesting new knowledge, is welcome. Often industrial practitioners will identify the risky and uncertain parts of a project and deliberately leave them out, because they don't know how to tackle them, or cannot within the time available. Similarly undergraduate students may choose to concentrate on the straightforward parts of their development projects and omit what they don't yet know how to do. A researcher, on the other hand, will focus on the risky and uncertain areas, because if the uncertainties are successfully tackled, it will lead to new knowledge. You can therefore claim to be doing research rather than 'normal' design and creation through the novelty and risk-taking of your software product or the process used. You can further strengthen your claim by justifying your design rationale in terms of its theoretical underpinnings via the literature, mathematical logic and formal methods and/or data from the field. You should also be able to say how the knowledge acquired from your design and creation research could be generalizable to other situations.

How far do you go?

Some institutions require that a project demonstrate the whole development life cycle: analysis, design, implementation and testing. However, such a requirement is more common at undergraduate and masters level than at PhD level.

At PhD level, a design and creation project might involve analysis and design for a new type of IT system, but no implementation need be done, because the implementation is relatively trivial once an effective design has been produced. For other PhD projects it may be necessary to develop a design into an implementation, because the researcher wants to study what happens next when it is used in the real world. However, the programming work need not be carried out by the PhD researcher, but can be delegated to someone else, because the coding is straightforward and therefore not in itself a contribution to knowledge.

It is rare for any IT system developed in design and creation research to be a full-grown system that can be used immediately by practitioners without any further researcher involvement. Instead, the system's role is usually that of a prototype to illustrate ideas and define and demonstrate the constructs, models and methods by which efficient and effective working systems (involving both people and technology) might be achieved.

Evaluation

Having developed an IT artefact, it must be evaluated. There are many criteria for evaluating an IT artefact: functionality, completeness, consistency, accuracy, performance, reliability, usability, accessibility, aesthetics, entertainment, fit with organization, and so on. The criteria you use depend on the reason you developed the artefact in the first place – they will be related to your original research objectives. The evaluation can lead to conclusions about the design process as well as the design product, and may suggest that further modifications to either or both are needed.

Concentrating on the technical aspects of a system, black box and white box testing can be used to identify bugs and check out execution paths. Black box testing, as its name suggests, treats a program or program module as a black box, which cannot be looked into, and concentrates on testing whether particular inputs to this black box produce the anticipated outputs. White box testing looks at the program code and tests different pathways through it, for example, to make sure that the system behaves correctly when a 'repeat … until …' command is reached. Mathematical techniques can be used to evaluate costs, response times, mean time between failures, data recall and data precision. For safety critical or mission critical systems, formal verification procedures can be used to check a program for correctness. Sometimes logic and argument (rhetoric) can be used to build a convincing case for the artefact's quality, for example by showing how it meets existing international standards for such an artefact.

Many computing researchers do not evaluate whether the artefact does work in a real-life context. Their objective is to show '*proof of concept*' only, via a functioning prototype. The prototype's purpose is to show that the researcher's design solution has certain properties or that, under certain conditions, it behaves in a particular way. For example, if previously it was not known whether a particular process could be automated, a working prototype demonstrates that it is indeed feasible. Sometimes the implementation will need to be compared with existing technical implementations to demonstrate an improvement. In some cases, an implementation may be run using a set of test data and the results compared with those produced by a human expert analysing the same test data.

Some computing researchers go further, and evaluate the artefact in use, but in a restricted context, in order to establish '*proof by demonstration*'. For example:

- The researchers try out the artefact on students rather than real-life practitioners.
- The researchers use the artefact on a carefully restricted task that may not scale up to a typical industry-based task.
- The researchers carry out a user evaluation survey of potential, rather than actual, end-users, often involving only a small number of respondents meaning proper statistical analysis is not feasible.

IS researchers, on the other hand, may find that their IT artefact is expected to undergo *real-world evaluation* – its use is examined in a real-life context, and not just a rather artificial university context. For this, you will need one of the other strategies described in this book, for example, a case study (see Chapter 10) or a survey (Chapter 7) or, especially for a new method, action research (Chapter 11).

As explained in Chapter 1, in software engineering research there is increasing recognition of the need not just for technical evaluation of an IT artefact, but also for empirical evaluation in a real-life context. In future, the software engineering research community *might* therefore expect real-world evaluation of IT artefacts to the same level as the IS research community.

You should discuss with your supervisor how much, if any, real-world evaluation will be expected for your IT artefact. Of course, the more that is required, the more time you will have to allocate for it in your project schedule.

Use of data generation methods

Design and creation research often makes use of the data generation methods discussed in this book: interviews, observations, questionnaires and documents (see Chapters 13–16). For example, interviews and questionnaires are often used to find out from a client or intended end-users the requirements specification or design brief. They can also be used to find out how people evaluate the IT artefact you develop. You might use observations to watch how people currently work, before proposing, designing and implementing a computer-based system to support them. You might also study existing documents, such as an organization's procedures manual or people's job descriptions, to understand the context in which your proposed IT artefact will be expected to work. There will certainly be your own researcher-generated documents, such as analysis and design models, testing logs, user guides and your personal journal – all of these help to document and capture your design and creation research strategy.

It has to be said that many researchers who choose to use the design and creation strategy pay little attention to using properly the various data generation methods. Many interviews are inadequately documented and analysed, for example, and many questionnaires are poorly designed. Perhaps it is too easy to be seduced by the thrill of creating an IT artefact, so other aspects of the research are overlooked. You would be well advised, therefore, to read and act upon the advice in the relevant chapters on data generation methods in this book.

Having a client

Some research projects are sponsored by a client. Having a client means that someone other than you thinks the research topic is worthwhile. A client can also offer suggestions of problems drawn from the world outside academia, which will enhance the likely relevance of your research outcomes. However, differences between clients' interests and researchers' interests can sometimes cause difficulties and conflict. This is a particular danger for design and creation research leading to the development of a new computer-based system.

Problems can arise when the client is only interested in the tangible IT product, usually a computer system, and is just tolerating your need and desire to create some new knowledge as well as a new system. It is essential that the different goals of the client and the researcher are identified and discussed, so that some way of accommodating both interests is found. The client may ask you to abandon one area of development in order to have an IT system that has fewer functions but is available for use. You, on the other hand, may think that particular area of development is the most interesting and the one most likely to lead to new knowledge. There can also be difficulties if the researcher runs out of time and realizes that it is necessary to stop working on the computer system in order to write up the academic report, but the client wants the system to be finished. These possible scenarios should be discussed at the beginning of the project. The priority of academic issues over practical issues should be agreed at the outset – otherwise there is a danger that your work will produce something useful for the client but not for your academic qualification or career. Once a project is underway, if client problems occur, you should discuss them with your supervisor, who, if necessary, will remind your client of the agreed priority of academic issues.

There must also be agreement before the project starts about intellectual property rights and confidentiality – often set out in a written contract. You might develop an amazing new system doing something never before achieved, but if you are not able to discuss its design and development in your thesis or conference or journal articles, then it is of little use to your academic goals. Find out if your university has standard agreements to be used that set out 'who owns what, and who can write about what'.

Finally, you may find that a client is willing to let you develop an IT system to address a problem but does not want you to evaluate the system in use in the organization, perhaps because of fears of disrupting the work of the employees. This is probably not a problem for many computing researchers, who, as we have seen, will be happy to demonstrate just a 'proof of concept' via the IT system. But it could cause a problem, particularly for those in IS, where reviewers and examiners often expect to see an evaluation of a system in its real-life context. Again, this is something you should think about, and obtain agreement on, before undertaking a design and creation project with a client.

Creative Computing and Digital Art

In recent years, the potential of computers has been explored by artists, who use digital technology to question or illuminate aspects of our world. They have used multimedia systems, computer visualization and computer music to express their creative ideas via digital technologies. A new branch of computing research is therefore emerging: digital art, where the artist's own creative work forms, as a point of origin or reference, a significant part of the intellectual enquiry. Of course, any design and creation activity involves creative, artistic work. Rather than a binary divide between IT developers and digital artists, there is therefore a spectrum, with mathematically oriented computer scientists at one end and expression- and aesthetics-oriented artists at the other.

Different approaches to IT development

One way of defining different approaches to the design and creation of IT artefacts might be as follows:

- **Artists** develop IT artefacts to challenge or change people's individual perceptions.
- **IS researchers** develop IT artefacts to make people more efficient or effective.
- **Computing** researchers develop IT artefacts to explore the functional capabilities of digital technology.

Do you agree or can you suggest a better way of characterizing the differences?

For digital artists, there is less emphasis on the use of good engineering principles involving modelling, documentation and testing, so that their IT artefact will be reliable and maintainable. It may not matter if a piece of digital art is a bit flaky and prone to crashing under certain conditions. Nor is it likely that someone else will need to come along and modify a piece of digital art in the future, so thorough documentation is less important. Nevertheless, if the production of digital art is to be considered as research, it is still important that readers can see how the artist moved from initial awareness of an idea or a potential through explorations of alternative artistic expressions, through to the final piece or portfolio or performance. The documents produced by the artist therefore become important data generation methods: the storyboards, moodboards, personal reflective journal, and so on.

As well as giving a performance or providing a corpus of creative work, the researcher-artist is expected to write a thesis or article that analyses and contextualizes the work as a contribution to knowledge. This should show how it relates to and extends what has previously been done by artists or analysed by art critics and art historians. The work should also be evaluated. Evaluation of an artistic piece of work is often more subjective than the technical evaluation of a software artefact. Evaluation of digital art is further hampered, since the rhetoric and assessment criteria for its aesthetic, social or economic value are still being developed. The artist can give a personal reflection and evaluation of the artwork. Further evaluation can come from, for example, staging an exhibition and surveying the audience's reactions via interviews, questionnaires and observations, and from art critics' reviews.

The Internet and Design and Creation Research

Design and creation research has led to the development and spread of the Internet and the World-Wide Web. Such research led to the Arpanet, which became the Internet, and Tim Berners-Lee's proposal for a document transfer system, which became the World Wide Web, and to the subsequent development of e-commerce systems, online communities, Intranets, extranets, software bots, web development methods, and so on – the list goes on and on. There are still many potential research topics involving design and creation research on some aspect of the Internet or web. Current areas of interest include mobile or ubiquitous computing, the semantic web, grid computing and web engineering.

However, you should also be aware of possible difficulties if you want to do design and creation research on some aspect of the Internet. Because institutions need to protect their networks from intruders and viruses, you may find it difficult to develop a working version of your proposed system. Your university or sponsoring client will be reluctant to allow you to do anything that might breach their system's firewall or otherwise interfere with the smooth running of their network systems. You might find you have to set up your own home computer as a webserver in order to demonstrate an IT artefact – making the prototype less realistic and raising questions about your work's scalability. Also, if you are designing for the Internet and web, rather than an organization's Intranet, your users will be less accessible – they could be anywhere in the world – and you will not know many, if any, of them. This means you will have to think carefully about how you will gain understanding of your users and obtain their evaluations of your IT artefact. To help you, all the other chapters in this book on strategies and data generation methods include a section on how to use that approach over the Internet.

Examples of Design and Creation Research in IS and Computing

Many of the modelling techniques and design processes routinely taught to IS and computing students were originally proposed by researchers using the design and creation research strategy. For example, data modelling, structured analysis, object-oriented programming and software inspections. As indicated earlier, it is the normal form of research for computing. It is therefore difficult to pick out a few examples – there are too many to choose from! Some recent examples include:

- Costagliola, Deufemia and Polese (2004) present a framework for modelling visual notations (such as entity-relationship diagrams, flow charts, class diagrams). The IT artefact of their research is therefore a *model*. They claim this framework/ model will enable the next generation of CASE tools to support systems modelling and the syntactic and semantic correction of any models produced. They found their argument on formal logic and mathematics, and show 'proof of concept' by explaining how the framework has been incorporated into a computer-based system to model some diagrammatic notations that is, an *instantiation.*
- Mukherjee, Ramakrishnan and Kifer (2004) propose a new *construct*: 'semantic bookmarks'. These are aimed at visually handicapped users of the web. Such users are presented with the logical structure of a web page organized around an 'ontology', or set of semantic concepts relevant to a particular domain. If a particular concept is of interest, a user can ask for it to be bookmarked. Unlike the bookmarks provided in conventional browsers aimed at non-visually impaired users, semantic bookmarks are not closely tied to the physical structure of webpages, and so are resilient even if a webpage changes structurally. The researchers argue the need for semantic bookmarks and explain how they might be used. They

evaluate the concept via 'proof by demonstration': they have developed an *instantiation* that supports semantic bookmarks, and they discuss its use by just four users accessing three websites.

- Petinot et al. (2004) describe an *instantiation*. They explain CiteSeer, an automated service that finds academic publications on the Web and allows users to browse the documents and follow links to other documents cited in them. Their design and creation research focussed on how to integrate CiteSeer into the emerging semantic Web. The article explains the methods and functions incorporated into a new system, CiteSeer-API, which sits on top of the existing CiteSeer software. No evaluation of the system in use is provided.

IS research has also seen a lot of design and creation work. One noticeable strand in the 1980s and early 1990s was a focus on systems development methodologies, that is, new IT *methods* were proposed and evaluated, for example, SSM (Checkland, 1981), ETHICS (Mumford, 1983) and many more. From the mid 1990s, IS research seemed to focus more on the *use* of IT artefacts in organizations and the implications of such use, with a shift from design and creation to managerial and organizational issues. However, recently there have been calls for IS researchers to return to exploring the IT that underlies all IS research and therefore to do more design and creation research (Hevner, March, Park, & Ram, 2004; Orlikowski & Iacono, 2001; Vaishnavi & Kuechler, 2004).

Digital art as research is only now emerging. Some examples of web-based art can be found in, for example, Daniel Brown's work (www.danielbrowns.com), London Design Museum's Designer of the Year 2004. Some of his original experimental works are held at the San Francisco Museum of Modern Art.

Evaluating Design and Creation Research

Advantages of the design and creation research strategy include:

- You have something tangible to show for your efforts – some kind of IT artefact – rather than just abstract theories or other knowledge.
- It appeals to people who enjoy technical and creative development work.
- It is the normally expected mode of research in some computing areas such as computer science and software engineering.
- Because the use of IT and computers is still relatively new in many domains, and because the technology is advancing rapidly, there is plenty of scope for proposing and developing new IT artefacts and therefore making a contribution to knowledge.

Disadvantages of the design and creation research strategy include:

- You may be challenged to justify why your work is not just 'normal' design and creation.
- It is risky if you do not have the necessary technical or artistic skills. Enthusiasm is no substitute.
- It can be difficult to generalize to different settings from the use of an IT artefact in a single situation.
- The (apparent) success of an IT artefact may depend on the researchers being present – once they've gone, an IT method or system may not work so effectively.
- It may produce perishable research. Rapid advances in technology can invalidate the research results before they have been tried out in a real-life context or even before they have been written up and published.

Use the 'Evaluation Guide' below to help you analyse and evaluate research based on the design and creation strategy. If there is insufficient information for you to answer some questions, you should not completely reject the research report, but you should treat the findings with caution and be wary about relying on the report for evidence.

EVALUATION GUIDE: DESIGN AND CREATION

1   What kind of IT artefact(s) did the researchers design and create? (Construct, model, method, instantiation?)
2   What makes this piece of work research and not 'normal' design and development work?
3   What information is given about the researchers' development methodology, if any? Is this enough information? Is it an appropriate methodology?
4   Do the researchers discuss all stages of the systems development life cycle, or just some stages? Are enough stages discussed, or too many?
5   Do the researchers describe their use of any data generation methods during their design and creation work? Is the description satisfactory?
6   What do the researchers tell you about how they evaluated their IT artefact? (Proof of concept? Proof by demonstration? Real-world evaluation?) What evaluation criteria do they use? Are these appropriate?
7   Do the researchers use their results to make generalizations about the use of their IT artefact in other situations? Is this appropriate?
8   What limitations in their design and creation strategy do the researchers recognize?
9   Given your current state of knowledge, can you identify other flaws or omissions in the researchers' reporting of their design and creation strategy?
10 Overall, how effectively do you think the design and creation strategy has been reported and used?

PRACTICAL WORK

1   Obtain an issue of *Communications of the ACM,* a highly-rated computing journal. Answer the following questions:

    a   How many of the research articles are based on the design and creation research strategy?

    b   How many of these articles propose a new construct? How many a model, method or instantiation?

    c   How many of the research articles are based on another of the research strategies described in this book?

2   Now repeat the exercise above using a highly rated IS journal, such as *MIS Quarterly* or *Information Systems Research.*

3   Answer the questions above about the dissertations or theses recently produced by research students in your department. What conclusions can you draw from your answers in these three exercises?

4   Practise analysing and evaluating research based on the design and creation strategy. Study a piece of research which used this strategy. Answer the questions in the 'Evaluation Guide' above, using the material in this chapter to help you.

FURTHER READING

March and Smith (1995) is a widely cited article that discusses the different types of IT artefacts that can be the products of design research, and contrasts design research with natural science research. Hevner et al. (2004) provide a conceptual framework and guidelines for IS researchers on understanding, performing and evaluating design research. They do assume that any IT artefact is aimed at a business environment, which, of course, is not always the case, but their discussion of the relationship between what they call 'design science' and 'behavioural science', is very useful, as are their seven guidelines for design research. Hughes and Wood-Harper (1999) discuss how systems developers working in organizations can be seen as researchers. Vaishnavi and Kuechler (2004) provide an online working document on the ISWorld website that discusses design research and its philosophical underpinnings. The document includes a resources section with a growing bibliography of references on design research in general as well as design research in IS. Another useful bibliography of references on design research in many disciplines – including computing – with commentary on the most popular references, is a special issue of the *Visible Language* journal (VL, 2002).

Overviews of digital art and Internet art are given by Paul (2003) and Greene (2004). Publications on digital arts media and their relationship to earlier media such as painting, photography, film, television and oral story-telling include Manovich (2001), Bolter and Grusin (2000), Lunenfeld (2000) and Murray (1998). Sunderland University (UK) has a webpage, ▶

▶ 'Materials for Art Practice-led researchers' (www.sunderland.ac.uk/~as0bgr/learnmat.html), that is useful for digital art researchers. The Research Training Initiative (RTI) is a project based at Birmingham Institute of Art and Design. It aims to develop and support research education and training in art, design and media and to encourage debate about research skills, methods and approaches (www.biad.uce.ac.uk/research/rti/). Its website includes an online journal, *Research Issues in Art, Design and Media.*

References

Bolter, D.J., & Grusin, R. (2000). *Remediation: Understanding new media.* Cambridge, MA: MIT Press.

Checkland, P. (1981). *Systems thinking, systems practice.* Chichester: Wiley.

Checkland, P., & Scholes, J. (1990). *Soft systems methodology in action.* Chichester: Wiley.

Costagliola, G., Deufemia, V., & Polese, G. (2004). A framework for modeling and implementing visual notations with applications to software engineering. *ACM Transactions on Software Engineering and Methodology, 13*(4), 431–487.

December, J. (2005). *Web development.* Retrieved 27 April 2005 from www.december.com/web/develop.html

Greene, R. (2004). *Internet art.* London: Thames & Hudson.

Hevner, A.R., March, S.T., Park, J., & Ram, S. (2004). Design science in information systems research. *MIS Quarterly, 28*(1), 75–105.

Hughes, J., & Wood-Harper, A.T. (1999). Systems development as a research act. *Journal of Information Technology, 14*(1), 83–94.

Lunenfeld, P. (Ed.). (2000). *The digital dialectic: New essays on new media* (paperback ed.). Cambridge, MA: MIT Press.

Manovich, L. (2001). *The language of new media.* Cambridge, MA: MIT Press.

March, S., & Smith, G. (1995). Design and natural science research on information technology. *Decision Support Systems, 15*, 251–266.

Martin, J. (1989). *Information engineering.* Englewood Cliffs, NJ: Prentice-Hall.

Mukherjee, S., Ramakrishnan, I.V., & Kifer, M. (2004). Semantic bookmarking for non-visual web access. In J.A. Jacko & A. Seers (Eds.), *Assets'04 (6th International Conference on Computers and Accessibility)* (pp. 185–192). Atlanta, GA: ACM.

Mumford, E. (1983). *Designing human systems.* Manchester: Manchester Business School.

Murray, J. (1998). *Hamlet on the holodeck: The future of narrative in cyberspace.* Cambridge, MA: MIT Press.

Orlikowski, W.J., & Iacono, C. (2001). Desperately seeking the 'IT' in IT research – A call to theorizing the IT artifact. *Information Systems Research, 12*(2), 121–134.

Paul, C. (2003). *Digital art.* London: Thames & Hudson.

Petinot, Y., Giles, C.L., Bhatnagar, V., Teregowda, P.B., Han, H., & Councill, I. (2004). A service-oriented architecture for digital libraries. In *ICSOC'04 (2nd International Conference on Service Oriented Computing)* (pp. 263–268). New York: ACM.

Rumbaugh, J., Jacobson, I., & Booch, G. (1999). *The Unified Modeling Language reference manual*. Englewood Cliffs, NJ: Prentice Hall.

Vaishnavi, V., & Kuechler, W. (2004). *Design research in information systems*. Retrieved 27 April 2005 from www.isworld.org/Researchdesign/drisISworld.htm

Vidgen, R., Avison, D.E., Wood, B., & Wood-Harper, T. (2002). *Developing web information systems*. Oxford: Butterworth-Heinemann.

VL. (2002). An annotated design research bibliography: By and for the design community. *Visible Language, 36*(2), 97–240.

Yourdon, E. (1989). *Modern structured analysis*. Englewood Cliffs, NJ: Yourdon Press/Prentice-Hall.

9 Experiments

In this chapter you will learn about:

- what is meant by an experimental research strategy;
- issues to address in planning and performing experimental research;
- how experiment-based research might be applied to the Internet;
- how experiments have been used in IS and computing;
- the advantages and disadvantages of experiment-based research;
- analysing and evaluating experiment-based research.

Defining Experiments

In everyday language, we often speak of doing an experiment when we mean we will try something out and find out what happens. For example, I wondered if taking a different route to work would reduce my journey time. Yesterday I carried out an 'experiment' to find out – I took the different route and timed my journey. It took me 10 minutes less than my normal average journey, so I *might* conclude that my experiment showed the new route was quicker. However, my experiment could be criticized. How can I be certain that there were no other factors affecting yesterday's journey that might have caused my shorter journey time? Did I set off for work at exactly the same time as normal, or was my departure later than usual, so I missed the rush hour traffic and had a quicker journey? Was it the first day of the school holidays, so there was less traffic on the roads? Had an accident occurred on a road feeding into my route, so fewer cars were able to join my route? Had there been an item on the radio warning of possible disruptions on my route and advising drivers to take a different road? Academic researchers would therefore criticize my experiment because I had not paid attention to the many variables that could affect my journey, and so I am not justified in saying that my new route *caused* my shorter journey time.

In academic research, an experiment is a strategy that investigates cause and effect relationships, seeking to prove or disprove a causal link between a factor and an observed outcome. It is often associated with research in the physical sciences (for example, physics, chemistry and metallurgy) and is at the heart of the scientific method and positivism (see Chapter 19). Researchers start by developing a theory about their topic of interest, which leads to a statement based on the theory that can be tested empirically via an experiment. This statement is of the form 'Factor A causes B', and is known as a *hypothesis*. For example:

- Hypothesis: the Watson–Klein–Bloggs algorithm enables quicker data processing than our current algorithm.
- Hypothesis: smoking cigarettes causes lung cancer.
- Hypothesis: students pay more attention in lectures if you don't give them handouts.

An experiment is then designed to prove or disprove the hypothesis. All factors that might affect the results are excluded from the study, other than the one factor that is thought to cause a particular outcome. The experiment is run and careful measurements or other observations are made of the outcomes. If the researchers are confident that no other factor could have caused the observed results, their hypothesis that factor A causes outcome B is proven. However, even the most carefully designed laboratory-based experiment might have been contaminated by some unrecognized other factor. Good researchers would not therefore draw firm conclusions from experiments until they have been repeated many times by both themselves and other researchers. (This need for *repeatability* of experiments and outcomes is discussed further in Chapter 19.)

A research strategy based on experiments is typically characterized by:

- Observation and measurement. The researchers make precise and detailed observation of outcomes and changes that occur when a particular factor is introduced or removed.
- A process of (1) observation or measurement of a factor; (2) manipulation of circumstances; and (3) re-observation or re-measurement of the factor to identify any changes.
- Proving or disproving a relationship between two or more factors.
- Identification of causal factors. The researchers do not just identify that two factors appear to be linked, that is, they occur at the same time or always happen in sequence. The researchers aim to discover which factor is the cause (called the 'independent variable') and which the effect (called the 'dependent variable(s)').
- Explanation and prediction. The researchers are able to *explain* the causal link between two factors by means of the theory from which their hypothesis was

derived or, in some cases, by means of a new theory that they propose. They are able to *predict* future events if their experiment proves that a factor will always cause a particular outcome.

- Repetition. Experiments are typically repeated many times, and under varying conditions, to be certain that the observed/measured outcomes are not caused by some other factor, for example, faulty equipment.

Warning: Terms and definitions

Note that a few writers use the term 'experiment' to mean *any* piece of field research including surveys and case studies, and so on. They use the term 'formal experiment' to mean the kind of experimental research described in this chapter.

In this book an experiment is defined as a particular kind of research strategy that aims to isolate cause and effect by manipulation of what is thought to be the causal, or independent, variable and measurement of its effect on the dependent variable(s).

Planning and Conducting Experiments

When designing an experiment you have to think about the hypothesis to be tested, the variables to be controlled and measured, and internal and external validity. There are also different kinds of experiments: true experiments, quasi experiments and uncontrolled trials. All of these are explained in this section.

Hypotheses

An experiment is based on a hypothesis to be tested. A hypothesis is a statement that has not yet been tested empirically (that is, by gathering field data) but for which it is *possible* to devise empirical tests that will provide clear evidence to support it or reject it. It is written as a kind of prediction, for example:

- When factor A occurs B will happen.
- An increase in D causes a decrease in C.
- Water will freeze when the temperature drops to 32 degrees Fahrenheit (0 degrees centigrade).

A hypothesis must be testable and it must always be possible to disprove, or falsify, the hypothesis. For example, the statement 'All squares have four sides of equal length and contain four right angles' is not falsifiable, (because something only gets called a square if it meets that definition) and so is not a hypothesis.

Independent and dependent variables

It is important to distinguish between *dependent* and *independent* variables. The independent variable affects one or more dependent variables: its size, number, length or whatever exists independently and is not affected by the other variable. A dependent variable changes as a result of changes to the independent variable (see the box below). An experiment will be based on manipulation of the independent variable to observe the changes in the dependent variable(s). You might introduce an independent variable into a situation, or remove one, or change the size of one. For example, the introduction of a new teaching and learning approach might lead to improved examination results. This could be investigated via an experiment, where the independent variable is the new approach and the dependent variable is the exam results.

Sometimes an experiment is designed to manipulate more than one independent variable. However, the more independent variables that are measured, the more complex the statistical analysis required. Unless you are already highly skilled in statistics, I recommend you stick to one independent variable, two at most.

Variables in experiments

Independent variable	Dependent variable
Cause	*Effect*

Controls

The aim of a research strategy based on experiments is to show that one factor *only* causes an observed change. The researcher therefore tries to control all the variables, either all at once or in a sequence of experiments so that in the end just one factor remains as the only viable cause of the observed change. For example, in the experiment mentioned above, to examine the link between a new teaching approach and examination results, it would be necessary for the examination and the marker to be exactly the same as before the introduction of the new approach, otherwise it is possible that an easier examination or a more generous marker caused the improved results. Ways of controlling variables that might affect your outcomes include:

- **Eliminate the factor from the experiment:** for example, if students are to be used as subjects in an experiment about how people can be helped to learn programming skills, it might be necessary to exclude from the study any students who have previous computing experience, to ensure that all the participants have comparable previous experience.
- **Hold the factor constant:** this is used if it is not possible to eliminate a factor from a situation. For example, if the age of the people participating in an experiment might have a possible effect on the results, choose participants who are all the same age.
- **Use random selection of subjects:** if sufficient research subjects are chosen on a random basis, any factors associated with individuals that might interfere with the results (age, weight, gender, beliefs, and so on) should cancel each other out across the whole group.
- **Use control groups:** two groups are set up where the members are equally balanced: numbers, gender, age, previous relevant experience, and so on. For one group, the control group, no manipulation of the independent variable occurs. For the other, the independent variable is manipulated. Outcomes are measured for each group. Providing the groups have been chosen properly and the experiment designed and conducted properly, any variation in the outcomes between the two groups must be attributable to the variable that was manipulated.
- **Make the researchers and subjects blind:** don't panic – only metaphorically speaking. This approach tries to ensure people don't influence the results because of their expectations. When testing a new drug, medical researchers make sure that neither the researchers nor the patient subjects know who is receiving the drug under trial and who is receiving a placebo, a sugar-pill with no effect. In IS and computing, a computer program rather than a researcher could allocate test materials to groups, and researchers could measure outcomes and statistically analyse them without knowing which group was the control group and which received the manipulation.

Observation and measurement

The experiment strategy involves observations, making measurements of the dependent variables and observing change. Typical things which are observed and measured include:

- project data, for example, number of person-hours, cost, time to completion;
- self-report responses (for example, the subjects of the experiment complete a questionnaire about their feelings or how they rate a concept);
- behavioural counts – the number of times a certain kind of behaviour occurs (for example, number of times someone asks for help or accesses an online help system);
- number of bugs in a piece of code;
- time to process a file of data.

There should be a 'before' and 'after' measurement, (called *pre-test* and *post-test*) otherwise no change, which might be attributable to the manipulation of the independent variable, can be observed. For example, if a new computerized system for customer orders is introduced, it is not sufficient to measure customers' satisfaction with the system by means of a post-implementation questionnaire and then say that their satisfaction was *caused* by the new system. Customer satisfaction questionnaires would need to be completed before and after the introduction of the new system, to see if any change (hopefully improvement) is detected. (Of course, customer satisfaction could really be dependent on the quality of goods, speed of delivery, match to catalogue description, and so on.)

Normally quantitative data is used, because we need to measure change and use statistical analysis. Sometimes, we have to find a variable to measure that only approximates to what we really want to measure. For example, most IS and computing researchers do not have access or the expertise to use medical equipment that can measure stress levels in humans (for example, heart rate, blood pressure, skin conductance). Instead, we might have to ask people to fill out a questionnaire where they rate their stress levels on a scale of 1–10.

In IS and computing research, many outcome measures are related to each other. For example, productivity rates, code defects and delivery times. An experiment could be designed, for instance, to show that a new development method decreases the time taken to deliver the finished product. However, as well as the delivery time, it would be important to measure other factors, such as code defect rates or analyst stress, to see if they are adversely affected by adoption of the new method.

Results are usually analysed using statistics. It is important that you decide *before* carrying out an experiment exactly what will be measured and what statistical tests you will use on the results (some help is available in Chapter 17 on quantitative data analysis).

Internal validity

Your experiment has good *internal validity* if the measurements you obtain are indeed due to your manipulations of the independent variable, and not to any other factors. Common threats to the internal validity of experiments include:

- **Differences between the experimental and control group**: if they were different to start with, any differences you subsequently measure might not be attributable to your manipulation of the experimental group.
- **History**: events you do not notice interfere between your pre-test and post-test observations. For example, a researcher monitors stress levels in a group of systems analysts in an organization. After implementation of a new timesheet system the researcher measures again and finds a huge increase in stress. However, what the researcher does not know is that between the two tests, the organization

announced a large number of redundancies and plans to relocate their main offices to another country. Many of the analysts are concerned about their future, which is likely to have affected their stress levels.

- **Maturation**: participants change between tests. An obvious example is any experiment involving children. You could test 4-year-olds' competency at some task, and test them again at 6 years old – their performance is likely to have improved regardless of any manipulation you had done during the past 2 years. Maturation can also be a problem with experiments involving adults. The first test might give them practice, or cause boredom or fatigue, or alert them to the purpose of the study. Any of these effects might influence their performance in the second test.

- **Instrumentation**: faulty instruments used to measure the dependent variable will affect the results. This could be inaccurate measuring devices, or interviewers becoming more bored, or more practised, with experience.

- **Experimental mortality**: some subjects might drop out before a study is complete (not necessarily through death). They might leave the company, or be reassigned to another project, or use their right to withdraw from your research. Such dropouts often lead to bias in your remaining sample of participants. For example, if all the people who drop out are those who are most familiar with a particular technology in a company, you can no longer compare the use of that technology with any new technology. Similarly, some systems development projects may also 'die' – they are abandoned before completion. If you are collecting data about the historical costs of projects, to compare with current or future costs, how will you decide the costs of incomplete projects? Will you take their costs up to the time of abandonment, or estimate costs likely to be incurred if they had continued? It is always important to note who or what dropped out from your study, to see if they bias any subsequent analysis.

- **Reactivity and experimenter effects**: people might change their behaviour as a reaction to being tested. For example, someone tested for speed of data input might subsequently decide to undertake keyboard skills training, and show a much better result in later tests. Participants also often want to help the researcher, or to look good, and so try to give what they hope is the 'right' data – a particular concern when the researcher has more power than the subjects, for example, a teacher carrying out experiments on her students. Experimenters can also unconsciously bias the results they obtain, because of the way they interact with their participants. The psychology literature also discusses the ways in which experimenters' age, race or sex may affect the results they obtain from participants.

External validity

Your experiment has good *external validity* if your results are not unique to a particular set of circumstances but are *generalizable*, that is, the same results can be predicted for subsequent occasions and in other situations. Experimenters seek high external validity. The best way of demonstrating generalizability is to repeat the experiment many times in many situations. You can also design your experiment carefully so that it is likely to have high external validity. The main threat to external validity comes from non-representativeness – using a test case or sample of participants that is not typical of those found elsewhere. For example:

- **Over-reliance on special types of participants**: researchers often use students as the subjects of their experiments. But students are often younger and better educated than the general population, with different personal values and motivations. An experiment's results might be generalizable to other students, but not to people in general. Researchers have sometimes used students in experiments as substitutes for managers, but students have not had the same experiences as most managers and are not subject to the same work pressures and politics as managers, so again such experiments' results are unlikely to be generalizable to managers in organizations.

  Researchers often ask for volunteers to take part in their experiments, but the psychology literature shows that volunteers have certain characteristics that differentiate them from the general population (for example, more intelligent, more sociable, higher respect for scientific researchers). Again results found from an experiment involving volunteer participants may not be generalizable to a wider population.
- **Too few participants**: sometimes researchers do not have enough participants, so that it is impossible to show that a result is statistically significant.
- **Non-representative participants**: we have already seen that students and volunteers may not be representative of a wider population. You need to make sure that your group of participants is typical of the population that you wish to make statements about. You do this by selecting a representative sample by, for example, random sampling or stratified sampling (see Chapter 7 on surveys).
- **Non-representative test cases**: similarly, a researcher investigating, say, the efficiency of a new data processing algorithm, would need to ensure that data files on which an experiment is based are typical of the kinds of data files used in a real-life context.

Quasi- or field experiments

So far our discussion has concentrated on true experiments involving manipulation of the independent variable, pre- and post-test measurement of the dependent variable(s), and control or removal of all other variables. Such experiments usually have to take place in a laboratory so that all variables can be carefully controlled. However, a laboratory is, by its very nature, an artificial situation and may not be typical of situations found elsewhere. This is a particular problem for many IS researchers who are interested in the social context in which information systems are designed and used, and which is usually not replicable in a lab. But if researchers move to a more natural setting, they lose control over the variables and find it far harder to manipulate an independent variable. For example, IS researchers could not deliberately engineer the take-over of one business by another to monitor how that affected information flows within an organization. Some researchers therefore use *quasi-experiments* (quasi means 'as if'). They try to remain true to the spirit of classic laboratory experiments, but concentrate on observing events in real-life settings where there is a 'naturally occurring' experiment. Supposing, for example, a new user input device is invented, to replace the mouse and keyboard. Laboratory experiments may show that users find it comfortable and efficient. However, only long-term use will show whether it causes an increase in cases of repetitive strain injury (RSI). A quasi-experiment (also called a *field experiment*) could therefore be designed. Researchers examine how many cases of RSI were found over the previous five years and then monitor how many cases are found once the new input device is put into use. Any increase in RSI cases *could* be attributable to the new device. However, other causes might be possible, such as an increase in the amount of daily inputs required, or a change in the workforce with less attention given to training employees in how to sit and hold their arms correctly to avoid RSI. In quasi-experiments, there are often variables that the researchers cannot control and that might have caused the measured effect. They can never, therefore, establish cause and effect as conclusively as a true experiment.

The uncontrolled trial

Novice IS and computing researchers sometimes talk of the introduction of a new computer system or a new method as being an experiment. They are making a change and want to see what happens. However, such activity does not meet the tenets of either a true or a quasi-experiment. A systems developer could, for example, introduce a new systems development method. But how will they know the effect of the introduction of the new method? They need to measure something before the introduction of the new method, and again afterwards, and they need to measure and account for other things in the environment that might also cause any change (for example, other variables, the passing of time and so on). Without these measurements and analysis, the developer cannot say that the new method has caused any effect, so they are *not* conducting an experiment, they are conducting an uncontrolled trial, from which little can be concluded. (If you do want to explore what happens when a new computer system or a new method is introduced, case study and action research are often more appropriate strategies. See Chapters 10 and 11.)

Experimental designs

Many different kinds of experimental designs are possible. A particular design is chosen by researchers to ensure that any change in the dependent variable can only be attributable to the independent variable and nothing else. Some possible designs include:

- **One group, pre-test and post-test:** the participants' performance is measured (for example, data modelling ability), the researchers then apply some treatment (for example, a new method of teaching data modelling), they then measure the participants' performance again. By comparing the before and after scores, the researchers can assess the effects of the treatment. However, they cannot know whether time had an effect – the participants might just have got better over time anyway, without the researchers doing anything.
- **Static group comparison:** the participants are divided into two groups. The researchers apply the treatment to one group and do nothing to the other group. (For example, one class is taught by a traditional method, another via a new method of data modelling.) The performance of both groups is then measured. Differences in outcomes between the groups could be explained by the treatment. However, if participants were not assigned randomly to the two groups, any difference *might* be caused by other factors than the treatment – perhaps all the good students were in just one of the groups.
- **Pre-test/post-test control group:** participants are randomly assigned to one of two groups. Performance is measured before intervention – both groups should perform in the same way if the random assignment has been carried out correctly. Treatment is given to one group. Performance of both groups is again measured. Any difference is assumed to be caused by the treatment. However, pre-testing of the participants might have affected their subsequent performance.
- **Solomon four-group design:** this design controls for the possibility of pre-testing affecting subsequent performance, but it is expensive because of the number of participants needed. Participants are randomly assigned to four groups:

  - Group A is pre-tested, treated and post-tested.
  - Group B is pre-tested, receives no treatment, and post-tested.
  - Group C receives the treatment and is post-tested.
  - Group D receives no treatment and is tested.

Many more designs are possible – see, for example Field and Hole (2003).

The Internet and Experiments

Experiments are possible on how users interact with particular websites, that is, the experiments focus on human–computer interaction. You would need to be certain, however, that each user was seeing the website in the same way – remember different browsers can display websites differently, and some users will have configured their own browsers to their own preferences. It is often best to place the users in a laboratory where you could ensure that all saw the same.

Web-based experiments *are* possible. Usually participants are invited to visit a webpage where they are asked to follow a set of instructions. Their responses and actions are monitored using cookies or the log of a web-server. This means that much of the experiment is automated, and so needs low maintenance and is little affected by the researcher-experimenter. Such web-based experiments are useful where many participants are required, more than could be reached by the researcher in their own neighbourhood, or where specific kinds of subjects are needed, that are geographically dispersed.

Experiments involving computer programs that run over the Internet are, however, difficult because the Internet is not under the control of the researcher – connections, network availability, upload and download speeds, and so on. A researcher cannot even be certain that two emails sent almost simultaneously will take the same route over the Internet to their intended recipient. The difficulties are compounded for researchers who want to experiment on people via the Internet because these users have an offline existence as well as an online existence, and that offline existence cannot be monitored or controlled by the researcher. At best, therefore, researchers will probably have to content themselves with quasi-experiments, and recognize the limitations and possibility of alternative explanations for any cause–effect explanation they offer. For example, a researcher might monitor the number of incidents of flaming (abusive messages) in an online discussion group before and after the posting of a set of 'netiquette' rules. Any decrease might be attributable to the posting of the rules, but the researcher would have to look for other causes such as the main flamers not taking part in the discussion during the time of the experiment (on holiday? not interested? too busy?), or the topic under discussion being one where there was little disagreement anyway among the participants.

Examples of Experiments in IS and Computing Research

Experiments have been used extensively in IS and computing research to investigate human–computer interaction. For example, when the computer mouse was first introduced, a number of studies investigated users' speed of data input, comparing those using a mouse and drop-down menus and those using keyboard control keys.

More recent examples of the use of experiments in IS and computing research include:

- Zendler, Horn, Schwaertzel and Ploedereder (2001) investigated how an expert programmer retrieved reusable software components from a library. They compared different representation techniques used for software components, in order to see whether one representation technique was more effective in aiding retrieval than the other types. They only had one experimental subject, but in their article argue that such a single-case design can be a valid experimental approach.

- Smith, Keil and Depledge (2001) investigated the problem of 'runaway' information systems, where people in an organization are reluctant to report negative news about a project, so it continues, running over time and budget. They used an experiment strategy to find out what factors influence people's willingness to report bad news about a project. This experiment involved role-playing by business students – the researchers discuss whether they think this limits the generalizability of their findings.
- Fencott, van Schaik, Ling and Shafiullah (2002) investigated how users move around in a virtual environment. Their experiments were based in a computer laboratory where some psychology undergraduates were observed navigating around a virtual environment. Each subject was faced with four doors in the virtual environment and had free choice over which door to go through. The doors were identical, except that each had a single black circle moving across its surface in one of four directions: vertically, horizontally, diagonally up or diagonally down. Via experiment the researchers investigated whether a particular type of movement caused more people to use that particular door. A second experiment investigated whether the types of 'reward' found in the different rooms beyond each door induced people to stay longer in that room.

Evaluating Experiment-based Research

Advantages of experiments as a research strategy include:

- They are a well-established strategy, seen by many as the most 'scientific' and therefore most acceptable approach. Where people have not received any formal research methods training, this is often the only research strategy they know.
- They are the only research strategy that can prove causal relationships.
- Laboratory experiments permit high levels of precision in measuring outcomes and analysing the data.
- Laboratory experiments allow researchers to remain at their normal place of work, without the time and costs incurred in visiting field sites.

Disadvantages of experiments include:

- Laboratory experiments often create artificial situations, which are not comparable with real-world situations.
- It is often difficult or impossible to control all the relevant variables.

- It is often difficult to recruit a representative sample of participants.
- It may be necessary to conceal from the participants the purpose of the research, so that they do not skew the results by, for example, performing in the way they think you want them to. However, deception of participants is normally viewed as unethical (see Chapter 5).

Use the 'Evaluation Guide' below to help you analyse and evaluate experiment-based research. If there is insufficient information for you to answer some questions, you should not completely reject the research report, but you should treat the findings with caution and be wary about relying on the report for evidence.

EVALUATION GUIDE: EXPERIMENTS

1   Was a hypothesis or predicted outcome of the experiment clearly stated in the introduction to the research?
2   Was the research a true experiment, a quasi-experiment or an uncontrolled trial?
3   What information is given about the independent and dependent variables manipulated or measured in the study? What additional information would you like?
4   What information is given about any participants and how they were found? What additional information would you like?
5   What information is given about how representative the sample is of the wider population about which conclusions are drawn? Are you satisfied that the sample is representative?
6   What information is given about the apparatus and the process the researchers used to make measurements? What additional information would you like?
7   What limitations in their experiment strategy do the researchers recognize?
8   Given your current state of knowledge, can you identify other flaws or omissions in the researchers' reporting of their experiment?
9   Assuming their statistical analysis is correct, have the researchers convinced you that they have demonstrated cause and effect?
10 Overall, how effectively do you think the experiment strategy has been reported and used?

Experiments involve observations and measurements and analysis of quantitative data. You should therefore also read Chapters 14 ('Observations') and 17 ('Quantitative Data Analysis'). If your experiments involve people as participants, there are clearly limits to what you can ask them to do as compared to what you might do to a computer or a program. You must therefore read Chapter 5 on research participants and ethics.

PRACTICAL WORK

1   Study the following statements and write down the independent and dependent variables in each:

   a   Frequent computer crashes create frustration.
   b   Children learn more from interactive multimedia CDs than from books.
   c   Men are better programmers than women.
   d   Novice programmers spot fewer bugs than experienced programmers.

2   Study the following statements and decide which ones are falsifiable and could therefore be used as hypotheses:

   a   It always rains on the first day of the school holidays.
   b   Women are better at multi-tasking than men.
   c   Either it is sunny or it is not sunny.
   d   All triangles have three sides.
   e   The number of bugs already found in a program is related to the number of bugs still to be discovered.
   f   Companies without a website will suffer reduced sales.

3   Design an experiment (true, quasi- or uncontrolled trial) to investigate each of the following:

   a   Whether a lecturer's use of PowerPoint® slides in a lecture increases students' recall of the subject matter.
   b   Whether managers' use of email increases or decreases when stress levels are high.
   c   Whether object-oriented models are produced quicker than entity-relationship diagrams.
   d   Whether the use of a computer-based knowledge management system leads to better management decision-making.

4   Practise analysing and evaluating experiment-based research. Study a piece of research that used experiments. (Concentrate on the approach used rather than on any statistical analysis of the data.) Answer the questions in the 'Evaluation Guide' above, using the material in this chapter to help you.

FURTHER READING

Field and Hole (2003) is an easy to read, practical and humorous guide to designing and conducting experiments. The book is aimed at psychology students but is useful for researchers in other disciplines too. It covers different experimental designs, how to analyse and interpret the data using statistics, and how to write up the experimental research.

   Jarvenpaa, Dickson and DeSanctis (1985) discuss common methodological problems in experimental IS studies, particularly those concerning internal validity. They provide some useful guidelines for experimental IS researchers. Similarly Kitchenham et al. (2001, 2002) argue that empirical studies in software engineering often have poor experimental design, ▶

▶ inappropriate use of statistical techniques and conclusions that do not follow from the results. They therefore offer guidelines for empirical research in software engineering, concentrating on experiments and statistical analysis and drawing from advice written for medical researchers. These guidelines are relevant to other branches of IS and computing too. Tichy (1998) discusses several arguments *against* the use of experiments in computer science, and refutes each of them. Finally, Reips (2002) summarizes what is known so far about the conduct of Internet-based experiments, and gives recommendations on how they can be used effectively.

References

Fencott, C., van Schaik, P., Ling, J., & Shafiullah, M. (2002). The effects of movement of attractors and pictorial content of rewards on users' behaviour in virtual environments. *Interacting with Computers, 15*, 121–140.

Field, A., & Hole, G. (2003). *How to design and report experiments*. London: Sage.

Jarvenpaa, S.L., Dickson, G., & DeSanctis, G. (1985). Methodological issues in experimental IS research: Experiences and recommendations. *MIS Quarterly, 9*(2), 141–156.

Kitchenham, B.A., Pfleeger, S.L., Pickard, L.M., Jones, P.W., Hoaglin, D.C., El-Emam, K., et al. (2001). *Preliminary guidelines for empirical research in software engineering*. Ottawa: National Research Council of Canada.

Kitchenham, B.A., Pfleeger, S.L., Pickard, L.M., Jones, P.W., Hoaglin, D.C., El-Emam, K., et al. (2002). Preliminary guidelines for empirical research in software engineering. *IEEE Transactions on Software Engineering, 28*(8), 721–734.

Reips, U.-D. (2002). Standards for Internet-based experimenting. *Experimental Psychology, 49*(4), 243–256.

Smith, H.J., Keil, M., & Depledge, G. (2001). Keeping mum as the project goes under: Towards an explanatory model. *Journal of Management Information Systems, 18*(2), 189–227.

Tichy, W.F. (1998). Should computer scientists experiment more? *IEEE Computer, 31*(5), 32–40.

Zendler, A., Horn, E., Schwaertzel, H., & Ploedereder, E. (2001). Demonstrating the usage of single-case designs in experimental software engineering. *Information and Software Technology, 43*, 681–691.

10 Case Studies

In this chapter you will learn about:

- what is meant by a case study research strategy;
- issues to address in planning and undertaking case study research;
- how case study research might be applied to the Internet;
- how case studies have been used in IS and computing;
- the advantages and disadvantages of case study research;
- analysing and evaluating case study research.

Defining Case Studies

A case study focuses on one instance of the 'thing' that is to be investigated: an organization, a department, an information system, a discussion forum, a systems developer, a development project, a decision, and so on. This one instance, or case, is studied in depth, using a variety of data generation methods (interviewing, observation, document analysis and/or questionnaires – see Chapters 13–16). The aim is to obtain a rich, detailed insight into the 'life' of that case and its complex relationships and processes.

If using a survey (see Chapter 7), a researcher is able to take a wide but only shallow view of lots of instances of the phenomenon under investigation and is unlikely to obtain much information about the *context* of the phenomenon for each instance. If using an experiment (see Chapter 9), the researcher must divorce a phenomenon from its context, in order to establish that the measured outcomes can only have been caused by the researcher's manipulation of an independent variable and not by anything else. Both survey and experiment therefore simplify the complexities of the real world. A case study, on the other hand, looks at the chosen case within its real-life context, and focuses on all the factors, issues, politics, processes and relationships that constitute the messiness of the real world. By exploring all these factors and painting a detailed picture of how they link together, a researcher will try to explain *how* and *why* certain outcomes might occur in a particular situation. A case study approach does not test hypotheses, as in experiments (see Chapter 9), but from studying a particular instance, insight can be gained and knowledge generated that might also be relevant to other situations. Research based on a case study can have an underlying philosophical paradigm of either positivism, interpretivism or critical research (see Chapters 19–20).

DEFINITION: Case study

A case study is an empirical inquiry that investigates a contemporary phenomenon within its real-life context, especially when the boundaries between phenomenon and context are not clearly evident. (Yin, 2003b)

A case study is characterized by:

- **Focus on depth rather than breadth**: the researcher obtains as much detail as possible about one instance of the phenomenon under investigation.
- **Natural setting**: the instance, or case, is examined in its natural setting, not in a laboratory or other artificial situation. The case existed prior to the researcher arriving on the scene, and, normally, continues to exist after the researcher has moved on. The researcher seeks to disturb the setting as little as possible.
- **Holistic study**: the researcher focuses on the complexity of relationships and processes and how they are interconnected and inter-related, rather than trying to isolate individual factors.
- **Multiple sources and methods**: the researcher uses a wide range of data sources. For example, if studying a department, a researcher will try to talk to as many people as possible about life and work in that department, rather than just one or two people, to obtain multiple perceptions about the department and how it operates. Both quantitative and qualitative data can be used, obtained via a large range of data generation methods: interviewing and observing people, questionnaires if the researcher can pose some standardized questions, and document analysis such as minutes of departmental meetings, internal briefing notes and the researcher's own field notes and personal journal (for more on field notes see Chapter 12 on their use in ethnography).

Warning: Definition of terms

Some people confuse case study research with case study teaching. Case study teaching is used in some disciplines, for example, business studies, where students study a particular instance and analyse what happened. In case study teaching, however, the case may be altered or simplified to bring out key learning points about something, which should not occur in case study research.

Others, particularly in the computing disciplines, use the term case study when they mean a scenario to which they have applied their proposed modelling technique, method or program. This scenario is often artificial and typically much simpler than normally occurs in real life. Case study research, on the other hand, concentrates on finding out about the complexities of the real world.

Planning and Conducting Case Studies

Types of case studies

It is suggested there are three basic types of case studies (Yin, 2003b): exploratory, descriptive and explanatory.

- An **exploratory study** is used to define the questions or hypotheses to be used in a subsequent study. It is used to help a researcher understand a research problem. It might be used, for example, where there is little in the literature about a topic, so a real-life instance is investigated, in order to identify the topics to be covered in a subsequent research project. For example, an exploratory case study might help you work out what questions to pose in a questionnaire to be used in a survey.
- A **descriptive study** leads to a rich, detailed analysis of a particular phenomenon and its context. The analysis tells a story, including discussion of what occurred and how different people perceive what occurred.
- An **explanatory study** goes further than a descriptive study in trying to explain why events happened as they did or particular outcomes occurred. The case study analysis seeks to identify the multiple, often inter-linked, factors that had an effect, or compares what was found in the case to theories from the literature in order to see whether one theory matches the case better than others.

A case study approach, whether exploratory, descriptive or explanatory, can use a single case or multiple cases. The most common approach is to examine one case only. If a multiple case study approach is adopted, each case is written up separately, but then the researcher looks for similarities or differences between the different cases. Readers often find similar evidence and outcomes from several case studies more compelling than conclusions drawn from just one case study. However, any differences between two or more cases can also be useful. The first case study may lead the researcher to suggest a theoretical framework to explain what has been found. This framework might suggest the circumstances when another case will *not* be like the first. The researcher can therefore examine data from a second, differing case to see whether the theoretical framework's predictions are correct. Multiple case study approaches are, of course, more time consuming to perform than single-case study approaches, and result in much more data to analyse.

Case studies also vary in their approach to time:

- A **historical study** examines what happened in the past by asking people what they remember about earlier events and analysing documents produced at the time. Of course, such a study is dependent on people's memories; the researcher must also recognize that documents such as minutes of meetings are always produced for a purpose and with a particular audience in mind – they are rarely an objective description of what occurred.
- A **short-term, contemporary study** examines what is occurring in the case *now*. The researcher observes what occurs and asks people to talk about and explain what is going on.
- A **longitudinal study** involves the researcher investigating the case over time, anything from one month to several years, analysing those processes and relationships that are continuous and those that change.

Selection of cases

Since a case study focuses on one instance of the 'thing' that is to be investigated, it is important to choose the right instance in the first place and to be able to justify this choice to readers of your research. Your choice of a particular case might be based on:

- **Typical instance**: the chosen case is typical of many others and can therefore stand as representative of the whole class. Findings from the one case should be generalizable to the whole class.
- **Extreme instance**: the case is not typical of others but provides a contrast with the norm.
- **Test-bed for theory**: the case contains elements that make it suitable for testing an existing theory. You would then investigate whether the theory holds true in this particular case, or whether the theory must be challenged or modified.

- **Convenience**: people in the chosen case have agreed to give you access, and it is convenient in terms of time and resources. Of course, this should not be your main reason for choosing a particular case.
- **Unique opportunity**: the chance arises to study something that you had not previously planned for, and that may not occur again. Perhaps you were in the right place at the right time, or happened to talk to the right person. Good researchers watch out for such opportunities.

In 2001 foot-and-mouth disease (FMD) struck animals on British farms. This was a harrowing time for many farmers and the businesses that served them. However, I realized that this dreadful event also presented me with a unique opportunity. I carried out four case studies, looking at how some local governments used their websites during the FMD outbreak: the information presented and the different audiences addressed. The data provided empirical evidence for a theory about website audiences being a 'construction' of website developers, and I also made recommendations for how local governments could make better use of their websites during any future crisis. (Oates, 2002, 2003)

**CASE STUDY
Seizing a unique opportunity –
an example**

Generalizations

Some people criticize case studies for producing knowledge that only relates to the case under study. However, it is possible to generate broader conclusions that are relevant beyond the case itself, known as *generalizations*. Although some factors in the case may be unique, other factors will typically be found in other cases too. Generalizations can therefore be made, to the extent that your chosen case is typical of other cases. For example, if you have studied a small manufacturing company's use of IT, your findings may also apply to other small manufacturing companies. It's important that you inform your readers to what extent you judge your chosen case is typical of other cases in its class, or whether you feel your chosen case is unique, interesting in its own right but whose findings are unlikely to be generalized to others. You should also give your readers sufficient detail about the case so that *they* can decide if your case is similar to one which they are familiar. Cases might be similar on the basis of their physical location, history, social mix, technical basis or organizational type. Walsham (1995) suggests that four main types of generalisations are possible from case study research – concepts, theory, implications and rich insight – or a combination of these.

- **A concept** is a new idea or notion that emerges from the analysis, and which sometimes may even require a new word to be added to the vocabulary of the research discipline. For example, in her ethnographic work (see Chapter 12) Zuboff (1988) introduced the verb, 'to informate' to express the concept of IT producing new information for an organization and making visible activities, events and objects via the information produced about them.

- A **theory** is a coherent collection of concepts and propositions with an underlying world-view. This might be expressed as a 'conceptual framework' and is often presented via a diagrammatic model. For example, Orlikowski (1993) developed a framework for conceptualizing the organizational issues around the adoption and use of CASE tools.
- **Implications** arising from a case study are suggestions about what might happen in other similar instances, possibly with specific recommendations for action. For example, Walsham (1993) discusses several case studies, and concludes with implications for future IS research, education and practice.
- **Rich insight** is what we might glean from reading a case study that does not fit neatly into the three categories of concept, theory or implications, but nevertheless give us important new understanding about a situation.

Relationship to theory

There are various ways of linking theory to case study research. The case study can be used to:

- **Build a new theory**: as the previous section explained, a case study can lead to the development of a new concept, theory, framework or model. These can then be applied by researchers to other situations, possibly via another research strategy. For example, a case study could lead to a conceptual framework that could be used to analyse another case study, or to new hypotheses that could be explored via experiments or a survey.
- **Test an existing theory**: a researcher could take an existing theory and use a case study to see if the empirical evidence gained confirms the theory, implies necessary modifications to it, or contradicts it. For example, there is a substantial amount in the literature about technology acceptance – under what circumstances a new IT-based system will be accepted by the users, building on Davis' (1989) technology acceptance model. A case study could look at one instance of the introduction and implementation of a new technical system, and see whether the pattern of user acceptance (or not) conforms with what the theory suggests.
- **Evaluate alternative theories**: a researcher could examine all the factors in a case and see which pre-existing theory or model best matches what was found in the case.

Also, the *theory can shape the case study*. A pre-existing theory or model can be used to help the researcher decide which case to choose, what data to collect, which questions to ask and what themes to look for during data analysis. Of course, the danger of this is that the researcher might be too rigid in sticking to the chosen theory, and so not see other interesting and relevant issues in the case.

Some therefore argue that a researcher should not start off with an existing theory, but follow a *grounded theory* approach (Glaser & Strauss, 1967). The researcher tries to enter the situation with no pre-conceived ideas about theory, collects some data, analyses it for emerging patterns and themes, and then starts to develop a theory. This emerging theory is used to guide what further data is collected, which in turn leads to further modification of the emerging theory. Only when new data seems to confirm the researcher's theory, rather than add anything new, does the case study come to an end. At this point, the researcher's theory can be compared with existing theories in the literature. The argument for this approach is that any explanations or models or frameworks that the researcher proposes as outcomes from the case study are well grounded in empirical data, rather than being dreamt up by some armchair theorizing and only afterwards checked to see if they work in reality. Chapter 18 describes grounded theory in more detail.

Warning: Grounded theory

Some researchers claim that they are using grounded theory to justify sloppy research, where they have not thought through their research topic or reasons for choosing a particular case, and have just leapt into their field research to see what emerges. Grounded theory has its own literature discussing how it should be done in a careful and rigorous way (see Chapter 18).

Underlying philosophy

As indicated earlier, unlike some research strategies (for example, experiments) the case study strategy is not associated with just one underlying research philosophy. It can be used in research that has an underlying philosophy of positivism, interpretivism or critical thinking. If you want to use a case study approach, you should therefore first study Chapters 19 and 20 on philosophical paradigms, and be clear about which paradigm you are working in. Each paradigm has a different set of criteria for judging what makes a case study one of high quality. The 'Further Reading' section suggests sources on case studies within the different philosophical paradigms.

Reporting

It is unlikely that readers of your research report based on a case study will be able to visit the same case and make their own observations and analysis. They are dependent on your account of what was found and how it should be interpreted. It is therefore essential that you describe in some detail the nature of the case and how you arrived at your conclusions. You should give background information about the case and why it was chosen, who you interviewed or observed, what documents you used, and the timescale of your research. You should also explain how you recorded the data, how you analysed it and how you moved between theory and empirical data.

You should also recognize that there may be more than one interpretation or explanation for the data that you generated. You explore alternative interpretations and make an argument for what you consider to be the one that best explains your data. Such explanations may be of your own devising (if you are building a new theory) or may be pre-existing theories from the literature (if you are testing and evaluating existing theories).

The need to report all of this means that your final account may be very lengthy. This is not so much of a problem if your case study forms the major part of your PhD thesis, but it is if you want to write it up as a journal article or conference paper, where word number restrictions are much lower. For a journal article or conference paper, you may find you have to concentrate on just one or two findings, possibly publishing the full case study research later in a book.

The Internet and Case Studies

The case study strategy can be appropriate for studying 'life' on the Internet. For example, researchers can study an instance of online communities such as those participating in a particular online discussion forum, or using a particular service (for example, the eBay 'community'), or working together (for example, the open source community). These people can be studied by use of online interviews, observations, questionnaires and documents. For example, in an often-cited study, Lee (1994) adopts a case study approach and examines email exchanges among managers in a particular organization. He uses an existing theory (information richness theory) and studies how richness of communication occurs in the case, and how the users themselves experience and understand the use of email.

Researchers can also study online artefacts as cases. For example, you could study one particular website and observe how it evolves over time, perhaps linking the evolution to factors in the website's environment (online or offline) that might influence the web-developers to change it. Of course, to understand fully the evolution, you would probably need to interview the developers themselves, either face-to-face or via email. Two particular issues for Internet-based case studies are the problems of boundary and offline/online existence:

- **The problem of boundary**: where do you draw the line between the case you are studying and all its interlinking components, and its outside world or context? This can be a problem for real-world case studies too, but is emphasized in online studies because everything on the web is readily linked to something else via hyperlinks. So, if studying a website, for example, do you include other sites that 'your' site links to? If studying an online discussion group's communications, do you include the webpage that a contributor recommends others to look at? There is no hard and fast rule – you have to decide for yourself what is 'inside' and outside' your case study, and be able to explain and justify this to your readers.

- **The problem of offline/online existence**: people and communities do not just exist online. They have an offline existence too. If you only study what they do online, you may be missing important factors in their offline world that influence how they behave online. For example, in studying an organization's email communications, you might have to know about the company's culture and hierarchy, which are known to those sending emails, but not made explicit in their communications. As an outsider, you might not realize the hidden, shared meanings in some of the emails. Similarly, if studying the contribution patterns of people in an online discussion group, you may not know that one person has a regular commitment that affects how often they are able to submit messages, even though the current topic might be one to which they would like to contribute. You may be able to deal with this offline/online problem by interviewing people (face-to-face or via email) and finding out how their offline existence has an effect on their online activities. If not, you should acknowledge the problem and the possible limitations it places on your research findings.

Examples of Case Studies in IS and Computing Research

A case study approach is particularly suited to research into the development, implementation and ongoing use of information systems, because it enables researchers to study all the factors and their inter-relationships (managers, users, developers, technology, legislation, group dynamics, power and politics, and so on). It has therefore been widely used in the IS discipline. It has been less used in the computing disciplines, but *could* be a very useful research strategy in computing research. For example, many researchers who use the 'design and creation' strategy consider their research completed when their system is judged to be bug-free. However, they could follow up with a case study of their system in use, to see if the intended benefits, as set out in the design brief or requirements specification (that is, the original theory of why the system was a good idea), are experienced in practice, and what unforeseen modifications are needed once the system is used in real life.

Some examples of the use of a case study strategy in IS and computing research are:

- Markus (1983) uses a case study to investigate user resistance to the implementation of management information systems. She looks at three different theories of the causes of user resistance and shows how the data demonstrated the superiority of one of the theories. This is viewed as one of the classic case studies in IS research. It was discussed in a panel session at ICIS 2000 (International Conference on Information Systems), where panel members debated how it would be reviewed if submitted for publication in 2000. Their presentations are available online at: www.people.vcu.edu/~aslee/ICIS2000/ICIS2000-Panel-Markus1983.htm

- Star and Ruhleder (1996) look at the case of the development of a large-scale CSCW (computer-supported collaborative work) system, designed for a group of geneticists who were geographically separated. The researchers use an existing theory (Bateson's model of levels of learning) to help analyse and interpret their data. A later study (Barrett & Walsham, 2004) has taken their article as a case study and looks at how it has since been cited in the IS literature, that is, how the authors' contributions to knowledge (concept, theory, specific implications or rich insight) have subsequently been used.
- Orlikowski (1993) uses the case study strategy to explore the paradox that some studies report improvements in productivity from the use of CASE tools, whereas others report no improvement.
- Tapia (2004) examines a small software development company during the dot.com boom and bust era. She analyses how the owners and managers used various techniques to increase their control over the employees, and how the developers at first accepted but later resisted those techniques.

Evaluating Case Study-based Research

Advantages of the case study research strategy include:

- It can deal with complex situations where it is difficult to study a single factor in isolation.
- It is appropriate for situations where the researcher has little control over events.
- It is suitable for both theory building and theory testing.
- It allows the researcher to show the complexities of life and to explore alternative meanings and explanations.
- It produces data that is close to people's experiences and can be more accessible than highly numeric studies – most people enjoy reading stories.

Disadvantages of the case study research strategy include:

- It is sometimes perceived (especially by positivist researchers – see Chapter 19) as lacking rigour and leading to generalizations with poor credibility.
- It can be difficult and time-consuming to negotiate access to the necessary settings, people and documents.

- The presence of the researcher can affect how people behave so that you end up not being able to study what you wanted to.
- There are no set rules to follow and you cannot know in advance whether you are naturally any good at it.

Use the 'Evaluation Guide' below to help you analyse and evaluate case study-based research. If there is insufficient information for you to answer some questions, you should not completely reject the research report, but you should treat the findings with caution and be wary about relying on the report for evidence.

EVALUATION GUIDE: CASE STUDIES

1 Have the criteria for choosing the particular case(s) been described and justified?
2 What kind of case study strategy is used? (For example, 'exploratory, multiple and longitudinal'.)
3 What data generation methods were used? Do you think enough methods were used and enough data collected?
4 How long did the researcher spend in the field? Do you think this was long enough?
5 Does the research look at relationships and processes and provide a holistic perspective?
6 What kind of generalizations are reported, if any?
7 How does the researcher link theory to the case study?
8 What limitations in the case study research does the researcher recognize?
9 Can you identify other flaws or omissions in the researcher's reporting of the case study?
10 Overall, how effectively do you think the case study strategy has been reported and used?

PRACTICAL WORK

1 Think of a research question that could be addressed via a case study research strategy. Now think about how a survey could be used to address the same question. What aspects of the question could the survey answer? What aspects could the case study answer? What would the advantages be of using a case study rather than a survey to address your question?
2 Imagine you are on the interview panel for a researcher who will undertake some case study-based research. List the skills that the successful candidate will need to possess. How could you find out at the interview whether each candidate has them? If no candidate possesses all the necessary skills, for which ones would it be possible ▶

▶ to provide training before the successful applicant starts the research? Are there some skills which can't be taught?

3 Practise analysing and evaluating research based on a case study strategy. Study a piece of research that used a case study. Analyse and evaluate it using the 'Evaluation Guide' above and referring to the material in this chapter as necessary.

FURTHER READING

The classic texts on case study research are by Yin (2003a, 2003b). He takes a positivist approach to case studies as do the IS researchers Benbasat, Goldstein and Mead (1987) and Dubé and Paré (2003). Walsham, on the other hand, makes extensive use of interpretive case studies in IS. Walsham (1995) discusses the nature of interpretive case studies and his two books (1993, 2001) provide many case studies concerning the use of IT within organizations and in an increasingly globalized world. For an approach to adopting the critical paradigm within a case study strategy, see Ngwenyama and Lee (1997).

Michael Myers' (1997) online living document on qualitative research methods in information systems includes a section on case studies and many useful references (www.qual.auckland.ac.nz).

Finally, for lighter reading, Kidder (1982) tells an interesting story of the development of a new computer in a particular company (Data General Corporation), where a team of young engineers was given one year to design and build a new machine. As Yin points out (2003b, p. 25), this is an excellent example of a case study, although aimed at a popular rather than academic audience.

References

Barrett, M., & Walsham, G. (2004). Making contributions from interpretive case studies: Examining processes of construction and use. In B. Kaplan, D.P.I. Truex, D. Wastell, T. Wood-Harper, & J.I. DeGross (Eds.), *Information systems research. Relevant theory and informed practice* (pp. 293–312). Boston, MA: Kluwer Academic.

Benbasat, I., Goldstein, D.K., & Mead, M. (1987). The case research strategy in studies of information systems. *MIS Quarterly, 11*(3), 369–386.

Davis, F.D. (1989). Perceived usefulness, perceived ease of use, and user acceptance of information technology. *MIS Quarterly, 13*(3), 319–340.

Dubé, L., & Paré, G. (2003). Rigor in information systems positivist case research: Current practices, trends, and recommendations. *MIS Quarterly, 27*(4), 597–636.

Glaser, B., & Strauss, A. (1967). *The discovery of grounded theory*. Chicago, IL: Aldine.

Kidder, T. (1982). *The soul of a new machine*. London: Penguin.

Lee, A.S. (1994). Electronic mail as a medium for rich communication: An empirical investigation using hermeneutic interpretation. *MIS Quarterly, 18*(2), 143–157.

Markus, M.L. (1983). Power, politics and MIS implementation. *Communications of the ACM, 26*(6), 430–445.

Myers, M.L. (1997). Qualitative research in information systems. *MIS Quarterly, 21*(2), 241–242. *MISQ Discovery* archive version, June 1997, www.misq.org/discovery/MISQD_isworld. Updated version retrieved 8 July 2005 from www.qual.auckland.ac.nz

Ngwenyama, O.K., & Lee, A.S. (1997). Communication richness in electronic mail: Critical social theory and the contextuality of meaning. *MIS Quarterly, 21*(2), 145–167.

Oates, B.J. (2002). Foot and mouth disease: Constructing and serving multiple audiences. In *Proceedings of the UKAIS 2002 conference [UK Academy of Information Systems]*. Leeds: Leeds Metropolitan University.

Oates, B.J. (2003). Foot and mouth disease: Informing the community? *Informing Science, 6*, 103–114.

Orlikowski, W.J. (1993). CASE tools as organizational change: Investigating incremental and radical changes in systems development. *MIS Quarterly, 17*(3), 309–340.

Star, S.L., & Ruhleder, K. (1996). Steps towards an ecology of infrastructure: Design and access for large information spaces. *Information Systems Research, 7*(1), 111–134.

Tapia, A.H. (2004). Resistance or deviance: A high-tech workplace during the bursting of the dot-com bubble. In B. Kaplan, D.P.I. Truex, D. Wastell, T. Wood-Harper, & J.I. DeGross (Eds.), *Information systems research. Relevant theory and informed practice* (pp. 577–596). Boston, IL: Kluwer Academic.

Walsham, G. (1993). *Interpreting information systems in organizations*. Chichester: Wiley.

Walsham, G. (1995). Interpretive case studies in IS research: Nature and method. *European Journal of Information Systems, 4*, 74–81.

Walsham, G. (2001). *Making a world of difference. IT in a global context*. Chichester: Wiley.

Yin, R.K. (2003a). *Applications of case study research* (2nd ed.). Thousand Oaks, CA: Sage.

Yin, R.K. (2003b). *Case study research. Design and methods* (3rd ed.). Thousand Oaks, CA: Sage.

Zuboff, S. (1988). *In the age of the smart machine*. New York: Basic Books.

11 Action Research

In this chapter you will learn about:

- what is meant by action research;
- issues to address in planning and designing action research;
- developments in action research;
- how action research might be carried out via the Internet;
- how action research has been used in IS and computing;
- the advantages and disadvantages of action research;
- analysing and evaluating action research.

Defining Action Research

The roots of the action research method are generally traced back to Lewin in the USA in the 1940s and 1950s and similar but independent work by the Tavistock Institute in the UK in the 1950s and 1960s. Lewin was concerned to make social scientists' activities 'useful' by applying social psychology techniques to practical social problems, rather than doing research just to write books or papers that only other academics would read. Scientists at the Tavistock Institute worked with patients suffering from psychological and social disorders arising from their World War II experiences. The scientists had no initial theory of treatment, but planned, acted and reflected upon their interventions with the patients, and gradually developed a body of knowledge about how to help people suffering from war-induced trauma.

From its origins, action research has been used particularly by professionals who want to investigate and improve their *own* working practices. For example, nurses might enquire into their interactions with patients and try different approaches to improving their work, or teachers might research into different strategies for maintaining discipline in the classroom and examine which seem to be the most effective. This implies that people doing their everyday jobs are able to carry out research into their own actions and moves research away from the clutches of a highly-trained and specialized academic elite. Academics carrying out action research into a situation would be expected to collaborate with the people in that setting. Their role might change so that rather than coming in as experts to analyse, diagnose and suggest changes, they are facilitators who enable practitioners to do their own research. However, this participative approach and democratization of research is not always apparent in many examples of action research in IS and computing.

Action research is characterized by:

- **Concentration on practical issues**: rather than dealing with abstract hypotheses, experiments in a laboratory, software programs or mathematical proofs, it addresses the concerns and complex problems expressed by people living, working and acting in the real-world. It therefore requires researchers to work in the field, in the messiness of human affairs.
- **An iterative cycle of plan–act–reflect**: the researchers plan to do something in a real-world situation, do it, and then reflect on what happened or was learnt, and then begin another cycle of plan–act–reflect. As its name suggests, action research is about research into *action*.
- **An emphasis on change**: researchers do not simply observe and describe. They are concerned with doing things that make a difference, and learning about how they effected the change.
- **Collaboration with practitioners**: people living and working in the situation under study are active participants in the research.
- **Multiple data generation methods**: there are no restrictions on the types of data appropriate to action research. Both quantitative and qualitative data can be used. Researchers might decide to interview and observe, issue questionnaires, and collect documents produced by themselves (for example, their own field notes or personal journals) or by others in the situation (for example, minutes of departmental meetings, web-server logs or internal briefing notes).
- **Action outcomes plus research outcomes**: action research outcomes can relate to both *action* (practical achievements in the problem situation) and *research* (learning about the processes of problem-solving and acting in a situation). Ideally, both types of outcome should be achieved. However, sometimes projects may not lead to practical achievement but can still be judged as successful by academic researchers if learning is made about models and theories and/or the process of problem-solving, including possible reasons for the failure to alleviate the problem situation. Similarly, practitioners may feel a project was successful for them if practical improvements have been made in a situation, but without any contribution to academic knowledge.

Like case study research (see Chapter 10), action research can have an underlying philosophical paradigm of either positivism or interpretivism or critical research (see Chapters 19–20). Before carrying out an action research project you will need to be certain about which paradigm you are working in, since each has a different set of criteria for judging the quality of action research.

Planning and Conducting Action Research

Action research as practised and described in the IS and computing literature often has a rather narrower meaning than that understood across the social sciences and other professions. In this section, we concentrate on action research as it is commonly used in our disciplines. In the following section, we look at the way in which action research is now understood and used in some other disciplines – which could also be relevant to IS and computing.

F, M and A

Peter Checkland has been a very influential action researcher in IS. He and his colleagues created and refined SSM using action research to address problems in organizational situations (Checkland, 1981; Checkland & Scholes, 1990). He suggests researchers should conceptualize action research in terms of F, M and A:

- **F**: a *framework of ideas* that acts as a theory base for the research in a particular action research project.
- **M**: a *problem-solving methodology* that the researchers create or adopt, which embodies F, enabling the theory base to be put into use.
- **A**: an *area of application*, that is, a real-world problem situation where researchers use M, aiming to help people in that situation bring about changes that they agree to be improvements. While acting in A, action researchers should reflect upon the declared F and M, modifying them as necessary.

For example, in Checkland's work, F is general systems theory, M is SSM and A is a number of organizations, both public and private, in which SSM has been developed, used and refined.

The concepts of F, M and A help action researchers to define how knowledge and practical outcomes from the research will be created and expressed. They help to make the process of intervening in a situation and generating research conclusions explicit, rather than their seeming to be based on hidden hunches and intuition, and are useful for structuring action research reports.

Some researchers argue that F, the framework of ideas or theory base, should whenever possible be derived from the existing literature (for example, structuration theory, actor network theory or the technology acceptance model). That is, the theory is a set of constructs that have already been peer reviewed and accepted into the academic community. Others use the term 'theory' more loosely, to mean the initial ideas that the researchers have about a situation. Whichever view is adopted, it is essential that action researchers have explicit theoretical foundations for their intervention in a setting, otherwise it will not be accepted as research.

The research process

As stated already, action research is based on an iterative process of plan–act–reflect. This cycle is often expressed as five stages (Susman & Evered, 1978):

1 **Diagnosis**: identifying the nature of the problem situation, including all interrelated factors, and developing a working theory (F) about the situation and how it might be changed.
2 **Planning**: specifying actions that should alleviate the situation (M).
3 **Intervention**: taking action in the agreed area of application (A) in line with the plan.
4 **Evaluation**: establishing whether the theoretical effects of the action were realized, and whether they did indeed relieve the problem(s).
5 **Reflection**: deciding what has been achieved in terms of both practical outcomes and new knowledge, and whether a new action research cycle is required.

Because social practices and interactions are being studied, it is usually difficult to plan action research projects in detail and in advance. They can't be designed in the same way as an experiment, for example. Once under way, an action research project is not completely under the control of the researchers – events in the problem situation may disrupt their plans, which must therefore be flexible and adaptable. Nevertheless, the action research process still needs to be structured and managed to avoid criticisms about lack of rigour. Researchers should be clear about whether they are currently planning, acting or reflecting, and must generate data systematically throughout the research stages (via interviews, observations, questionnaires or documents). This data should be recorded in a form that can be referred to both during and after the completion of the action part of the research, and that can be analysed by people other than those directly involved in order to judge the validity or soundness of the claimed outcomes. In other words, as well as conceptualizing your action research in terms of F, M and A, you should add a further concept, R, the actual research process adopted in your particular study. The more information you can give in your research reports about R, the happier your audience will be that it was indeed a planned, structured piece of academic research, not an ad hoc set of activities written up later as if they were action research.

Distinguishing action research from consultancy

It is important that you understand the differences between action research and consultancy. Both involve working in organizations to effect changes, but the differences are as follows (Baskerville & Wood-Harper, 1996):

- Researchers require more rigorous documentation than consultants.
- Researchers require theoretical justifications and consultants require empirical justifications.
- The consultation process is usually linear, while the action research process is cyclical.
- Consultants operate under tighter time and budget restraints.

You need to be clear at the start of a project whether you are undertaking action research or consultancy. Papers submitted to research journals are rejected if they look as though they were originally consultancy projects that the authors later tried to write up as if they had been action research.

Mutually acceptable research protocol

In action research, academic researchers and practitioners work together. It is unlike, say, a case study of an organization, where the organizational members can often simply get on with their normal jobs, ignoring the academic researchers and allowing them to merge into the background. The research agenda is strongly influenced by the day-to-day concerns of those in the organization. They must agree to make changes, and then evaluate honestly whether those changes have any effect – at the same time as carrying out their normal roles and dealing with the everyday pressures and demands. They must, therefore, be committed both to the research objectives and also to trying out and evaluating new things suggested by researchers.

To ensure that all those taking part work together successfully, it is essential that a mutually acceptable research protocol be developed and agreed between all those involved in the action research. This should be based on the normal ethical research guidelines such as the right to withdraw, the right to anonymity, and so on (see Chapter 5 on participants and research ethics), but should also make explicit:

- the objectives of the project and how it will be evaluated;
- the roles and responsibilities of the various participants;
- any organizational constraints (for example, no changes to be implemented during the peak trading season).

Developing such a protocol, whether a formal written document or a word-of-mouth agreement, takes time. However, the process of development is useful in its own right. It provides the opportunity for academic researchers to explain the nature of action research, and how it differs from consultancy or case study research, and for all to examine their different motivations for taking part. From your own standpoint, it helps you to clarify expectations about your involvement in the work – whether you will be *collaborative* (an equal co-worker with the subjects), *facilitative* (the organizational members solve the immediate problem, supported by your advice) or *expert* (you bear the responsibility for solving the immediate problem).

Participation

Participation is an important theme in the IS literature on action research. For example:

> A major strand of action research is that the practitioners should participate in the analysis, design and implementation processes and contribute at least as much as researchers in any decision making. (Avison & Wood-Harper, 1990, p. 180)

But it is not clear from the IS literature that those practitioners have always been active and equal partners for all aspects of an action research project. Instead, lip service may be being paid to the idea of participation, but in practice the academic researchers may make many of the decisions. You should ask of any piece of action research claiming participation by practitioners whether they took part in all decisions and reflections about the methodology (M), framework (F) and action research process (R) used, or was their involvement limited to sharing knowledge about the area of application (A), following the researchers' suggestions and identifying practical outcomes? And have they been involved in the writing up and dissemination of the research findings? Control over the formulation of the research questions, strategy and dissemination determines who really owns the research.

66 Participation in research

Research tends to be owned and controlled by researchers, or by those who, in turn, own and control the researchers. Those who remain powerless to influence the processes of information gathering, the identification of truth, and the dissemination of findings are usually the subjects of the research, those very people whose interests the research may purport to serve. (Brechin, 1993, p. 73) 99

Some action researchers work with their students on action research projects. The students intervene in organizations and make changes, and report back to their supervisor, who then helps them reflect on what has been learnt and plan for another cycle. This can be a successful strategy. However, it does raise more questions about the true extent of participation. Does the students' lower status and authority (compared with their supervisor) militate against authentic collaboration? How can academic supervisors guard against students reporting outcomes supportive of an academic's favoured theory or methodology in the hope of gaining approval and/or better assessment grades?

Many writers on action research in the IS literature assume there will be a traditional professional–client relationship. For example, they describe the research protocol (see above) as a researcher–client agreement. But who *is* the client? Often the client is a budget-holder within an organization – if they are not happy, the action research project does not continue. Such a client's interests and needs do not always coincide, however, with the interests and needs of people lower down the company hierarchy. How are their interests represented in the action research project? Also, where the client has greater political power, for example if academic researchers are being paid by the client to achieve practical outcomes, the researchers could be reluctant to be fully open, fearing losing the contract, or not being awarded further work. Again, this works against full participation by all affected.

I suggest that in writing about and reading about action research projects, attention should be paid to the extent of participation achieved. Readers should know the degree of involvement of those affected, the political relationships between the participants and any constraints on the free exchange of views and hence on the claimed outcomes.

Self-delusion and group-think

There is a danger in action research that researchers, perhaps subconsciously, want to show that the exercise is useful, and that their theory or method is valid. They may be deluding themselves. Psychologists have shown that it is difficult for people to be aware of the processes influencing their behaviour. Afterwards they tend to produce a post-rationalization of their acts, using retrospective interpretations about information that had probably not been fully attended to at the time. There could be an increased danger of this if an action researcher uses and reflects on F and M alone, without the benefit of fellow academics to challenge any assumptions or assertions. If action researchers do work alone, they should explain what steps were taken to avoid self-delusion.

However, even where others are involved, there is the possibility of 'group-think' where all concerned state something to be true simply because they want to believe it to be so, or because nobody in the group challenges the emerging group consensus. Co-researchers, either consciously or subconsciously, do not notice or mention aspects of their experience that indicate the limitations of an idea in practice. The group tacitly agrees to construct a pseudo-reality. To counter this, an explicit 'devil's advocate' procedure (Heron, 1996, pp. 146–148) can be built into the research process. One or more group members regularly try to show that a theory does not apply, or a method is not working, or that someone's evaluation is not really based on empirical evidence.

I have rarely seen the problems of self-delusion and group-think addressed in reports of action research projects, but I do advise you to address them in your own action research and explain in your reports how you guarded against them. Otherwise, your outcomes might not be accepted by those who are already dubious about the legitimacy of action research as a research strategy.

Outcomes

As stated earlier, action research outcomes can relate to both *action* (practical achievements in the problem situation and *research* (learning about the processes of problem-solving and acting in a situation). Successful practical outcomes might include improved efficiency, greater effectiveness or enhanced communication and understanding. Similar to case study research (see Chapter 10), action research can contribute to academic research by confirming, modifying or rejecting existing theories, or building new ones.

Generalizations

Just as for case studies, it is important not to make broad generalizations from one action research study that might have unique features not found in other situations. However, you should reflect upon the extent to which your chosen problem situation is typical of other settings, so your outcomes might be applicable elsewhere. You should also give sufficient information about the problem situation for *readers* to make their own assessment of whether the approach and findings could be applied in another setting with which they are familiar. Models, theories and methods, developed from the action research, are all forms of generalizations that often have wider applicability.

Developments in Action Research

Action research is still evolving as a research strategy. It therefore does not have a fixed meaning but one that is *emergent*. The previous section discussed the conduct of action research as commonly understood in IS and computing. In this section, we look at how it is now understood by some researchers in other disciplines. I call it here 'new action research', but must stress that is not really so very new. It has been developed over at least the last 20 years, but it is fairly new to IS and computing.

Definition

A recent definition of new action research is:

> ... a participatory, democratic process concerned with developing practical know-ing in the pursuit of worthwhile human purposes, grounded in a participatory worldview which we believe is emerging at this historical moment. It seeks to bring together action and reflection, theory and practice, in participation with others, in the pursuit of practical solutions to issues of pressing concern to people, and more generally the flourishing of individual persons and their communities. (Reason & Bradbury, 2001a, p. 1)

We can compare this with Rapoport's definition of action research, which is often cited in the IS literature:

> Action research aims to contribute both to the practical concerns of people in an immediate problematic situation and to the goals of social science by joint collab-oration within a mutually acceptable ethical framework. (Rapoport, 1970, p. 499)

or with a definition from an IS action researcher:

> A general term to refer to research methodologies and projects where the researcher(s) tries to directly improve the participating organization(s) and, at the same time, to generate scientific knowledge. (Kock, 1997)

The first definition places less emphasis than the other two on contribution to scien-tific knowledge and greater emphasis on worthwhile purposes, participation and indi-vidual human (rather than organizational) flourishing.

Currently the most detailed exposition of the emerging new action research is provided by Reason and Bradbury (2001b). They suggest researchers should address five quality issues in the new action research: relational praxis, reflexive-practical out-come, plurality of knowing, significant work, and new and enduring consequences/infrastructure. Each of these is briefly explained in this section, and some implications for action research in IS and computing are also indicated.

Relational praxis

'Praxis' is another word for 'practice'. The defining characteristic of the emergent worldview of the new action research is participation in the world. This world is not made up of separate things, but of *relationships*, which we co-create, participate in and maintain. We can't stand outside our world as dispassionate observers, we're necessarily already acting in it, forming relationships as we live and breathe. The aim of the new action research is therefore to support and enhance skills for being-in-the-world. Since we're *all* acting and being in the world, the new action research seeks to remove the researcher–subject distinction, or academic–practitioner distinction, and calls instead on a joint inquiry where people who share a problem come together to resolve it. This implies that everyone is capable of being a researcher; research is not the exclusive preserve of those in labs and universities. Research is undertaken *with*, *for* and *by* people.

The previous section has already questioned the true extent of participation in many IS and computing action research projects. Many of the discussions of action research in IS and computing also seem to conflate the interests of an action researcher's co-participants with the interests of an organization as, for example, in Kock's definition of action research at the beginning of this section (see above) or Baskerville (1999, p. 11):

> The researcher is *actively involved*, with expected benefit for both *researcher* and *organization*. (Baskerville's italics.)

But really there is no such thing as 'the organization', which might benefit from action research. It's a collection of people with many differing and conflicting needs or problems. What are called 'organizational needs' are formulated by powerful groups within the organization, such as senior managers representing the shareholders' interests, possibly to the detriment of others in the organization. For new action research in business organizations, a goal of improved business performance would *not* be superior to that of human flourishing. This could cause problems for IS action researchers who are based in business schools where managers are normally seen as the primary clients and research is often focused on economic goals.

There has also been a tradition of participatory design (by the end-users) in the development of information systems. These approaches have often been developed via action research. However, such participatory design approaches are also criticized for not addressing conflict problems arising from the unequal distribution of power and the irreconcilability of management and worker needs, and for often being managerialist in not challenging the power or legitimacy of managers' right to manage (for example, Howcroft & Wilson, 2003).

The 'relational-praxis' issue, if addressed more fully in IS and computing, could lead to more focus on genuine participation by all affected and studied, a move away from seeing managers as the primary clients and a goal of human flourishing rather than economic and efficiency objectives. In the longer term this might mean research into the development and use of information systems would move away from a primarily business focus towards more studying of such things as the information society, the digital divide, community informatics and e-democracy.

Reflexive-practical outcome

The new action research, like conventional action research, aims at practical outcomes, as well as academic knowledge. Practical outcomes, though, are less concerned with whether organizational benefits have been achieved (remember, *who* in the organization benefits? Just the powerful?). Instead, it asks, 'Do people whose reputations and livelihoods are affected act differently as a result of the inquiry?' This applies as much to the academic researchers as to other participants, implying the need for researchers to provide confessional accounts of their action research and how it changed *them*. Such reflexive accounts by action researchers are currently rare in the IS and computing literature.

Kemmis (2001) suggests there are three kinds of action research and outcomes: technical, practical and emancipatory.

- **Technical**: concentrates on functional improvements, that is, doing things better – probably the majority of action research projects. For example, Kock, McQueen and Scott (1997) discuss an action research study that investigated the thesis that 'groupware systems would positively affect productivity and quality of project-related activities'. This kind of action research would not normally question the goals themselves (that is, is improved productivity necessarily always a Good Thing? For whom?). Nor would it examine the history of how people got themselves into their current (perceived) problem situation.
- **Practical**: the research participants aim to improve their functional practice, as above, but also to reflect on and understand how their goals, and the criteria they use for evaluating their practice, are shaped by their own ways of seeing themselves and their context. The study becomes a form of *self-education* (perhaps a better term than Kemmis' confusing use of 'practical') and the focus is as much on people changing themselves as changing the outcomes of their practice. For example, Mumford (2001) discusses some of the personal lessons she has learnt over a long career of using action research in IS.
- **Emancipatory**: aims to improve technical performance, and the self-understanding of those involved, but also to help them critically evaluate their social or organizational context. They come to see how their functional goals may be limited or inappropriate within a wider view of the situation in which they live or work, and how their self-understandings may be shaped by shared misunderstandings about the nature and consequences of what they do. Such action research also aims to *empower* the participants to overcome the barriers (structures, conventions, discrimination) that prevent human flourishing. In other words, participants are enabled to overcome the injustices of oppression and domination (see Chapter 20 on critical research for more discussion.) Examples of this type of action research can be found in the women's, civil rights and land rights movements. In IS, Waring (2004), for example, describes an action research project involving the design and procurement of a computerized and integrated payroll and personnel system, where she empowered the participants to challenge the assumptions and dominance of the finance director and IT professionals.

The 'reflexive-practical outcome' issue therefore challenges IS and computing researchers to include accounts of how they themselves are changed by their action research, and to go beyond technical outcomes to include self-education and emancipatory outcomes.

Plurality of knowing

The new action research argues that using the full range of human sensibilities is appropriate to investigate being and acting in the world. As we live, we do not always use words and rational thinking. We also use, for example, art, emotions and intuition. This means that at least four different types of knowledge can emerge from action research: experiential, presentational, propositional and practical (Heron, 1996):

- **Experiential knowledge:** gained by direct encounter; almost impossible to put into words, being tacit and based on empathy, intuition and feeling.
- **Presentational knowledge:** emerges from experiential knowledge. Gives the first expression of knowing something, through stories, drawings, sculpture, music, dance, and so on.
- **Propositional knowledge:** knowledge 'about' something in the form of logically organized ideas and theories, as in most academic research.
- **Practical knowledge:** evident in knowing 'how to' exercise a skill (note this is different from Kemmis' use of 'practical', discussed above).

The 'plurality of knowing' issue therefore challenges action researchers to include emotional, intuitive and artistic skills in their work and acknowledge (and remove?) academics' bias towards text-based, propositional knowledge. Papers and conference presentations could include pictures or drama performances, for example, if they convey the knowledge that was gained.

Significant work

In the new action research, significant and worthwhile work is that which is well-grounded in the everyday concerns of people, and which ideally moves beyond the technical to developing people's capacity to ask fundamental questions about their world. A goal might be that people say, 'That work is inspiring. It helps me live a better life' (Bradbury & Reason, 2001, p. 449).

Conventional IS and computing action researchers, who are accustomed to providing knowledge to support organizational objectives (or objectives of the organization's powerful – see above), may therefore find their research challenged by new action researchers who question whether it is worthwhile research. Explicit attention to the 'significant work' issue focuses attention on the kind of research questions we choose to address.

New and enduring consequences/infrastructure

New action research should also have consequences that endure. These can include new practical and academic knowledge but there are other possibilities too. Bradbury and Reason (2001) ask whether:

- those involved can say, 'This work continues to develop and help us';
- the work has been seeded so that it can be continued participatively if the initiating researcher moves away;
- it leaves behind new patterns of behaviour within a group, or new structures such as centres for action research;
- others can say, 'We can use your work to develop our own.'

Conventional action research in IS and computing is judged as successful if it leads to practical achievements in the problem situation, and/or learning about the processes of problem solving and acting in a situation. Attention to the 'new and enduring consequences' issue could enrich our action research by recognizing more types of consequences beyond answering the original research question, such as community ties or other forms of social capital, sustainability and critical awareness.

How brave do you feel?

Action research as conventionally practised is not yet well established in IS. Many IS researchers still do not accept it as 'proper' research. It is even less well-accepted in the computing disciplines. The new action research, as described here, is likely to be viewed even less favourably by supervisors, reviewers and those with power in the IS and computing disciplines. It challenges our ideas about knowledge and worthwhile research.

You therefore have to be brave to use action research, of whichever form. But if it accords with your personal beliefs, have courage. It can be a worthwhile pursuit.

The Internet and Action Research

So far there have not been many studies involving the Internet and action research, but there are many possibilities. Action research can be used to develop and refine the methods people use for developing web- or Internet-based systems. For example, the web development methodology WISDM was developed using action research (Vidgen,

Avison, Wood, & Wood-Harper, 2002). It can also be used to design and implement new ways of using Internet technology. For example, Tang, Yasa and Forrester (2004) discuss using action research to help a manufacturing business (egg production) to plan and implement an e-business infrastructure to gain a competitive edge, and Bailey and Moar (2001) use action research to explore the possibilities and challenges of Internet-based 3D virtual environments as creative learning tools for children. Action research can also be used to find out about the interactions of people using the Internet, that is, to understand and change people's behaviour in online groups. For example, Horelli and Kaaja (2002) examine whether use of the Internet can enable children to participate more in decision-making on urban planning and neighbourhood development.

As with online case study research (see Chapter 10), the drawback of online action research is that the people you work with online have an offline existence too, which might influence their online practices. If you study only the online aspects of your action research, your analysis may be incomplete.

Examples of Action Research in IS and Computing

There is a growing body of work involving action research in the IS literature, but so far its use has been rarely reported in the computing literature. In IS, an important use of action research has been in the exploration of better systems development methods or methodologies. For example:

- SSM (Checkland, 1981; Checkland & Scholes, 1990).
- The Multiview methodology (Avison & Wood-Harper, 1990).
- The ETHICS methodology (Mumford, 1995).
- WISDM, a web development methodology (Vidgen et al., 2002).

Indeed Baskerville and Wood-Harper argue (1996, p. 240):

> The relevance of action research to systems development methodology has not been forcefully stated in the past. We suggest that action research, as a research method in the study of human methods, is the most scientifically legitimate approach available. Indeed, where a specific new methodology or an improvement to a methodologies [sic] is being studied, the action research method may be the only relevant research method presently available.

This implies that those computing researchers examining software engineering or web engineering methods should consider whether action research is the most appropriate strategy for them. However, you should discuss this with your supervisor, since its lack of recognition in computing could cause you problems in getting your work accepted.

In IS, action research has been more widely practised and accepted in Europe than in the USA, although that situation may now be changing. Other examples of its use include Scandinavian research aimed at empowering trade unions and users (Bjerknes, Ehn, & Kyng, 1987), and the work of Mathiassen and colleagues who collaborated with practitioners in four organizations over 3 years to understand, support and improve systems development practices (Mathiassen, 2002).

Prototyping of IT systems can also be seen as a form of action research, although such work rarely makes reference to the action research literature. Perhaps researchers who design and create IT artefacts and use prototyping to evaluate them could make their practice more visible and increase their opportunities for publication in the research literature if they followed the guidelines of action research.

Evaluating Action Research

Advantages of action research as a research strategy include:

- It concentrates on research that is relevant to people in the real world, bringing about actual improvements in practice, not just models and theories described in little-read academic publications.
- It can bridge the gap between the rarefied academic world and the everyday world of most people.
- It is particularly suited to the creation and refinement of systems development and problem-solving methods.
- It can democratize the research process and engender a greater appreciation of all types of knowledge and ways of knowing.
- It can have higher goals than other research strategies, such as enabling people to change the way they live, and improving social justice.

Disadvantages of action research as a research strategy include:

- It is not yet known and accepted by many computing researchers and some IS researchers.
- It is criticized by some (especially by positivist researchers – see Chapter 19) for lack of rigour, inability to establish cause and effect and outcomes that may not be generalizable to other situations.
- It is sometimes confused with consultancy.
- It is not suited to people who are unwilling to work democratically with others in complex, problematic and unpredictable real-world situations.
- It can be difficult to meet the needs and expectations of everyone involved.

Use the 'Evaluation Guide' to help you analyse and evaluate a project based on action research. If there is insufficient information for you to answer some questions, you should not completely reject the research report, but you should treat the findings with caution and be wary about relying on the report for evidence.

EVALUATION GUIDE: ACTION RESEARCH

1   Did the work involve an iterative cycle of plan–act–reflect? How many cycles are described? Do you think this is enough?
2   Do the researchers make explicit their framework of ideas (F), methodology (M) and area of application (A)?
3   What data generation methods were used? Do you think enough methods were used and enough data collected?
4   Do the researchers discuss the extent of participation achieved, and any limitations in their claimed outcomes caused by lack of full participation?
5   Do the researchers recognize the problems of self-delusion or group-think, and explain adequately how they addressed them?
6   What practical and research outcomes and generalizations do the researchers claim from the action research?
7   How does the research measure up against the quality issues for new action research?
8   What limitations in the action research do the researchers recognize?
9   Can you identify other flaws or omissions in the researchers' reporting of the action research study?
10 Overall, how effectively do you think the action research strategy has been reported and used?

PRACTICAL WORK

1   Try some action research in your own practice. Think of a household chore that you dislike (cleaning? cooking? doing the grocery shopping?). Plan what you could do to make it more enjoyable, and the criteria you will use to evaluate whether it is more enjoyable. Put your plan into effect. Evaluate the outcome(s). Reflect on what you have learnt – about doing the chore, yourself and action research.
2   Find some reports of actual action research projects in IS and computing. For example, look at a journal's special issue on action research (see 'Further Reading' below). How many of the projects involved bringing practical benefits to *business* organizations, and how many were concerned with non-business benefits? Consider whether the balance in the range of articles between a business and non-business focus is appropriate.
3   Practise analysing and evaluating action research. Study a piece of research that used it. Answer the questions in the 'Evaluation Guide' above, using the material in this chapter to help you.

FURTHER READING

As noted already, action research is rarely reported in the computing literature. In the IS literature, however, special issues on it in *Information Technology & People* (*IT&P*, 2001) and *MIS Quarterly* (*MISQ*, 2004) are evidence of interest in it. Checkland both describes the nature of action research (1991) and also illustrates its use (1981; Checkland & Scholes, 1990). Further guidance on the strategy is given by Baskerville (1999), Baskerville and Wood-Harper (1996) and Davison, Martinsons and Kock (2004). Reviews of its use in IS are given by Baskerville and Wood-Harper (1998) and Lau (1997). Myers (1997) is an online living (that is, regularly updated) document covering qualitative research methods in IS, including a section on action research and many useful references (currently available at: www.qual.auckland.ac.nz). Note that McKay and Marshall (2001) criticize many authors for failing to distinguish between the problem-solving method used in a situation (called M in this chapter) with the action research strategy used to investigate that problem-solving method (called R in this chapter).

Reason and Bradbury (2001b) discuss what this chapter has called 'new action research' and give many examples of its use in different disciplines. Oates (2004) discusses their five quality issues (see above) and implications for IS action research, and uses the issues to analyse and evaluate an action research project. This project used Heron's cooperative inquiry approach (Heron, 1996), one type of new action research.

References

Avison, D.E., & Wood-Harper, A.T. (1990). *Multiview: An exploration in information systems development*. Oxford: Blackwell Scientific.

Bailey, F., & Moar, M. (2001). The Vertex Project: Children creating and populating 3D virtual worlds. *Journal of Art & Design Education, 20*(1), 19–30.

Baskerville, R.L. (1999). Investigating information systems with action research. *Communications of the Association for Information Systems, 2*(Article 19), 1–31.

Baskerville, R.L., & Wood-Harper, A.T. (1996). A critical perspective on action research as a method for information systems research. *Journal of Information Technology, 11*, 235–246.

Baskerville, R.L., & Wood-Harper, A.T. (1998). Diversity in information systems action research methods. *European Journal of Information Systems, 7*, 90–107.

Bjerknes, G., Ehn, P., & Kyng, M. (1987). *Computers and democracy*. Aldershot: Avebury.

Bradbury, H., & Reason, P. (2001). Conclusion: Broadening the bandwidth of validity: Issues and choice-points for improving the quality of action research. In H. Bradbury & P. Reason (Eds.), *Handbook of action research. Participatory inquiry & practice* (pp. 447–455). London: Sage.

Brechin, A. (1993). Sharing. In P. Shakespeare, D. Atkinson, & S. French (Eds.), *Reflecting on research practice. Issues in health and social welfare* (pp. 70–82). Buckingham: Open University Press.

Checkland, P. (1981). *Systems thinking, systems practice*. Chichester: Wiley.

Checkland, P. (1991). From framework through experience to learning: The essential nature of action research. In H.-E. Nissen, H.-K. Klein, & R.A. Hirschheim (Eds.), *Information systems research: Contemporary approaches & emergent traditions* (pp. 397–403). Amsterdam: North-Holland.

Checkland, P., & Scholes, J. (1990). *Soft systems methodology in action*. Chichester: Wiley.

Davison, R.M., Martinsons, M.G., & Kock, N. (2004). Principles of canonical action research. *Information Systems Journal, 14*(1), 65–86.

Heron, J. (1996). *Co-operative inquiry: Research into the human condition*. London: Sage.

Horelli, L., & Kaaja, M. (2002). Opportunities and constraints of 'Internet-assisted urban planning' with young people. *Journal of Environmental Psychology, 22*(1–2), 191–200.

Howcroft, D., & Wilson, M. (2003). Paradoxes of participatory practices: The Janus role of the systems developer. *Information and Organization, 13*(1), 1–24.

IT&P. (2001). Special issue on action research in information systems. *Information Technology & People, 14*(1).

Kemmis, S. (2001). Exploring the relevance of critical theory for action research: Emancipatory action research in the footsteps of Juergen Habermas. In P. Reason & H. Bradbury (Eds.), *Handbook of action research. Participatory inquiry & practice* (pp. 91–102). London: Sage.

Kock, N.F. (1997). Myths in organizational action research: Reflections on a study of computer-supported process redesign groups. *Organizations and Society, 4*(9), 65–91.

Kock, N.F., McQueen, R.J., & Scott, J.L. (1997). Can action research be made more rigorous in a positivist sense? The contribution of an iterative approach. *Journal of Systems and Information Technology, 1*(1), 1–24.

Lau, F. (1997). A review on the use of action research in information systems studies. In A. Lee, J. Liebenau, & J. DeGross (Eds.), *Information systems and qualitative research* (pp. 31–68). London: Chapman & Hall.

Mathiassen, L. (2002). Collaborative practice research. *Information Technology & People, 15*(4), 321–345.

McKay, J., & Marshall, P. (2001). The dual imperatives of action research. *Information Technology & People, 14*(1), 46–59.

MISQ. (2004). Special issue on action research. *MIS Quarterly, 28*(3).

Mumford, E. (1995). *Effective systems design and requirements analysis: The ETHICS approach*. Basingstoke: Macmillan.

Mumford, E. (2001). Advice for an action researcher. *Information Technology & People, 14*(1), 12–27.

Myers, M. (1997). Qualitative research in information systems. *MIS Quarterly, 21*(2), 241–242. *MISQ Discovery* archive version, June 1997, www.misq.org/discovery/MISQD_isworld. Updated version retrieved 8 July 2005 from www.qual.auckland.ac.nz.

Oates, B.J. (2004). Action research: Time to take a turn? In B. Kaplan, D. Truex, D. Wastell, T. Wood-Harper & J. DeGross (Eds.), *Information systems research. Relevant theory and informed practice* (pp. 315–333). Boston, MA: Kluwer.

Rapoport, R.N. (1970). Three dilemmas of action research. *Human Relations, 23*(6), 499–513.

Reason, P., & Bradbury, H. (2001a). Introduction: Inquiry and participation in search of a world worthy of human aspiration. In P. Reason & H. Bradbury (Eds.), *Handbook of action research. Participatory inquiry & practice* (pp. 1–14). London: Sage.

Reason, P., & Bradbury, H. (Eds.). (2001b). *Handbook of action research: Participatory inquiry & practice.* London: Sage.

Susman, G.I., & Evered, R.D. (1978). An assessment of the scientific merits of action research. *Administrative Science Quarterly, 23*(December), 582–603.

Tang, N.K.H., Yasa, P.R., & Forrester, P.L. (2004). An application of the Delta Model and BPR in transforming electronic business – The case of a food ingredients company in UK. *Information Systems Journal, 14*(2), 111–130.

Vidgen, R., Avison, D.E., Wood, B., & Wood-Harper, T. (2002). *Developing web information systems.* Oxford: Butterworth-Heinemann.

Waring, T. (2004). From critical theory into information systems practice: A case study of a payroll–personnel system. In B. Kaplan, D. Truex, D. Wastell, T. Wood-Harper, & J. DeGross (Eds.), *Information systems research. Relevant theory and informed practice* (pp. 555–575). Boston, MA: Kluwer.

12 Ethnography

In this chapter you will learn about:

- what is meant by ethnography;
- issues to address in planning and designing an ethnography;
- how an ethnography might be carried out via the Internet;
- how ethnography has been used in IS and computing;
- the advantages and disadvantages of ethnography;
- analysing and evaluating research based on ethnography.

Defining Ethnography

Ethnography means a description of peoples or cultures. Think back to when you started your university studies. You had to learn about the culture of your university and department: the norms of behaviour, appropriate dress and all kinds of unwritten rules and tacit assumptions about how to 'be' a student at your institution. Similarly, anyone starting a new job, or moving to a new country, has to learn about the culture and ways of acting of the people already there, who rarely have to think about such things because they seem perfectly natural to them, it's just 'the way things are done around here'. Whenever we are faced with learning about a new culture, we could be said to be acting as ethnographers. What makes an ethnography a piece of academic research, rather than simple, everyday coping with new contexts, is that ethnographic researchers gather and record data about the culture being studied, reflect on the process of how they came to understand the culture, acknowledge how they might have impacted on the people of that culture, link what they have observed to previous literature and write up the process and findings as academic books or articles.

The initial research question for an ethnographer can be summarized as, 'What is life like for these people?' Ethnography originated in anthropology. Researchers would visit some exotic foreign tribe for a lengthy stay, and try to live like 'the natives', so that they could learn about how these different people lived, worked and perceived their world (for example, Mead, 1943). From the mid-20th century, researchers found they did not have to live for a long time in far-off countries, there were also interesting cultures or sub-cultures that were closer to home and might be studied for a shorter time. Attention turned to groups that were relatively small in number (so easily studied) and that were, often, somewhat outside the mainstream of society. For example, ethnographic studies have been done of drug users, street gangs or football club supporters. More recently, ethnographers have turned their attention to more mundane aspects of social life, recognizing that even 'normal' groups have their own particular codes of behaviour and ways of seeing the world, and have studied, for example, life in a school classroom or in an air traffic control department. All these different types of ethnographies have some characteristics in common:

- The ethnographer spends time in the field, taking part in the life of the people there, that is, carrying out participant observation (see Chapter 14) rather than being a detached observer.
- The ethnography does not take place in an artificial experimental setting, but in the natural setting of the subjects, which, as far as possible, should be undisturbed by the presence of the ethnographer.
- The ethnographer becomes the research instrument, using multiple data generation methods such as interviews, observations and documents (Chapters 13–16) and, especially, copious personal field notes about what they see, feel and experience.
- The ethnographer tries to construct a representation of the world as perceived by the people who live in that world. The test of success of this is whether those people recognize the ethnographer's description of familiar features of their own culture.
- The ethnographer tries to produce a holistic description of the culture, including social, cultural and economic aspects of the situation, rather than just concentrating on one or two aspects of life in that world.

Because the outcomes of an ethnography are so dependent on the researcher as the research instrument, some people find it hard to accept that an ethnography is 'proper' research. Critics point out that the researcher is not detached and objective, and the findings are unlikely to be repeated by someone else, because someone else would, no doubt, experience different things during their time in the studied culture. This argument arises from different ideas about what we mean by research and knowledge, and how we should carry out research to produce knowledge. In other words, the argument is about the underlying philosophical paradigm of different research strategies. Ethnographers tend to be based in the interpretive or critical paradigms, whereas their critics are usually based in the positivist paradigm. These are explained in Chapters 19 and 20, which you must read if you intend to carry out an ethnography.

Planning and Conducting an Ethnography

It is difficult to provide a hard and fast set of rules or sequence of tasks for designing and conducting an ethnography. So much depends on the people in the culture being studied. The researcher must be willing to be flexible, to seize opportunities to learn whenever they present themselves, and to abandon avenues if they seem to be leading nowhere or are unwelcome to the people being studied.

" Being an ethnographer

Fieldworkers, it seems, learn to move among strangers while holding themselves in readiness for episodes of embarrassment, affection, misfortune, partial or vague revelation, deceit, confusion, isolation, warmth, adventure, fear, concealment, pleasure, surprise, insult and always possible deportation. Accident and happenstance shapes fieldworkers' studies as much as planning and foresight; numbing routine as much as live theatre; impulse as much as rational choice; mistaken judgements as much as accurate ones. This may not be the way fieldwork is reported, but it is the way it is done. (Van Maanen, 1988, p. 2) "

This lack of defined procedures, together with no formal mechanisms for judging the accuracy of an ethnographer's results, has made ethnographers vulnerable to criticisms of being 'unscientific' from researchers from other traditions with their array of experiments, surveys and statistical techniques. As ethnographers have turned their attention to more familiar and nearby cultures, rather than the exotic and far away tribes, ethnographers have also had to reflect on whether it is really possible to suspend belief in what they normally take for granted in their own cultures. They have also struggled with how to negotiate access to, act within and report on a setting where the people may be more powerful than they are. Ethnographers have, therefore, debated at great length the nature of their research and how they believe it is valid, examining what Van Maanen (1995) describes as the 'ethnography of ethnography'. Rather than providing a step-by-step guide to conducting an ethnography, this section therefore reviews the issues with which established ethnographers continue to grapple, and which each new ethnographer must find a way to address.

Types of ethnography

There are several different types of ethnography. Here we'll briefly look at three of them: the holistic, semiotic and critical schools (Harvey & Myers, 1995; Myers, 1999 [citing Sanday, 1979]).

- Ethnographers from the **holistic** school say that the researchers must have empathy and identification with the group being observed, that is, they should 'go native' and live like the local people (for example, Evans-Pritchard, 1950). If they do this properly they can act like a sponge and absorb the language and culture of the people they are studying. Others criticize this approach, arguing that we can never set aside all our previous experiences and our own cultural ways of seeing things to put ourselves fully in the shoes of another.
- Ethnographers from the **semiotic** or **thick description** school say that researchers need not identify with and have empathy with their subjects. Instead, the role of the ethnographer is to examine the symbolic forms used by the people under study (words, images, institutions, rituals, behaviours) and analyse them with respect to one another and to the whole culture that they comprise (Geertz, 1973). Ethnographers therefore examine the 'webs of significance' that people in any culture weave. The researcher then communicates these webs of significance by providing an extremely rich or 'thick' description of the situation and its context.
- Ethnographers from the **critical** school assume that the social order that they observe is influenced by individual and group politics, hidden agendas, power centres and unstated assumptions that serve to repress or hide realities. Researchers therefore must get to what is hidden behind the language and other symbolic forms. Critical ethnographers try to uncover what is normally hidden and unspoken in the culture and question the assumptions (Thomas, 1993).

Field notes

In addition to data generation methods such as interviews and observations, ethnographers make detailed field notes. These notes can contain anything and everything that the researcher feels might be relevant. For example, you would normally keep notes on:

- **Substance**: your recording of things that are said or events that happen, including what, where, when and who, as well as the emotional atmosphere at the time.
- **Methodology**: your thoughts and comments on the research process, for example, difficulties in gaining access to someone, justification for changing your research approach, personal hunches to follow up.
- **Analysis**: your reflections on how your other two sections relate to your original research questions or things you have read in the literature, or that lead to new theories or working models.

The notes become a source of evidence and a basis for data analysis in the writing up of the ethnography.

It is essential that you write field notes regularly. Don't worry about whether something is relevant, just write it down anyway. Many ethnographers have commented that what they noted as unusual at the beginning of the study seemed quite normal by the end. If they had not noted it down they would have lost that sense of strangeness. Also, the sooner you write something down, the better. Memories are fallible, and they can distort our recall by re-structuring events to fit in with our latest models or theories. Field notes can also serve as a crutch – by making notes when nothing much seems to be happening, or by going through your previous notes and writing new comments, you still feel like you're an ethnographer.

You can use a notebook where you write everything down and just indicate in the margin whether the note is substantive, methodological or analytic. Or, you might prepare a template in a word processor, with sections for different types of notes.

Example of field notes

Ulrike Schultze (2001) carried out an ethnographic study of people engaged in creating information and knowledge in a large US company. She created a template in her word processor to capture field notes for each day using the headings:

Date	Calendar of today's events
Location	Detailed discussion of main event
Project phase	About my research: People
To do	About my research: Process
Main events	About my research: Academic thoughts
Small/odd events	About my research: Mistakes I made
What I learned	Personal notes
Plans for tomorrow	

Description, theory and generalization

Some people see the role of the ethnographer as to produce a rich, detailed picture of events or cultures. These descriptions should be *standalone* studies. The researcher need not be concerned about whether the situation is representative of other situations, or examine the broader implications of their findings for other events or cultures, or discuss how the work contributes to wider theories. However, others question the usefulness of many standalone descriptions if they do not contribute to the accumulation of any generalized knowledge. Some therefore argue that an ethnography should be undertaken in order to *produce* a theory, one that is grounded in the detailed observations that occur. Others argue that an ethnography should serve as a *test-bed* for theories that have already been advanced, to see whether they hold true in a particular context. A compromise position is to argue that the detailed descriptions of an ethnography are useful in their own right, but the ethnography should also be placed in a theoretical context, for example (Denscombe, 2003, p. 88):

- analysis of how the findings confirm or refute existing theories;
- discussion of why the event or culture was selected in terms of its relevance to concerns in the researcher's own culture;
- consideration of how the findings compare with those of other similar ethnographies.

Reflexivity

Reflexivity is concerned with the relationship between the researcher, the participants and the research process. Ethnographers think a lot about reflexivity. It is relevant to all types of research and is usually explicitly discussed in interpretive and critical studies (see Chapter 20). In early ethnographies, researchers portrayed themselves as objective observers of a situation. However, the possibility of an ethnographer ever being entirely objective is now rejected. We can never suspend all of our prejudices or be gender neutral; what we see is shaped by *our* culture, not the culture of those we are observing. Since researchers themselves are the main research instrument in ethnography, it is now seen as crucial that they reflect on:

- their pre-conceptions, age, gender, race, background, education and experiences;
- how they might be perceived by the people in their study;
- how they might influence the setting and what they observe;
- how their cultural and educational background and prejudices might affect what they observe and report;
- how their background might influence the structuring mechanisms they use to impose sense on their observations.

Ethnographers must therefore observe others and participate with them, and, at the same time, stand back and observe themselves observing and participating.

In reporting their findings, ethnographers include a discussion of their self, and how their personal experiences, beliefs and values may have shaped what was observed and how it was interpreted. It can be difficult, however, to decide how much to reveal about yourself. Too little and readers will argue that they cannot judge whether your findings are just a reflection of your own prejudices; too much and readers will argue that your ethnography is really an autobiography, with too much about you and too little about the group you were studying. Many reviewers, accustomed to a more objective style of research, feel uncomfortable reading a subjective, reflexive account. Ethnographers are also aware that they make themselves vulnerable by discarding the conventional authorial power, and possibly revealing aspects of themselves that they might prefer to remain confidential. You have to decide how much detail about yourself to give, depending on the nature of the research topic, the methods, the setting and the audience for whom the ethnography is written.

Writing

Ethnographers also recognize that the act of writing up their research is not a selfless, objective act. It is a creative act. Ethnographers cannot reproduce everything they saw, heard or experienced, so by choosing to concentrate on some aspects and omitting others, they are constructing a *partial* account of a culture. They also decide what detail to give about themselves and their own experiences, meaning that the ethnography becomes a form of self-presentation and identity construction. The same can be argued for any piece of research, but ethnographers, in their combined roles of research instruments, data analysts and ethnography writers, are particularly aware of the partial and possibly one-sided nature of their accounts.

The problem of what to write about and what to leave out is particularly difficult when writing up an ethnography as a journal article, because journals normally set a maximum length of 20–25 pages. Ethnographers find that it is difficult to reduce an immersion experience that lasted several months or years into 20 pages. But if they write about just one or two aspects of their ethnography, they lose the holistic picture that they wish to paint. Many ethnographies are therefore written up as books rather than journal articles.

Tests of success

An ethnography is said to be successful if its readers are able to understand the activities of people in another culture (or sub-culture) and see that they make sense *within the context of that culture*. The activities might previously have seemed to the readers absurd or irrational, but after reading the ethnography they don't any more. The readers must also be presented with enough evidence to be assured that the phenomena being described do exist outside the ethnographer's mind (for example, photographs, written documents, film, audio-tape transcripts). Also, the members of the culture being studied should recognize the description and agree that it explains how they live or work.

If you have thought about all of the issues discussed in this section, and this kind of research appeals, you can begin to plan your ethnography. You also need to read Chapter 5 on participants, to ensure that you work ethically – particularly if you are thinking of undertaking covert observation of other people. You also need to think about how you will use questionnaires, conduct interviews, make observations and collect documents (see Chapters 13–16). You then need to analyse your data and make interpretations, (see Chapters 17 and 18) and present your findings (see Chapter 21).

The Internet and Ethnography

For ethnographers there are two different ways of viewing the Internet (Hine, 2000): as a culture or as a cultural artefact.

- The *culture* view sees the Internet as a (virtual) *place* where people form and re-form a culture or set of practices and meanings. Instead of travelling to a geographical place, an ethnographer can go online and examine what people do in cyberspace: the interactions between them, the conventions they use (for example, the smiley face and other emoticons), the communities they form and the ways they make use of the technology available to them. An Internet ethnographer could investigate this culture by, for example, carrying out online interviews, observing interactions in chatrooms and collecting documents such as copies of websites visited.
- The *cultural artefact* view sees the Internet as a *product* of a culture – a technology produced by people in particular contexts and shaped by the ways in which people market, develop and use it. There is no fixed way for the Internet or World Wide Web to be – its shape and content depends on individuals and groups (for example, hardware producers, software vendors, website developers, newsgroup contributors). An Internet ethnographer could take one part of the Internet, say a company website, observe its structure and content and how they change over time, and use online or offline interviews to explore the social, political or organizational context shaping the website, how the site's audience was conceived by the site developers, and so on.

Neither of these views of the Internet is more appropriate than the other – the Internet can be seen in both ways. Any Internet ethnography that takes only one of the views would probably be incomplete. However, this poses a significant problem for the Internet ethnographer, who will need to find ways of switching between the two views.

One possible advantage of doing an Internet ethnography is that you do not need to travel – you can sit at a PC wherever you like and go online. However, the disadvantage of this is that you are not then immersed in a culture, as traditional ethnographers are, instead you have to move between an online and an offline world. On the other hand, other people you 'meet' on the Internet also have both an online and an offline presence – something that is often forgotten by those who only take the 'Internet as culture' view. As you try to fit your online and offline activities around each other, and think about the role you play online and whether that is who you are offline, you can reflect that others are experiencing the same conflicts and dilemmas – you are truly participating in Internet life!

Examples of Ethnography in IS and Computing Research

Zuboff's (1988) ground-breaking study looks at the introduction of IT-based systems into a range of organizations and explores how these systems were altering perceptions about the nature of work, the dynamics of the workplace, and appropriate management and organizational structures. Her studies started in 1978, when she realized that she was presented with a unique historical opportunity to study something, which, in a few years, would seem quite normal and just the way that work is done in a modern business.

Trauth (2000) is another book-length example of ethnography research in IS. She was concerned with the 'information economy' in Ireland, that is, companies and workers in the IT industries that produce hardware, software and information systems. She explored the two-way interaction between the cultural context and the information economy work, workers and workplaces in Ireland posing two research questions (p. 17):

- How does the socio-cultural context within which the information economy exists help to shape its structure?
- How are the effects of an information economy manifested in society?

Through her ethnographic study, she explored the thoughts, viewpoints and behaviours of particular people in certain organizations at a specific point in time: IS workers and managers in selected Irish and American-owned information sector firms, in Ireland, in the period 1989–99.

Other ethnographic studies have looked at the development of information systems (Bentley et al., 1992; Hughes, Randall, & Shapiro, 1992; Myers & Young, 1997; Orlikowski, 1991), the management of information technology (Davies, 1991; Davies & Nielsen, 1992), the creation of information and knowledge (Schultze, 2000) and the work practices of programmers (Robinson & Sharp, 2003).

Internet ethnographies include Turkle (1995) and Hine (2000). Turkle explores how people reconstruct their identities when they go online. Hine focuses on newsgroups and websites around the case of Louise Woodward, who was charged with the murder of a baby in her care.

Evaluating Ethnography-based Research

Advantages of ethnography as a research strategy include:

- It gives a rich, detailed picture of a particular situation or work practices, putting events or practices into context rather than abstracting one or two aspects in isolation.
- The findings do not emerge from an artificial experimental setting, but from the natural setting and lives of the people studied. It can therefore be used to challenge the findings from more artificial studies such as experiments.
- It can be used to study the institutional contexts of IS and computing practices, bringing into one study all the stakeholders and the human, social, organizational and technical aspects of IS development and application.

- It is good for studies where the topic of interest is complex and embedded in a social system that is not fully understood – as in much of information systems and software engineering research.
- It can be used to study something over a long period, for example, the introduction of a new information system and how people accommodate it and adapt it over time.

Disadvantages of an ethnography include:

- It makes high demands of the researcher: time, copious data to be managed, analysed and written up, being alone in a strange setting, handling social relations, persuading others to open up to you, dealing with the ethical aspects of observing others, and so on.
- Researchers can find it difficult to deal with the tension between providing an account of how things 'are' in the setting and yet also recognizing that all accounts are a construction of the author, who is inevitably biased.
- It can sometimes end up as 'story-telling', where a detailed account is given at the expense of developing any analytical insight or theoretical contribution.
- The in-depth study of one situation may not produce findings of relevance to any other situation.
- It is not as well-established as surveys and experiments and its approach and findings may be rejected by those accustomed to more 'scientific' approaches.

Use the 'Evaluation Guide' below to help you analyse and evaluate a project based on ethnography. If there is insufficient information for you to answer some questions, you should not completely reject the research report, but you should treat the findings with caution and be wary about relying on the report for evidence.

EVALUATION GUIDE: ETHNOGRAPHY

1   Did the research focus on lifestyles, meanings and beliefs?
2   What data generation methods were used? Do you think enough methods were used and enough data collected?
3   How long did the researcher spend in the field? Do you think this was long enough?
4   Does the work seem to belong to the holistic, semiotic or critical school?
5   Is the ethnography a standalone description, or is it linked to theory, other ethnographies or issues in the researcher's own culture?
6   Does the paper include an account of the researcher's self?
7   Has the researcher acknowledged that the ethnography is a construction rather than a literal description?
8   What limitations in the ethnography does the researcher recognize?
9   Can you identify other flaws or omissions in the researcher's reporting of the ethnography?
10 Overall, how effectively do you think the ethnography strategy has been reported and used?

PRACTICAL WORK

1   Over the next week, look at an organization with which you are familiar (for example, where you study or work) and try to see its culture through the eyes of a visiting Martian. Questions you could ask yourself include:

   a   What are the unwritten rules of behaviour or dress?
   b   What images or metaphors do people use to describe the organization?
   c   What beliefs and values dominate it – officially or unofficially?
   d   What ceremonies and rituals occur?
   e   Are there sub-cultures within the organization, with different values and practices?

2   Think about the concept of the Internet as a culture. When you are using the Internet find examples of online conventions or social norms that people have adopted. Are there different conventions in different areas, for example, newsgroups versus work-based email communications?
3   Think about the concept of the Internet as a cultural artefact. Watch out for mention of the Internet in newspaper articles or television programmes.

   a   What different visual images are used to portray the idea of the Internet? (For example, rear view of man sitting at computer, disembodied hand on mouse, …).
   b   What different metaphors are used to portray the Internet? (For example, a store of knowledge, a market place, …).
   c   What different beliefs about the Internet are given? (For example, a dangerous place for children, a place where terrorists plot, …).

4   Practise analysing and evaluating research based on ethnography. Study a piece of research that used it as its research strategy. Answer the questions in the 'Evaluation Guide' above, using the material in this chapter to help you.

FURTHER READING

Useful texts on ethnography that any budding ethnographer would be advised to study include Geertz (1973), Hammersley and Atkinson (1983) and Van Maanen (1988). Morgan (1997) discusses seeing organizations as cultures in Chapter 5.

   Myers (1997) is a living document on qualitative research methods in information systems (available online at: www.qual.auckland.ac.nz). It includes a section on ethnography and many useful references. The relevance of ethnographic research to IS and computing are discussed by Harvey and Myers (1995) and Myers (1999).

   In her book's appendix, Trauth (2000) reflects on her research methodology, including the problems she encountered and the worries she felt. Similarly Schultze (2000, 2001) reflects on her experiences of doing an ethnography in IS and suggests five necessary factors for a successful ethnography. Finally, Hine (2000) gives much food for thought about the changing meaning of ethnography when we study the Internet. You might find it easier to read her actual ethnography (2000, Chapters 4–7) before tackling the earlier, more theoretical chapters.

References

Bentley, R., Hughes, J.A., Randall, D., Rodden, T., Sawyer, P., Shapiro, D., et al. (1992). Ethnographically-informed systems design for air traffic control. In *CSCW '92. ACM 1992 conference on computer-supported cooperative work: Sharing perspectives* (pp. 123–129). New York: ACM Press.

Davies, L.J. (1991). Researching the organizational culture contexts of information systems strategy. In H.E. Nissen, H.K. Klein, & R. Hirschheim (Eds.), *Information systems research: Contemporary approaches and emergent traditions* (pp. 145–167). Amsterdam: Elsevier/North Holland.

Davies, L.J., & Nielsen, S. (1992). An ethnographic study of configuration management and documentation practices in an information technology centre. In K.E. Kendall, K. Lyytinen, & J. DeGross (Eds.), *The impact of computer supported technology on information systems development* (pp. 179–192). Amsterdam: Elsevier/North Holland.

Denscombe, M. (2003). *The good research guide for small-scale social research projects* (2nd ed.). Maidenhead: Open University Press.

Evans-Pritchard, E.E. (1950). *Witchcraft, oracles and magic among the Azende.* Oxford: Clarendon Press.

Geertz, C. (1973). *The interpretation of cultures.* New York: Basic Books.

Hammersley, M., & Atkinson, P. (1983). *Ethnography: Principles in practice.* London: Tavistock.

Harvey, L.J., & Myers, M.D. (1995). Scholarship and practice: The contribution of ethnographic research methods to bridging the gap. *Information Technology & People, 8*(3), 13–27.

Hine, C. (2000). *Virtual ethnography.* London: Sage.

Hughes, J.A., Randall, D., & Shapiro, D. (1992). Faltering from ethnography to design. In *CSCW '92. ACM 1992 conference on computer-supported cooperative work: Sharing perspectives* (pp. 115–123). New York: ACM.

Mead, M. (1943). *Coming of age in Samoa: A study of adolescence and sex in primitive societies.* Harmondsworth: Penguin.

Morgan, G. (1997). *Images of organization* (2nd revised ed.). Thousand Oaks, CA: Sage.

Myers, M.D. (1997). Qualitative research in information systems. *MIS Quarterly, 21*(2), 241–242. MISQ Discovery archive version, June 1997, www.misq.org/discovery/ MISQD_is world. Updated version retrieved 8 July 2005 from www.qual.auckland. ac.nz.

Myers, M.D. (1999). Investigating information systems with ethnographic research. *Communications of AIS, 2*(Article 23), 1–20.

Myers, M.D., & Young, L.W. (1997). Hidden agendas, power and managerial assumptions in information systems development: An ethnographic study. *Information Technology & People, 10*(3), 224–240.

Orlikowski, W.J. (1991). Integrated information environment or matrix of control. The contradictory implications of information technology. *Accounting, Management and Information Technologies, 1*(1), 9–42.

Robinson, H.M., & Sharp, H.C. (2003). An ethnography of XP practice. In *Proceedings of EASE/PPIG Conference April 2003* (pp. 15–27). Keele: University of Keele.

Sanday, P.R. (1979). The ethnographic paradigms. *Administrative Science Quarterly, 24*(4), 527–538.

Schultze, U. (2000). A confessional account of an ethnography about knowledge work. *MIS Quarterly, 24*(1), 3–41.

Schultze, U. (2001). Reflexive ethnography in information systems research. In E.M. Trauth (Ed.), *Qualitative research in IS: Issues and trends* (pp. 78–103). Hershey, PA: Idea Group.

Thomas, J. (1993). *Doing critical ethnography*. Newbury Park, CA: Sage.

Trauth, E.M. (2000). *The culture of an information economy. Influences and impacts in the Republic of Ireland*. Dordrecht: Kluwer Academic.

Turkle, S. (1995). *Life on the screen. Identity in the age of the Internet*. New York: Simon & Schuster.

Van Maanen, J. (1988). *Tales of the field: On writing ethnography*. Chicago, IL: University of Chicago Press.

Van Maanen, J. (1995). An end to innocence: The ethnography of ethnography. In J. Van Maanen (Ed.), *Representation in Ethnography* (pp. 1–35). Thousand Oaks, CA: Sage.

Zuboff, S. (1988). *In the age of the smart machine*. New York: Basic Books.

13 Interviews

In this chapter you will learn about:

- interviews as a data generation method;
- how to plan and conduct both individual and group interviews;
- how the Internet might be used for individual or group interviews;
- how interviews have been used in previous IS and computing research;
- the advantages and disadvantages of interviews as a data generation method;
- how to analyse and evaluate interview-based research.

Defining Interviews

Each research strategy (see Chapters 7–12) contains one or more data generation methods. We'll look now at the first of these – interviews. An interview is a particular kind of conversation between people. It has a set of assumptions (normally unspoken) that do not apply to 'normal' conversations. Usually, one person has a purpose for undertaking the interview: they want to gain information from the other(s). This means that the discussion does not occur by chance, but has been planned in some way by the researcher. They usually have an agenda – particular issues they want to find out about – so the discussion topics do not occur arbitrarily or randomly, with both sides free to choose topics at will. Instead, the researcher will steer the discussion onto their topics of interest. Since the researcher normally guides the discussion, it does not have a free-flowing form like other conversations. Rather, there is tacit agreement that, at least at the beginning of the interview if not all the way through, the researcher has the right to control both the agenda and the proceedings and will ask most of the questions. A research interview is not carried out covertly, for example, by secretly recording discussions, but is openly a meeting aiming to produce material for research purposes, and the interviewee knows this and agrees with it. It is also understood that the interviewee's words can normally be treated as 'on the record', so they can be used by the researcher later. Only if the interviewee specifies that some responses are not to be made publicly available are they treated as 'off the record'.

Interviews can be suitable data generation methods when a researcher wants to:

- obtain detailed information;
- ask questions that are complex, or open-ended, or whose order and logic might need to be different for different people;
- explore emotions, experiences or feelings that cannot easily be observed or described via pre-defined questionnaire responses;
- investigate sensitive issues, or privileged information, that respondents might not be willing to write about on paper for a researcher that they have not met.

Interviews are much used in case studies and ethnographies (Chapters 10 and 12), but can be used in other strategies too. For example, they can be used in surveys (Chapter 7), that is, interviewing people rather than asking them to complete a questionnaire. They are also often used to 'top-and-tail' a survey strategy – interviews are used to elicit themes that are then included in a questionnaire, and follow-up interviews are used to obtain more detail about some questionnaire responses. Similarly they can 'top-and-tail' a design and creation strategy (Chapter 8) by generating data for a requirements specification and eliciting user feedback on a finished design.

Although often one-to-one, interviews can also be undertaken with a group of respondents, as in focus groups that are used by politicians and market researchers. Both one-to-one and group interviews are therefore discussed in this chapter.

Planning and Conducting Interviews

Because we all regularly carry out conversations with others, it is tempting to think that we can all naturally carry out interviews. However, successful research interviews need planning and a particular set of skills, as explained below. This section concentrates on one-to-one interviews. The following section explains additional issues that arise in group interviews.

Types of interviews

Interviews can be divided into three types, so you need to decide which type you will use: structured, semi-structured or unstructured interviews.

- **Structured interviews**: these use pre-determined, standardized, identical questions for every interviewee. You read out the questions and note your interviewee's responses, often using pre-coded answers. Although there will be some social interaction between you and the respondent, such as if the respondent asks for and receives clarification, you do not really engage in a conversation and it is important that you read out all the questions in the same way and note the answers without comment, otherwise you might indicate your own views to the interviewee. In effect, you are asking your interviewees to complete a questionnaire, but you are doing the writing for them (or even entering their responses straight into a computer, if you use a laptop). For structured interviews, you should read Chapter 15 on questionnaires, which will help you plan a structured set of questions. The remainder of this chapter concentrates on the other two types of interview.

- **Semi-structured interviews**: you still have a list of themes to be covered and questions you want to ask, but you are willing to change the order of questions depending on the flow of the 'conversation' and you might ask additional questions if your interviewee brings up issues you had not prepared questions for. The interviewees are able to speak with more detail on the issues you raise, and introduce issues of their own that they think relevant to your themes.
- **Unstructured interviews**: the researcher has less control. You start things off by introducing a topic and then let the interviewees develop their ideas, talking freely about events, behaviour or beliefs, while you try not to interrupt and are as unintrusive as possible.

Both semi-structured and unstructured interviews allow interviewees to 'speak their minds' and so are used where the primary purpose is 'discovery', rather than 'checking'. They are therefore used for in-depth investigations, especially those aimed at exploring personal accounts and feelings. They are not useful, though, for situations where you want to draw research conclusions that are generalizations about the whole population (whatever this may be in relation to your research topic), because you will not have responses about the same topics from all your interviewees, and the time required means that you will usually only have a small number of cases from which to draw conclusions.

Researcher's role and identity

It has been shown that people respond differently depending on how they perceive the person asking the questions, that is, the data generated can depend on the perceived role and identity of the researcher. For example, they might answer you differently depending on whether they think you are a student or a journalist or a police detective. Your sex, age, ethnic origin, accent and status can also all influence the respondents when they decide what information to give you. You can, and should, aim to be professional, polite, punctual, receptive and neutral, but you cannot do much about many aspects of yourself that might influence your respondents. You should therefore ask yourself whether interviews are an appropriate data generation method for your topic, and whether you need to adjust how you present yourself. For example:

- Is there a likely age gap between you and your interviewees, and how might this affect the interviews?
- Given your research topic, will you find a lack of willingness to respond from people of the opposite sex or a different ethnic background?
- Is there a difference in social status or education between you and your interviewees, and how might this affect the interviews?
- Are there aspects of your appearance you might need to adjust to best fit in with the people being interviewed? (Blue hair and multiple earrings and studs might be perfectly acceptable when interviewing creative types in the computer games and animation industries, for example, but inappropriate when interviewing senior managers in a more conventional organization.)

Interview preparation

Obviously, you need to plan the issues you want to raise and the questions you want to ask. But your preparation should also include gathering background information on your interviewees and their context. For example, if you are to interview the employees of a particular organization, you could look at company reports and recent news articles on that organization. You could also find out about your interviewees, for example, their job title and department. This background research is useful because:

- It can highlight issues you might want to raise with the interviewee.
- It establishes your credibility as a professional in the eyes of interviewees, so they might be more willing to open up to you.
- It can help you assess the accuracy of some of the information given to you.

Sometimes it is useful to send your interviewees a list of topics or questions in advance, giving them time to think about their views, and again helping to establish your credibility as a serious researcher.

As part of your preparation, you should also carry out at least one practice interview with a willing friend, trying to follow all the points explained in this section.

Scheduling

You need to obtain agreement for an interview, telling your proposed interviewee the purpose of the interview and the likely duration. Be careful not to underestimate the time you will need – better to finish early and give your interviewees some unexpected free time than run over into their next planned activity. Carrying out interviews can be very tiring, and they need to be written up afterwards (see below), so a good rule of thumb is to schedule not more than three in one day. Similarly, interviewees should not normally be expected to make themselves available for more than two hours – if you know you will need longer, arrange to have a series of shorter interviews, otherwise you risk tiring and annoying your interviewees.

" Don't take up too much of your interviewee's time!

'I have answered three questions, and that is enough,'

Said his father, 'don't give yourself airs!

Do you think I can listen all day to such stuff?

Be off, or I'll kick you downstairs!'

(Lewis Carroll, 'You are old, Father William', *Alice's Adventures in Wonderland* [London: Penguin, 1994; first published 1865], Chapter 5)

"

The venue should be somewhere your interviewees feel comfortable – perhaps their office, a canteen or their home. Ideally, it should also be somewhere where you will not be disturbed, that is private and reasonably quiet.

Recording

You will need to somehow capture the discussion – relying on memory alone is not recommended, because our memories are unreliable and prone to bias and error. Recording methods include handwritten field notes, audio tape recording and videos. Most researchers use audio tape recording backed up by written field notes.

- **Field notes** are the minimum requirement. As well as noting what your interviewee says, you can note information about the context, such as the location or atmosphere, your own thoughts on what the interviewee's intent was behind some statements, or your observations of non-verbal communication, such as body language. Occasionally, an interviewee might refuse you permission to make notes during an interview – you must, of course, respect their wishes, but write up your recollections as best you can later. It's not easy to write notes, think about the interviewee's responses and ask questions all at the same time, so you should practise, and accept that your notes will not provide a complete record of everything said. As soon as possible after the interview you should write further notes on it, while the memory is still fresh in your mind.

- **Audio tape recording** provides you with a complete record of everything that is said, allowing you to concentrate on the process of the interview. The tapes can also be listened to by other researchers, which means they can check your work or analyse the data gathered. However, interviewees are often nervous about being recorded and may be more inhibited in their responses or even refuse permission. Also, tapes do not capture the non-verbal communication and context of the interview.
- **Video tape recording** can capture non-verbal communication and provides a more complete record of events during the interview. However, the equipment can be expensive and bulky, although costs are reducing and digital video cameras are much smaller than earlier analogue types. Video recording, however, is often intrusive and inhibiting, and many interviewees are reluctant to be filmed.

Seating and equipment

You should try to set up the seating arrangements to allow comfortable interaction – two people should ideally sit at 90 degrees to one another, which allows eye contact but without any suggestion of confrontation. Of course, if you are in someone's office, you might not be able to change the seating arrangement – is the seating arrangement chosen by your interviewee meaningful?

You need to be able to set up any equipment quickly, especially if you are in someone's private office and the interview 'clock' has already started running. You also need to be able to make small talk while setting up. For example, it is very off-putting for an interviewee if you start a conversation and then go quiet because you are watching your laptop booting up, which your interviewee cannot see.

Of course, you should thoroughly check your equipment before starting. Make sure it is functioning well, that batteries are fully charged up and, if possible, you have spares or some other backup in case of emergency. If audio taping, try to use tapes that are long enough on one side to cover the planned duration of the interview without the need to stop and turn them over. And finally, at the start of the interview – remember to switch off your mobile phone.

The interview

An interview normally begins with introductions, clarification about the purpose of the interview and the research, obtaining permission to record and giving assurances about confidentiality and anonymity. You should also make small talk, to help put the interviewee at ease, for example:

- comments about your journey to the interview (but do not moan);
- asking about any imminent holiday plans (but do not pry);
- remarks about the weather (always useful in the UK!).

As you move onto the main body of the interview, start with an easy question, one where the interviewee is likely already to have well-formed views. Then you can ask more questions about the response, or move onto your other topics. Questions about sensitive issues should be left until later in the interview, when your interviewee has had the chance to decide how much you can be trusted.

Your questions need to be clearly phrased and easily understood, not too long, nor two questions jumbled together, nor full of jargon or academic terms unfamiliar to your interviewee. Mostly you should use open rather than closed questions. Open questions often start with 'what', 'how' or 'why' and encourage the interviewee to provide an extensive answer. For example:

- 'What are your views about the potential of e-commerce for your organization?
- 'How could a knowledge management system help the company to meet its business goals?'
- 'Why have you chosen to develop your own in-house systems development method rather than use one that is available commercially?'

Closed questions elicit very short answers, often either 'Yes' or 'No', or they allow the interviewee to provide a fact or confirm a fact. For example:

- 'How many people work in your department?'
- 'Did I hear you say that the new computer system went live on the first of September?'

You can use aids to help you and your interviewee, for example, photographs, newspaper advertisements, screenshots, websites – anything that promotes a discussion about your research themes. Or you could describe a scenario and ask what the interviewee would do in such circumstances. Or you could ask the interviewee to describe a particularly interesting or challenging recent event that is relevant to your research topic. Your own behaviour can also help a discussion along. By leaning forward slightly and using eye contact, you can show that you are listening and interested. Use silence too – rather than rushing to fill gap in the conversation, wait and let your interviewee fill the gap.

You can also nudge the discussion along by using tactics that prompt, probe or check. Prompts are used to encourage your interviewee to say more. Probes are used when you want to pick up on something in more detail. Checks are used to make sure you have understood your interviewee correctly, and should be performed at regular points during the interview. They can also be used to conclude the discussion on one of your themes prior to moving on to the next (see the examples in the box).

Prompts, probes and checks

Examples of prompts:

- Remain silent.
- Repeat your question.
- Repeat the last few words said by your interviewee.

Examples of probes:

- 'Could you give me some examples of that?'
- 'Would an example of that be when …?'
- 'Can you give me more a bit more detail about what you mean by …?'

Examples of checks:

- 'So, let me see if I've understood you correctly …'
- 'What this means, then, is that …'
- 'If I can summarize what I think you've said …'

As far as possible, you should try to be non-judgemental, suspending your own views and not showing any reaction to your interviewee's comments other than polite interest. You should ask questions in a neutral tone of voice, to be careful you do not 'lead' the interviewees to give responses they think you want to hear. Watch your body language too – don't display disgust, surprise, anger or pleasure. Remember also to respect the rights of your interviewee – if someone does not want to answer a particular question, or seems to be becoming embarrassed or stressed, back off.

Finally, you should bring the interview to a close by inviting the interviewee to raise any points that have not been addressed so far, thanking the interviewee for their time, and asking whether you can send a summary or transcript of the interview for checking.

Transcribing

After an interview, you will need to transcribe your tapes, because it is much easier to search through and analyse the data once it is in written form. Many novice researchers underestimate how long transcription takes – assume something like 5 hours for every hour of tape, more if you are a slow writer or the tape quality is poor. Transcribing is laborious, but it is also rewarding because it brings the interview back to life again, and is your first real chance to start thinking about and analysing the data. As you transcribe the words, add your own informal notes and comments at the side, for example, gestures the interviewee made, uncomfortable atmospheres you sensed, or thoughts about what the comments might mean, how they relate to your themes or correspond with other interviews. It is important to capture the interviewee's words as spoken, because when you come to write up your findings, you will need to include quotations from them. Of course, most interviewees do not speak in complete, audible sentences, and there are false starts and pauses. Most researchers try to transcribe the words exactly as spoken, but may edit them slightly (to lose the 'erms' and 'uhs') when subsequently using quotations in their papers or thesis, while being careful not to distort the sense. Many researchers stick to transcribing just the words used, and lose the richness of intonation, pitch and non-verbal sounds. If it is important to your research topic that you do not lose this richness, there are established conventions about how to show such aspects in a written transcript (see, for example, O'Connell & Kowall, 1995; Potter & Wetherell, 1987). Be careful to label each transcript with the name of the interviewee, date and location of the interview, and number each line in the transcript so that you can easily find again each response.

Checking

If possible, you should take your interview notes or the transcript back to the interviewee for checking. This allows the interviewee to confirm that any facts are correct and that what was said was what was really meant. You should also check the interview data against other sources. For example, documents and observations can confirm statements in the interview or cast doubt on how seriously the interview responses should be taken. You should also look for themes that occur across more than one interview, rather than basing all your findings on one individual's views in one transcript.

Having planned and carried out your interviews, written up your notes and produced your transcripts, you can move onto data analysis, which can be either quantitative, for example, counting the number of times particular key words appear, or qualitative, for example, exploring the different themes that occur, or both (see Chapters 17 and 18).

Group Interviews

In a group interview, you would normally interview between three and six people together. This does not mean that you interview each individual in turn, working your way around the table. Instead, you want the group members to interact with each other and have a group discussion from which new insights might arise, which the individual members had not previously recognized. Advantages of a group interview include:

- They can help to generate consensus views.
- They can generate more responses, and more varied responses, as one participant's views are challenged by others or stimulate others to new ideas.
- They can brainstorm themes which can become the subject of a survey.

However, there are also disadvantages, including:

- Some members (often men or those higher up in a company hierarchy) might dominate the talk and the quieter ones (often women or those lower down in a company hierarchy) struggle to be heard.
- Some people might be reluctant to express their own views in front of the others.
- The opinions that are expressed might be those deemed to be 'acceptable' within the group.

When choosing your group members, it's a good idea to invite participants who are all of similar status, so that people are not worried about speaking up in front of someone senior to them. The seating should be arranged so that everyone is visible to everyone else, and the researcher should not be in a focal position.

If you decide to hold group interviews, all of the issues discussed in the previous section still apply. You will also have to have skills for facilitating a group discussion and ensuring that everyone is heard (see the box below).

Tactical questions for reducing dominance and involving others

- 'Jean, what do you think?'
- 'What do the rest of you think about this?'
- 'How does Mike's point relate to the one you raised, Sarah?'
- 'What do people think of Atta's suggestion?'

It is very hard to facilitate a group discussion and keep notes at the same time. Clearly audio recording is useful, but remember transcribing will take longer than for individual interviews because you will have people talking across each other and will need to spend longer deciphering what was said. It is a good idea to involve a second researcher, so that one can facilitate the discussion and one can observe and make notes.

Internet-based Interviews

Although there has been limited use so far, the Internet offers exciting possibilities for online individual and group interviews. Unless Voice-over-Internet telephony is being used, the interview is not spoken, but comprises a set of written questions and answers. Clearly this changes our understanding of 'interview'. Because responses have to be typed, they are likely to be shorter and less expansive than in a face-to-face interview. In online interviews, we also lose the richness of gestures and facial expressions and the context of a face-to-face interview. Researchers also have to either take on trust that their informants are who they say they are, or do some detective work to try and establish whether they are really qualified to speak on the subject. Similarly, informants need to be convinced about the identity and honesty of a researcher they have not met. However, online interviews can be cheaper than face-to-face interviews because there are no travel costs, they allow the researcher to reach informants across the world (or at least those people that have email access and the technical expertise), there are no tapes to transcribe and the data is already typed ready for analysis.

Opinion is still divided about whether online interviews are appropriate when the information sought requires the establishment of good inter-personal relationships. Some maintain that such intimacy cannot be achieved online because there are insufficient social cues for people to establish the human 'presence' of each other. Others argue that warm relationships can and do develop online, with a rapid increase in intimacy between people who were strangers a short while ago. (For a discussion of these two viewpoints, see Mann & Stewart, 2000.)

The simplest form of online interviews is via email to named individuals. An email can be sent introducing the researcher and the research topic and the recipient can be invited to answer some questions. Once those answers are received, the researcher follows up with more questions and a 'conversation' can ensue. Be careful if you are sending out the same questions via email to several people who do not know the identity of the other participants – use the 'Bcc' (blind copy) facility of your emailing software. For a group interview, all questions *and* responses are sent to the whole group. Alternatively, synchronous communication can be used, that is, real-time chat, where what one person types is immediately visible to everyone else. Some companies now offer virtual facilities for online focus groups with web-based 'rooms' for discussion sessions, and technical backup can also be provided for a fee.

If you do not know the names and email addresses of the people you want to invite to participate in your online interviews, you will have to appeal for volunteers via newsgroups or mailing lists – remember to obtain the permission of the list-owner or gatekeeper first.

You should be familiar with some of the shorthand notation used online (for example, LOL: laughs out loud, IMHO: in my humble opinion), but try not to use them yourself in case your interviewee does not know them. Similarly you should recognize the emoticons in common usage such as ;-) and :-(, but again use them carefully yourself because some people find them irritating. Remember, also, that different cultures might not know the emoticons, or have their own system (for example, Japan – see Mann and Stewart [2000] for examples).

Because they cannot see you nodding your head and looking interested, interviewees may need reassurance from you that they are supplying the kind of information you need. Remember, too, that participants can suddenly disappear – you do not know whether their emails have been lost in cyberspace, or they have decided to withdraw from your research, or they are ill, or …? Bear in mind that, currently at least, there is an expectation that email is answered quickly. This means that people will expect to hear back from you speedily, regardless of any other work or deadlines you might have. Online interviews can therefore be very demanding, and you will need to plan how you will schedule your online interview work alongside the rest of your commitments.

Finally, if you do intend to try online interviewing, you should read the 'Internet Research and Ethics' section in Chapter 5.

Examples of Interviews in IS and Computing Research

As noted earlier, interviews are used extensively in case studies and ethnographies, so IS and computing research based on these strategies is a good place to look for examples of interview use. For instance:

- Orlikowski (1993) carried out case studies of two organizations that adopted and used CASE tools. She developed a theoretical framework for conceptualizing the organizational issues around their adoption and use. She used unstructured and semi-structured interviews across all levels of the organization hierarchy: 119 in the first organization and 40 in the second organization. Her interviews were combined with observations and document study in a grounded theory approach (see Chapter 18). However, she gives us no information about how the interviews were conducted, or how her own role and identity might have impacted on the interviews. Her paper is, nevertheless, a good illustration of the kind of findings that can emerge from this type of research.
- Walsham (1993) has made extensive use of in-depth case studies to study IT in organizations, using semi-structured interviews alongside observations and document study. For example, Walsham explores the introduction of a new computer system into a UK manufacturing company, the strategy, development and use of a computer-based information system in a medium-sized UK building society, and three computer systems developed by a central government agency in a Third World country to monitor and control development projects. In each case, semi-structured interviews were the main data generation method.

- Hine (2000) used email 'interviews' to ask web developers about how and why they had developed their websites during the Louise Woodward case (who was accused of killing a baby in her care). Hine supplies the first email she sent out to web developers, which introduced herself and the purpose of her research before asking a set of questions. The recipients were invited to answer the questions as briefly or fully as they chose, or even to ignore some of them altogether if they wanted. She also gave the URL of her own website so that her potential informants could check her out first. Many of her informants did indeed visit her website – it gave them an opportunity to assess her and decide whether they would trust her, so going some way to replacing the cues an interviewee uses in assessing a face-to-face interviewer. She continued correspondence with some of her informants over time, so that the emails provided a series of 'interviews'. Hine includes reflections on how she might have been perceived by her informants, and how this might have impacted on the responses she obtained.

Evaluating Interview-based Research

Advantages of interviews as a data generation method in research include:

- They are good at dealing with topics in depth and in detail.
- They need relatively little equipment, and build on social skills that many researchers already have.
- The researcher can check the informant is the appropriate person to be answering the questions.
- They are flexible – the researcher can adjust a line of inquiry as the interview progresses.
- Interviewees often enjoy the opportunity to talk about their ideas to someone who is a non-critical listener.
- Some respondents prefer interviews to completing questionnaires, because they meet the researcher and it is easier to talk than to write down responses.

Disadvantages of interviews as a data generation method in research include:

- They are time-consuming for the researcher – the interview itself plus transcribing plus analysis of unstructured data.
- There can be a lack of reliability – the effect of the researcher and the context mean that consistency and objectivity are hard to achieve.
- They can be misleading – they focus on what the interviewees *say* they do or think, rather than what might really be the case.
- They are artificial – interviewees know they are speaking for the record, and they may find a type recorder or video recorder inhibiting, so a false impression may be given.

- They require good social skills and tact, otherwise they can be stressful and upsetting for both the interviewee and the researcher.
- Because of the time and effort involved, they are not usually suitable for circumstances where you want to make generalizations about a whole population, for which you would need a large number of interviewees (read about sample sizes in Chapter 7 on surveys).

Analysing and evaluating research based on interviews can be difficult because article length restrictions for journals and conference publications often prevent authors giving full details of how they conducted their interviews. This means that we have to take on trust that they carried out their interviews in an appropriate way, and that the interviews did indeed generate the data presented in the research report. You can use the 'Evaluation Guide' below to help you analyse and evaluate interview-based research. If there is insufficient information for you to answer the questions, you should not completely reject the research report, but you should treat the findings with some caution and be wary about relying on the report for evidence.

EVALUATION GUIDE: INTERVIEWS

1 What was the research topic? Were interviews an appropriate data generation method for this topic?
2 Were the interviews structured, semi-structured or unstructured? If they were completed in the real world, could online interviews have been used instead, and vice versa?
3 What information is given about the interviewer and how they might have affected the interview? Is this sufficient?
4 What information is given about the context of the interviews (location, ambience, and so on)? Is this sufficient?
5 What information is given about how the interview was recorded and how the record was checked? Is this sufficient?
6 Are sufficient quotations from the interviews used in the report of the research?
7 Do the researchers use the interview findings to make generalizations about a larger population? Is this appropriate?
8 What limitations in their interviews do the researchers recognize?
9 Can you identify other flaws or omissions in the researchers' reporting of their interviews?
10 Overall, how effectively do you think the interview-based approach has been reported and used?

PRACTICAL WORK

1   Practise conducting a semi-structured interview by carrying out the following activities:

   a   Devise 10 questions you could ask a colleague about their work (or, if your colleague is a full-time research student, about their research).
   b   Ask your colleague the questions and note down the answers.
   c   Where appropriate ask additional questions based on your colleague's responses – don't just stick rigidly to your 10 questions as you would in a structured interview.
   d   Now look at your notes and reflect. Did you find out what you wanted to find out? Did your questions produce the type of answers you expected? How could you improve your questions if you were to do another interview about someone's work? Did you manage to both ask questions and make notes at the same time? Do you think the interview felt like a natural conversation or was it more stilted? Does your colleague agree? Do you think you are a good interviewer?

2   Practise conducting an unstructured interview (as might occur in an ethnographic study, for instance) by carrying out the following activities:

   a   Ask a colleague to spare you ten minutes to tell you about their schooldays.
   b   Ask questions and prompt or probe, to help your colleague keep talking on the subject for 10 minutes.
   c   Make notes on your colleague's responses.
   d   Now look at your notes and reflect. Have you gained a detailed account of your colleague's schooldays? Did the conversation flow, or was it stilted and artificial? How much did *you* talk during the interview? How much did you influence the kind of answers your colleague gave? What does your colleague think about how you conducted the interview? What themes might you use in the analysis of your data? How does the content compare with the amount of detail and breadth you obtained in the first exercise?

3   You have decided to carry out some research into computer security and will interview some people about their personal approach and their company policy towards such issues as passwords, keeping backups, use of email and accessing company systems from off-site.

   a   How would your interviewees' responses differ if they believe you are: a student, an academic researcher, a journalist, a vendor of security systems or a police detective?
   b   Consider the advantages and disadvantages of using individual, group or Internet interviews for this research topic.

4   Study a piece of research that used interviews as a data generation method. Analyse and evaluate it using the 'Evaluation Guide' above and referring to the material in this chapter as necessary.

FURTHER READING

A detailed guide to conducting interviews is provided by Arksey and Knight (1999). Keats (2000) also provides valuable advice, including chapters on the special situations of interviewing children, adolescents, older people and people with disabilities, and interviewing across cultures and in stressful situations. Personal reflections on conducting interviews and analysing the data are given by Rapley (2004). Focus group interviews are covered in detail by Krueger and Casey (2000). Mann and Stewart (2000) provide two very useful chapters on online individual and group interviews, and cite various studies which have used them.

References

Arksey, H., & Knight, P.T. (1999). *Interviewing for social scientists. An introductory resource with examples*. London: Sage.

Hine, C. (2000). *Virtual ethnography*. London: Sage.

Keats, D. (2000). *Interviewing: A practical guide for students and professionals*. Buckingham: Open University Press.

Krueger, R.A., & Casey, M.A. (2000). *Focus groups. A practical guide for applied research* (3rd ed.). London: Sage.

Mann, C., & Stewart, F. (2000). *Internet communication and qualitative research. A handbook for researching online*. London: Sage.

O'Connell, D., & Kowall, S. (1995). Basic principles of transcription. In J.A. Smith, R. Harre, & L.V. Langenhove (Eds.), *Rethinking methods in psychology* (pp. 93–104). London: Sage.

Orlikowski, W.J. (1993). CASE tools as organizational change: Investigating incremental and radical changes in systems development. *MIS Quarterly, 17*(3), 309–340.

Potter, J., & Wetherell, M. (1987). *Discourse and social psychology*. London: Sage.

Rapley, T. (2004). Interviews. In C. Seale, G. Gobo, J.F. Gubrium, & D. Silverman (Eds.), *Qualitative research practice*. London: Sage.

Walsham, G. (1993). *Interpreting information systems in organizations*. Chichester: Wiley.

14 Observations

In this chapter you will learn about:

- observations as a data generation method;
- how to plan and conduct observations;
- how the Internet might be used for observation-based research;
- how observations have been used in IS and computing research;
- the advantages and disadvantages of observations for data generation;
- how to analyse and evaluate observation-based research.

Defining Observations

To observe means 'to watch' and 'to pay attention to'. Observing is something most of us do a lot of the time: seeing, hearing, noting, analysing, forming theories, making inferences, imposing meaning. Even something simple such as walking down the street involves us:

- watching what others are doing;
- trying to predict which way the oncoming people will move so that we don't bump into them;
- noting what they're wearing;
- deciding if we've seen someone we know or someone who might pose a risk to us;
- deducing why the harassed-looking woman is shouting at the little girl …

… and we've still barely covered 100 metres!

Researchers use observation as a data generation method to find out what people actually do, rather than what they report they do when questioned. Often observation

Highly systematic observations of pre-defined types of events	↔	Observations of anything and everything
Narrow concentration on particular type of event	↔	Broad focus
Observer takes no part in the proceedings	↔	Observer participates fully in the proceedings
Fact of observations taking place is known to all	↔	Fact of observations taking place is known to none except the researcher
No explanation, or false explanation, given for presence of observer-researcher	↔	Full explanation given for the presence of the observer–researcher
Short duration – could be as little as 5 minutes	↔	Long duration – possibly years
Record-keeping uses only simple note taking	↔	Record-keeping uses technology (e.g. audio tape, camera, stop watch, two-way mirror, computer program)
No feedback given afterwards to the observed	↔	Full feedback given afterwards to the observed

Figure 14.1   Different kinds of observation

involves looking, but it can involve senses other than sight: hearing, smelling, touching and tasting. For example, a researcher might look at the seating pattern in a group meeting, feel the texture or comfort of different chairs, listen to people's contributions (both the words and the tone), watch the body language, smell when people are becoming hot and bothered, even taste the orange juice that is handed round to help people cool down.

Observation as a data generation method can be used within any of the research strategies discussed in this book. It can be used in academic research to study, for example, behaviour at meetings or on a production line, or interactions between end-users and staff on an IT help-desk, or what students are really doing during a programming tutorial in a laboratory. It can also be used to study the behaviour of inanimate objects, such as software programs or computer-controlled devices.

There is a wide range of approaches to observation. They can be analysed by placing them on a number of spectrums, as Figure 14.1 shows.

One important distinction is between 'overt' and 'covert' research. In *covert* research, any people being observed do not know it. The researcher is like a spy. This approach is sometimes used by television reporters with hidden cameras to expose wrongdoers and/or provide entertainment for the viewers. The advantage of covert observation is that the setting is not disturbed and people behave naturally without putting on an act for the researchers. However, the disadvantage is that the observers have to make sure that no one realizes what they are doing, which means not asking too many questions, not criticizing anything that is seen as normal by those being observed, and not drawing attention to themselves in any way. If their cover is blown, they are likely to face angry people, and may even be in physical danger. Many people question whether covert observation is ethical, because those being observed have not given consent to the research. It *can* be acceptable if it occurs in a public place, where people know that strangers might be watching them, if everyone agrees that the observed and their interests are not harmed in any way, and if the observation techniques are as unobtrusive as possible. For example, at a digital art exhibition, rather than eavesdropping on people's conversations, researchers could identify the installations that aroused most interest by timing how long people spent studying them.

In *overt* research the people know that they are being observed. The advantage is that people can give consent, so that the research is more ethical. The researchers are less likely to cause upset and anger, and are free to ask as many questions as they like. They can also move around in the situation without being worried about looking out of place. However, some question whether people really are always able to give or refuse consent, even for overt observation. For example, if an IT manager arrives to assist an end-user with a problem and has a researcher in tow, the user may feel they cannot refuse the researcher's presence if they want the IT manager to help them, or if the IT manager is senior to them in the organization's hierarchy. Another important disadvantage of overt research is known as the 'Hawthorn Effect' – people modify their behaviour because they know they are being observed. They also have to work out how to treat the researcher – ignore or be friendly? – which can be stressful for them. They also need time to get used to being observed, and may become uncomfortable and defensive if they suspect the researcher does not approve of some of their behaviour.

Whether you use overt or covert research will depend on your objectives. It is safest and more ethically sound if you choose overt research. However, sometimes that just won't be possible. If you do want to use covert research, you must think carefully about the risks and ethics (see also Chapter 5 on research ethics).

Another important distinction in research approaches using observation is between *systematic* observation and *participant* observation. These are explained and discussed in the two sections that follow.

Planning and Conducting Systematic Observation

Systematic observation is where you decide in advance the particular type of events you want to observe, and use a pre-designed schedule to note their frequency or duration. In other words, you work with a pre-defined *system* of observations. This usually involves counting or timing, so leads to the generation of quantitative data. For example:

- observing a group meeting – number and type of contributions made by each member of the group;
- observing a queue at a university IT help-desk – time of arrival of each student, time student reaches head of queue, time taken to deal with the student's query;
- sample of people – observing everything one person does for a given time period, then switching to another person for the same length of time, and so on.

You could devise a schedule to observe, for example:

- frequency of events – counting how often the categories on the observation schedule occur in a given time period;
- timing of events – recording how long instances of events take, for example, the time taken for a computer program to process a given amount of data;
- events at a given time – logging everything that is happening at a specified time and repeating after a pre-defined interval (for example, every 15 minutes).

For example, Figure 14.2 shows an observation schedule used hourly each day for a week by technicians monitoring university computer labs.

Choosing or designing a schedule

By looking in the literature or on the web, you may find that someone has already designed a schedule that you could use. For example, many researchers have used a pre-defined schedule to observe the types of contribution people make to meetings

Date: Observer:

Lab number	Time	No. of students	No. of working computers	No. of out-of-order computers

Figure 14.2   Observation schedule for monitoring computer laboratories

(for example, making a new suggestion, acting as peace-maker, being obstructive and critical, summarizing ideas, drawing in other group members). If you can't find an 'off-the-shelf' schedule in the IS and computing literature, try the psychology literature, which has a long tradition of research based on observations, or, for more technical observations, the engineering literature.

If you have to design your own schedule, it's often worth initially spending time in the situation you are interested in, observing what goes on, before deciding exactly what kinds of events or activities to focus on. For all schedules, the items to be studied must be easily defined and obvious – you do not want to have to spend time deciding whether an action is really taking place. The items must also be relevant to your research objectives – there is no point generating data you are not going to use. You also need to make sure that your list of categories includes all possibilities – you do not want to notice relevant activities for which you have no place on your schedule. Your categories must also be unambiguous and not overlap with each other, so you can easily and quickly decide whether an item fits one category or another. Finally, the things to be observed must be easy to record – for example, it is easier to record isolated events than simultaneous ones. It is important to do a pilot study first, to see whether your observation schedule works.

You should include space in the schedule to note contextual factors that might be relevant to the situation. For example, a schedule to observe people in a meeting (Figure 14.3) includes a seating plan showing who was sitting where, and space to note such things as the time of day (if the meeting is late afternoon people may be more tired and irritable than at the start of the working day), the room temperature, background noise, even the weather outside the window. This contextual information may be needed to help explain the observations made.

Working with other observers

One advantage of using systematic observation is that you do not have to do all of it yourself. You can issue the schedules to others to do it for you. However, it is important that you train your assistants first, to make sure that they understand the schedule, the different categories of things they should observe and the method of recording. To ensure that the procedures are clear to everyone, and that they record the results in the same way, so that you have *inter-observer reliability*, a pilot run is essential. If two people observe the same situation and record different results on your schedule, then one of the following may apply:

- you have not trained your observers properly;
- your observers are not suited to the task;
- your schedule is not designed properly; or
- your research interest is not suited to systematic observation.

You can even get people to observe themselves, for example, by noting down the different kinds of activities they do during their working day. Of course, you will have

Date: Time: Observer:

Contextual factors:

Names of group members: Seating arrangements:

A:

B:

C:

D:

E:

Instructions: Note each time a group member does one of the activities

	A	B	C	D	E
Leading, e.g. proposing plans, seeking suggestions					
Constructive, e.g. making helpful suggestions, trying to solve problems					
Drawing in, e.g. encouraging others, supporting others, inviting others to contribute					
Obstructive, e.g. criticizing, disparaging, blocking contributions					
Clarifying/summarizing, e.g. rewording ideas/objectives, checking progress and time remaining					
Joking, e.g. being humorous					

Figure 14.3   Schedule for observing group meetings

to ask yourself how honestly and precisely they will record what they do, or whether they will provide you with a distorted picture of their activities.

Sampling

When you are observing many people or events, you are in effect doing a *survey* via observations. You therefore have to decide what kind of sample is to be used (see also Chapter 7 on surveys and sampling). Researchers using observation often use a set time period, for example, 1-hour periods. You must choose the appropriate time blocks and not introduce any bias into your results, to make sure that you are obtaining a representative sample of the things you want to observe. For example, if you want to observe how well used a university library facility is, you would not obtain representative results if you only observed on a Saturday evening when many students are socializing rather than studying.

Analysis and interpretation

When you have generated your observational data, you need to analyse it and interpret your results, with reasons. Then you should see if you can find alternative explanations. If you have more than one plausible explanation, you will probably have to carry out more research (for example, interviews, experiments) to establish which is the more plausible. Remember that from systematic observations you can only know *what* occurred, you cannot know for certain *why* the people you observed did what they did, or certain events occurred or particular measurements were taken.

Planning and Conducting Participant Observation

In *participant observation*, the researcher takes part in the situation under study, so that it can be experienced from the point of view of the others in that setting. This can be overt – people know that you are carrying out research into what they do. Or it can be covert – people think you are a 'normal' person, not a researcher. Rather than using a pre-defined observation schedule, the researcher notes down as much a possible about what occurs, producing a rich description of life in the setting. Your main piece of equipment is therefore yourself. You use your own senses – seeing, hearing, and so on – to experience and reflect on what people do in your chosen situation. Participant observation is often associated with ethnography (see Chapter 12), where the researcher tries to experience life in the setting from the inside, to gain understanding about what people do, why they do it, and the meanings they assign to activities.

Types of participation

We'll look at four types of participation: complete observer, complete participant, participant-observer and practitioner-researcher.

- A **complete observer** is present in the setting either overtly or covertly, observing everything that occurs, but takes no other part in the proceedings. For example, a researcher might sit in on a teacher's class to watch everything that occurs, but take no part in the lesson and class activities.
- At the other extreme, a **complete participant** uses covert observation and tries to become a member of the group being researched, to see the group's world from the inside. Of course, to fit into the research setting as a true participant, you require the necessary credentials. You may need to be of the right sex and age, and you may need particular skills and qualifications. For example, many readers of this book could quickly acquire the skills to participate as a supermarket shelf-stacker or car park attendant, but few will have the time to gain the necessary credentials to participate in the working lives of accountants or lawyers.
- A **participant-observer** shadows someone, and can be used if you don't have the necessary credentials to be a complete participant. You follow people as they go about their lives or jobs, observing the activities and interactions, taking part where you can (for example, making the coffee, doing some photocopying). If you gain the people's trust, so that they accept your presence and even forget that you are there sometimes, you can learn about what they do and how they feel about it.
- A **practitioner-researcher** is someone who already has a job and decides to put on a researcher's 'hat' as well and investigate their own work organization. Benefits of this approach are that you don't have to negotiate access into the setting – you are already there, and you don't have to spend a lot of time becoming familiar with it. However, such research does bring its own difficulties. You will probably need to obtain permission to research into your own organization, from both your bosses and colleagues – you do not want to risk losing your job if they find out only by accident. You must also somehow make yourself aware of the assumptions and pre-conceptions that you have about your own job and organization, other-wise you will overlook issues that an outsider would observe. You must also find the time to both continue to do your own job and also to be a researcher. Further difficulties are discussed below.

Process

Participant observation is time-consuming. The longer you can spend in a situation, the more you are likely to learn. Start by being non-selective in what you observe – try to observe everything that goes on rather than starting with pre-conceived ideas about what you are going to observe. In this way, you get a feel for the situation. Later, as things emerge that seem particularly significant to you, you can make more focused observations, concentrating on what seems important or strange, and start to form a tentative theoretical model of what is occurring. You might then look for unexpected or contradictory events, things that ought not to happen according to your emerging theory, meaning your theory needs revising. You should also look for the issues and problems that the participants see as important, so that you get an understanding of their views and beliefs. Remember that your purpose is to develop a theory about what is occurring – not just to tell a story about your time in the situation along the lines of 'What I did in the school-holidays'.

Field notes

Participant observation relies on the observer being able to make field notes – you can't possibly remember everything that you observe. You need to make notes as soon as you can after you have noticed something relevant. If you are a covert observer, this may mean you have to make frequent trips to the toilet to have the privacy to make notes! As well as noting what you have observed, you should note down your thoughts on the research process (for example, difficulties in forming a relationship with someone, or plans about what else to study) and your emerging analysis (for example, how what you are observing and experiencing relates to your research questions). You should also include reflections on yourself as a researcher (for example, how you feel, how you might be affecting the situation). (For further discussion of field notes see Chapter 12 on ethnography.)

Rules of the game

Even if people have given permission to be observed, they may not realize the rules of the game, that is, that *everything* they do and say might be recorded. For example, a group of systems developers might be happy for you to record what they do and say during official meetings at work, but not over the canteen table at lunchtime. Even if they say, 'this is not to be used', you have still heard the comment and cannot just erase it from your memory. When obtaining permission to observe, you should point out to people that you are interested in all aspects of their work or activities, not just the 'official' parts. You might need to remind them again later, once they have become used to your presence. But sometimes you and your conscience will have to weigh up whether you want to remind them you're observing, because reminding them may stop them doing precisely the things you are interested in.

Dangers and difficulties

Covert researchers risk being discovered by the people they are observing, as mentioned already. This could put you in physical danger. There are also other dangers and difficulties you may have to face when doing participant observation.

One of the biggest hazards is 'going native'. You lose your sense of detachment as an observer and identify fully with the other participants in the situation. No longer do things seem strange to you, they just seem like the natural way to do things. It is vital that you do not forget your research purpose and do not lose your researcher's independent way of seeing things. However, being required to operate at two levels – as a participant and a detached observer – is stressful. When you have come to know others in a situation, and possibly formed friendships with some, it can be difficult to separate yourself from them and write dispassionately about what you have observed and learnt. It can feel like a violation of their trust, causing stress for you. You should arrange to have regular meetings with your supervisor or a research support group to help you cope with your dual existence as participant and researcher.

Practitioner-researchers, as already explained, have to learn to recognize and discard their assumptions and pre-conceptions, to see themselves and their organizations as others would. If they are able to make the familiar seem strange, they can reveal and question the professional practices and priorities in their organization. However, there is a danger that once the research is over, they can't make the strange become familiar again, and can't go back to being a 'normal' practitioner. Practitioner-researchers can therefore end up unhappy and stressed in their jobs. The feelings experienced have even been compared to those of a priest, mullah or rabbi losing his faith. Again you should look to your supervisor or a support group to help you cope.

Finally if you are participating in a group that is acting unlawfully, you too may be expected to behave unlawfully. If caught, the plea of being a researcher is no defence.

Validity

For participant observation, there is often only one researcher, you. This means readers will wonder why they should take your word that what you claim to have observed would also have been observed by any other reasonable person, and you have not been biased. In other words, is your work and its outcomes valid? You *can't* guarantee that another person would observe the same as you. Each of us has:

- **selective recall**: our minds remember some things and forget others;
- **selective perception**: our minds notice some things and simply ignore others;
- **accentuated perception**: our minds are particularly sensitive to some things, based on previous experiences or our current state, and so take more notice of some things than others would.

Being selective and partisan is an inevitable part of most research. It's just that we become more aware of the problem in research based on personal observation because it is so dependent on the observer as the main piece of 'equipment'. You can strengthen your claim to validity by using:

- **Verbatim quotations** from the people in the setting, rather than summarizing what was said in your own words. Giving the actual words used reassures readers that you did indeed hear them.

- **Triangulation** of data or methods (see Chapter 3). You can observe several people doing the same thing, to see if they each do it in the same way, and you can use, say, interviews, to see if your findings derived from observation are confirmed by the participants.
- **Reflexivity** – you should constantly reflect upon yourself in the situation: how you might be affecting it, what you are taking for granted, assumptions you are making, and so on. Some of these reflections should be included when you write up your research, so that readers can judge whether they would observe the same as you if they were to enter the same setting.

The Internet and Observation

The scope for Internet-based observation is limited because mostly we can only 'see' the words people place on the Internet, or observe which webpages they visit. Given current technology, we cannot smell, touch or taste via the Internet. There is the possibility of hearing via Internet telephony – this has been little used so far in research, but is expanding rapidly, so it might be used more in future.

Up to now, researchers have concentrated on people's written linguistic behaviour. By observing the interactions in a newsgroup, chatroom or mailing list, researchers investigate *computer-mediated communication*. You could be a complete participant in a newsgroup, chatroom or mailing list by reading, interpreting and replying to messages. Because no one can see you, it does not matter what you look like. You can pretend to be a different age or gender. If people accept you as a legitimate member of that newsgroup, you are carrying out complete participant observation. However, you must consider the ethics of this. If other members eventually discover that you are a researcher and have been observing them covertly, and possibly deceiving them, they may feel harmed and that their privacy has been infringed.

You could, instead, introduce yourself as a researcher and ask the group's permission to observe and analyse their postings, as a participant-observer. You will need to explain your researcher role at the beginning of each of your own postings, because any new member of the group will not know about it. Be prepared for angry reactions. Many newsgroup members consider the group's online interactions as private (even though they are publicly available on the Internet), and there does seem to be a suspicion of, and even antagonism towards, academic researchers in cyberspace.

Alternatively you could lurk, not posting, merely observing – a covert complete observer. But then you are back with the ethical problems of covert observation.

Other ways of observing people using Internet technology are also possible. A webcam could be used to observe a setting, and the images sent over the Internet to a researcher who could be anywhere in the world. The participants might be aware of the camera's presence, and could choose when to switch it off, or they might be unaware, leading to ethical concerns about covert surveillance. Web-server logs, that monitor where website visitors come from and which pages they visit, and for how long, can also be analysed to learn more about people's web behaviour. Be wary of making unwarranted conclusions from the data in such a log. For example, if it shows that someone spent a long time on a particular webpage, it does not necessarily mean that they found that page interesting. They could have had a slow computer or network connection, or they could have turned away to speak to someone or make a cup of coffee.

Researchers are still discussing and evolving guidelines for Internet ethics and how and when researchers should obtain consent. See Chapter 5, on participants and ethics, for more information.

Examples of Observations in IS and Computing Research

Observations are often used by researchers in human–computer interaction. An early use was when GUIs (graphical user interfaces) and the mouse were first developed. Researchers would set data entry personnel a series of tasks and observe which produced the quicker and more accurate data entry: special keys or drop-down menus, keyboard or mouse. More recently, researchers have used eye-tracking equipment to observe, for example, how people's eyes move around a computer screen portraying a virtual reality environment.

Observations can be used to understand how people do their jobs, perhaps as part of systems analysis leading to the development of computer systems to help them perform more effectively. IS and computing researchers sometimes use a form of observation called *verbal protocol analysis*, especially when developing computer-based expert systems. The idea is that you watch an experienced person going about their work, but ask them to talk about it as they do it. (You may need to prompt them – 'what are you doing now?' – as they become engrossed in the task and forget to talk aloud.) This allows you to observe how an expert operates: the gathering and analysis of data, reasoning, theory formation and backtracking. This can then be incorporated into the mechanisms of a computer-based expert system. For example, Mao and Benbasat (1998) used verbal protocol analysis to investigate the interactions between some users and an expert system during an exercise to assess an organization's financial health.

Observation is often used within a case study or ethnography. For example:

- Nandhakumar and Jones (2001) investigated time management in project-based teams. One of the researchers was an overt participant-observer as a full-time member of the team developing an executive information system at a large manufacturing company. The researchers used a 'time-geography approach' to structure their interpretation of the management of time within the team and argue that traditional management accounting approaches to time management are too mechanistic to be able to capture the complexity of team-based work.

- Robinson and Sharp (2003) used observation in an ethnography based in a small company that used XP to develop web-based intelligent advertisements. They investigated whether the 12 practices of XP give rise to a culture that embodies the four values of XP (communication, simplicity, feedback and courage).

Examples of Internet-based observations include:

- Hine's (2000) study of newsgroups during the trial of Louise Woodward, who had been accused of the murder of a baby in her care;
- Denzin's (1999) covert observation of an online, self-help newsgroup for relatives of alcoholics.

Evaluating Observation-based Research

The advantages of *systematic observation* include:

- It discovers what people really do, rather than what they say they do.
- It is a means of collecting substantial amounts of quantitative data relatively quickly, and the data is pre-coded, so ready for analysis.
- After training, a schedule should be usable by anyone, enabling the delegation of work and the possibility of simultaneous observations in different locations.
- It can generate data about things that most participants are normally unaware of or would regard as mundane, such as the time wasted deleting spam from email inboxes or logging onto a network.

The advantages of *participant observation* include:

- It is cheap to carry out, since little equipment is needed.
- It provides a means of gaining rich insights into social settings; leading to holistic explanations of complex situations.
- It enables researchers to find out about people's beliefs and intentions as they see them.
- Practitioner-researchers can carry out research at the same time as undertaking their normal job.

The disadvantages of *systematic observation* include:

- It is restricted to studying overt behaviour, and cannot explain intentions, meanings or reasons.
- It assumes that overt behaviour can be readily broken down into easily observable and categorizable phenomena, so it can oversimplify a situation.

- It is often difficult to provide feedback to the people who have been observed, raising questions about the ethics of using people for the researcher's own ends with no benefit to the others involved.

The disadvantages of *participant observation* include:

- The observer must be there when the thing being investigated takes place – anything that happens in the observer's absence is not known.
- Some settings are not open to a researcher without the necessary credentials.
- It can lead the researcher into risky areas – physically, socially, legally or psychologically.
- It is sometimes criticized for lack of reliability, since the research depends on the researcher's 'self' and is difficult to repeat by another researcher.
- It is difficult to generalize from observations in one setting to others – any findings may be unique to the particular situation studied.

Two guides are necessary for analysing and evaluating observation research: one for systematic observation and one for participant observation. Use the appropriate one. If there is insufficient information for you to answer the questions, you should not completely reject the research report, but you should treat the findings with some caution.

EVALUATION GUIDE: SYSTEMATIC OBSERVATION

1 Was the observation schedule piloted?
2 Does the researcher provide the observation schedule? If not, how does this affect your confidence in the research?
3 Do you think the items observed were easily observable, unambiguous and independent from each other? Did they occur regularly enough to provide sufficient data, but without multiple simultaneous occurrences?
4 Do you think the items observed were the most appropriate for the research objectives?
5 How long did the researcher spend in the field? Do you think this was long enough? If there was more than one observer, how did they ensure inter-observer reliability?
6 Was the sample large enough and representative?
7 Did the research avoid disrupting the naturalness of the setting?
8 What limitations in the use of observation does the researcher recognize?
9 Can you identify other flaws or omissions in the researcher's reporting of the use of systematic observation?
10 Overall, how effectively do you think the use of observations for data generation has been reported and used?

EVALUATION GUIDE: PARTICIPANT OBSERVATION

1   What kind of participant observation was used?
2   How long did the researcher spend in the field? Do you think this was long enough?
3   Did the researcher avoid disrupting the naturalness of the setting?
4   Has the researcher reflected on self-identity and how it affected access, perception of events and the reactions of others?
5   Has the researcher discussed the ethics of the fieldwork and any personal difficulties encountered?
6   What methods has the researcher used to try to convince you of the validity of the observations?
7   Has the participant observation led to insights that would not be possible using other methods?
8   What limitations in the use of participant observation does the researcher recognize?
9   Can you identify other flaws or omissions in the researchers' reporting of the use of participant observation?
10 Overall, how effectively do you think the use of observations for data generation has been reported and used?

PRACTICAL WORK

1   Find a colleague to work with. Choose a public place where you can do some covert observation, such as a shopping centre or bus station. Do the following:

   a   Both of you watch the scene for 20 minutes, then leave the scene and separately write notes on what you saw. Analyse and compare your reports.
   b   Develop a schedule for systematic observation of some aspect of the situation you studied. Return to the scene and separately complete the schedule. Again anlayse and compare your results. Evaluate your schedule.
   c   Review what you have learnt from this exercise.

2   Write a short autobiographical essay. What are your goals, short term and long term? What do you like and dislike about being a research student? How is it different from undergraduate life? What keeps you going? What do you think motivates other people to be research students? Analyse what you have written for major themes and underlying assumptions.

   Now get a colleague to interview you using the same questions and pushing you to give your true views rather than statements which are simply socially acceptable. If possible, tape record the interview. Analyse your answers and compare them with what you wrote previously.

If you feel uncomfortable doing this exercise, you may have to conclude that you are not well-suited to the reflexivity required for participant observation.

3   Practise analysing and evaluating research that uses observation as a data generation method. Study a piece of research that used it. Answer the questions from the appropriate 'Evaluation Guide' above, using the material in this chapter to help you.

FURTHER READING

Although aimed at teachers studying children in the classroom, Boehm and Weinberg (1996) offer guidance on systematic observation that IS and computing researchers should also find useful. Advice on participant observation is offered by Jorgensen (1989), and Coghlan and Brannick (2004). Participant observation is often associated with ethnography (see Chapter 12), so texts on that strategy are also worth consulting, for example, Geertz (1973), Hammersley and Atkinson (1983) and Van Maanen (1988).

Mann and Stewart (2000) discuss the nature and ethics of Internet-based observations and cite many examples of such research. Denzin (1999) explains the 'method of instances' as an approach to analysing interactions in an online newsgroup, and Hine (2000) discusses participation in online communities and the problem of Internet researchers being unable to 'see' lurkers.

References

Boehm, A.E., & Weinberg, R.A. (1996). *The classroom observer: Developing observation skills in early childhood settings* (3rd ed.). New York: Teachers College Press.

Coghlan, D., & Brannick, T. (2004). *Doing action research in your own organization* (2nd ed.). London: Sage.

Denzin, N.K. (1999). Cybertalk and the method of instances. In S. Jones (Ed.), *Doing Internet research. Critical issues and methods for examining the Net* (pp. 107–125). Thousand Oaks, CA: Sage.

Geertz, C. (1973). *The interpretation of cultures*. New York: Basic Books.

Hammersley, M., & Atkinson, P. (1983). *Ethnography: Principles in practice*. London: Tavistock.

Hine, C. (2000). *Virtual ethnography*. London: Sage.

Jorgensen, D.L. (1989). *Participant observation. A methodology for human studies*. London: Sage.

Mann, C., & Stewart, F. (2000). *Internet communication and qualitative research. A handbook for researching online*. London: Sage.

Mao, J.-Y., & Benbasat, I. (1998). Contextualized access to knowledge: Theoretical perspectives and a process-tracing study. *Information Systems Journal, 8*(3), 217–239.

Nandhakumar, J., & Jones, M. (2001). Accounting for time: Managing time in project-based team working. *Accounting, Organizations and Society*, 26(3), 193–214.

Robinson, H., & Sharp, H. (2003). XP culture: Why the twelve practices both are and are not the most significant thing. In *Proceedings of the Agile Development Conference 2003* (pp. 12–21). Los Alamitos, CA: IEEE Computer society.

Van Maanen, J. (1988). *Tales of the field: On writing ethnography*. Chicago, IL: University of Chicago Press.

15 Questionnaires

In this chapter you will learn about:

- questionnaires as a method of generating data for your research;
- how to use questionnaires in research;
- how the Internet might be used for questionnaire-based research;
- how questionnaires have been used in previous IS and computing research;
- the advantages and disadvantages of questionnaires as a data generation method;
- how to analyse and evaluate questionnaire-based research.

Defining Questionnaires

A questionnaire is a pre-defined set of questions (sometimes called *items*), assembled in a pre-determined order. Respondents are asked to answer the questions, thus providing the researcher with data that can be analysed and interpreted. Questionnaires are frequently associated with the survey research strategy – often a questionnaire is sent out by post to a sample of people, who are asked to complete it and return it to the researcher. The researcher then analyses all the responses, looks for patterns and makes generalizations about the actions or views of a larger population than the sample. However, questionnaires can be used within other research strategies too, such as a case study, action research or design and creation.

Questionnaires can be *self-administered* – the respondent completes the questionnaire without the researcher being present. Or they can be *researcher-administered* – the researcher asks the respondent each question in turn and writes down the responses. The latter is a kind of structured interview (see Chapter 13) – and can be either face-to-face or over the telephone. If you intend to use a researcher-administered questionnaire, you should read this chapter in conjunction with Chapter 13 on interviews, considering especially how your appearance and interactions with your interviewees might affect the responses they give you.

Questionnaires are widely used in research because they provide an efficient way of collecting data from many people. They are best suited to situations where the researcher:

- wants to obtain data from a large number of people;
- wants to obtain relatively brief and uncontroversial information from people;
- needs to obtain standardized data, by posing identical questions to each respondent and pre-defining the range of answers which can be given;
- can expect the respondents to be able to read and understand the questions and possible answers;
- has the money to pay for printing, distributing and collecting questionnaires and the time to wait between posing the questions and getting the responses back.

Many novice researchers assume that they only have to produce a list of questions with multiple-choice answers and print them on a form to have a questionnaire. However, this is not the case. A questionnaire must be carefully designed and constructed so that valid, reliable data can be generated at reasonable cost. You need to write the questions so that all respondents understand them in the same way and decode the possible answers you provide in the way you intended. These questions and answers must also meet your research needs. This means that you must be clear how each question relates to your research questions or hypotheses, and you must know in advance how you intend to analyse the responses. Good researchers therefore spend a lot of time carefully constructing the questions they will use and assembling them in a structured way that will appear logical to the respondents. The next section will help you design a good questionnaire.

" Quality of questionnaires

Simply stated, the quality of the information obtained from a questionnaire is directly proportional to the quality of the questionnaire, which in turn is directly proportional to the quality of the construction process. (Peterson, 2000, p. 12)

"

Planning and Designing Questionnaires

With a questionnaire, you often don't get the chance to go back and ask further questions, so it's essential that you get its design right in the first place, before you issue it. A well-designed questionnaire can also increase the response rate, so that not too many just get thrown away by potential respondents. Let's consider the different aspects of questionnaires you will have to plan and design.

Form of administration

Most questionnaires are *self-administered*, which saves on the researcher's time and means that more people can be asked to complete the questionnaire. The respondents are also less likely to try to please the researcher by giving what they perceive to be the 'correct' or 'desired' answer. The researcher can also be confident that all respondents saw the same question.

In a *researcher-administered* questionnaire, there is a danger that respondents are asked the questions in a different manner, because the researcher varies their tone, or body language. Researcher-administration does, however, usually lead to a higher response rate – it is harder for people to refuse to complete the questionnaire when the researcher is standing in front of them. Researcher-administration also allows the researcher to put different sub-questions to respondents, depending on their previous answers.

Question content and wording

You have to make sure that your questionnaire will indeed generate data about the concept(s) you are interested in – known as *content validity*. For example, if you are interested in user satisfaction with a computer system, you have to think about all the different aspects of the 'user satisfaction' concept, and make sure that your questionnaire covers all of them (for example, timeliness of data, accuracy, relevance, ease-of-use, reliability of system, helpfulness of user manual and error messages). This means that you have to be familiar with the research domain and the relevant concepts before you start designing a questionnaire – usually by studying the literature (see Chapter 6).

It's usually worth looking at previously used questionnaires, where you might find questions that you can use or adapt. For example, ISWorld contains a data bank of questionnaires and questions that have been used in previous IS research (see 'Further Reading' below). Of course, you must not break any copyrights, and you should not reuse poorly designed questions.

Whether you reuse existing questions or design your own, each question you put into your questionnaire should be (Peterson, 2000, pp. 50–59):

- **Brief**: ideally 20 words or less, providing the question is still understandable.
- **Relevant**: each question must be relevant to the overall questionnaire and its purpose, and each word within a question must be relevant to the overall question you want to ask.

- **Unambiguous:** don't use words with multiple meanings (for example, 'Do you prefer nipple or mouse operations?') or words likely to be unfamiliar to the respondents, so that they have to guess what the question means (for example, 'Does your IT department subscribe to the CICO principle?').
- **Specific:** don't ask vague questions (for example, 'How many times have you logged onto the system recently?') and don't pose two questions within one item (for example, 'Is the user interface clear and user-friendly?').
- **Objective:** the wording of the question should not lead the respondents to a particular answer (for example, 'Do you agree with the majority of people in this country who say that those who unleash computer viruses on the Internet should be hanged?') or suggest that the answer is already known (for example, 'Do you agree that the user interface could be improved?').

Question types

Questions can be designed to generate two types of data: *factual data* (for example, date of birth, job title, number of children) and *opinions* (for example, what the respondent thinks about a computer animation, an information system or the information society). Both kinds of data can be collected within one questionnaire, although you need to be clear which kind of data each question is designed to collect.

Questions can also be divided into *open questions* and *closed questions* (see the box below for examples):

- **Open questions** leave the respondent to decide what answer to give – you just leave a blank space for them to fill in as they see fit.
- **Closed questions** force the respondent to choose from a range of answers that you have pre-defined.

Open and closed questions

- Open:

  What are your views on electronic voting?

- Closed:

  What are your views on electronic voting? Tick the ONE statement below that best matches your views on electronic voting.
  - ☐ A good idea.
  - ☐ A terrible idea.
  - ☐ Don't know.

For open questions, you need to decide how much space to leave for respondents' answers. If you leave too little space, they will be frustrated at not being able to give as full an answer as they want, and you will lose potentially useful data. If you leave too much space, they may find it off-putting and write nothing at all. Open questions enable you to grasp the full richness of people's views, expressed in their own words rather than yours. They take less time to prepare than closed questions. They are especially useful for questions where you realize there is a wide range of possible answers or you just don't know how the respondents are likely to answer. On the other hand, open questions require more effort than closed questions from the respondents. The responses are also harder to code and analyse than responses to closed questions.

Closed questions and their response formats take longer to design than open questions, because you have to make sure all possible answers are provided. However, the responses can be more quickly analysed, because they have, in effect, been pre-coded. If you allocate a numeric value to each pre-defined answer, statistical analysis of the responses is quick. Closed questions can save the respondents time in answering, but can also cause them frustration if they cannot find the pre-defined response that matches the answer they want to give. Closed questions can also be criticized for enabling respondents to answer quickly in a slapdash way without thinking much about their responses, and for putting answers into the respondents' minds that they might not otherwise have come up with.

Format of questions and responses

There are many different ways of designing questions and response formats. Here are some of them, with examples.

Yes/no answers

> Have you evaluated your company's website in the past 6 months? Yes/No
> Does your company use any open source software? Yes/No

Quantity questions

> How old were you at your last birthday?
> How many children aged 17 or less live in your house?

Agree/disagree with a statement
Do you agree or disagree with the following statement:

> The management introduces new computer-based systems here in a way that always takes account of employees' needs. Agree/Disagree.

Degree of agreement or disagreement – the 'Likert scale'
Please tick the ONE box that matches your view most closely:
> In my company decision-making is too centralized.

Agree strongly	Agree	Neither agree nor disagree	Disagree	Disagree strongly

Scale questions

For the following statements, please tick the box that matches your view most closely:
Communication between me and my immediate boss is:

Very bad	Bad	About right	Good	Very good

The use of frames in website design is:

Good practice	Bad practice	Don't know

The 'semantic differential scale'

On each of the lines below, place an X to show how you feel about the lectures on the Knowledge Management Module.

Pace too fast							Pace too slow
Interesting content							Boring content
Good use of slides							Poor use of slides
Too few handouts							Too many handouts

List questions

Please list the four most important IS problems your organization is currently facing.

Please list the three computer games you have played most in the past month.

Rank order questions

Please number each of the factors below in order of importance to you when you buy you next PC. Number the most important factor 1, the next 2 and so on.

Price   ...

On-site repair   ...

Familiar vendor's name   ...

Delivery within one week   ...

12-month warranty   ...

On-site initial set-up   ...

Make sure you don't use too many types of questions in one questionnaire – you are likely to confuse your respondents, and the overall design will look cluttered. On the other hand, some variety of question types can keep your respondents interested.

For questions where you provide a scale and respondents must choose one of the points on it, you need to think about how finely to tune that scale. Many researchers use a five-point scale (as in the Likert scale illustrated above), but up to nine points have been used. Many researchers include a 'don't know' or 'neither agree nor disagree' point in the scale. However, some argue that this enables respondents to put a line of ticks in the 'don't know' column, without really thinking about how they feel. If you don't allow a 'don't know' option, you force respondents to come off the fence and answer more definitely, but risk alienating those respondents who genuinely don't know.

Be careful also with the boundaries between points on a scale. For example, what is wrong with the following?

What is your age? Please tick ONE:

18 or less   ...

18–25   ...

25–35   ...

35–44   ...

46 or more   ...

What if the respondent is 18, 35 or 45 years old?

Layout and structure

Your questionnaire should have an introduction that explains its purpose, the sponsor of the research (if any), the return address and the date by which it should be returned.

Respondents should be reassured that their answers will be kept confidential and that completion of the questionnaire is voluntary. They should also be thanked for taking the time to complete it.

You need to include clear instructions about how to complete the questionnaire. Often, it is useful to give an example question and response, so that the respondents can see exactly what you mean.

When assembling your questionnaire, you need to put the questions in an order that will seem logical to the respondents – don't hop from topic to topic. Easier and less sensitive questions come first, the more complex or sensitive questions come later. However, this doesn't mean that you should start off with questions designed to generate demographic data about your respondents (for example, age, gender, where they live). Your introduction to the questionnaire will have explained its purpose and respondents have agreed to help you achieve that purpose, so they will be put off if the opening questions seem to bear no relation to it. Questions concerning such factual data can be placed at the end of the questionnaire.

Filter questions can be used to guide respondents through the questionnaire (for example, 'Do you have any children? If not, go to question 9.'). But make sure you don't make the respondents move forwards and backwards so that they feel lost within the questionnaire.

You also need to make sure the questionnaire is attractive – with a clear layout and adequate-sized font and good use of white space. It must be neither too long for people to complete, nor too short to provide you with all the data you need. If you intend to use optical character recognition to analyse the responses, you also need to make sure the form design matches the technical requirements of your machine-reader.

Pre-test and pilot

A questionnaire can be evaluated before use in a pre-test, where its content is shown to people who are experts in either your research domain or in questionnaire design. These experts should help you refine and improve the questionnaire.

It is also a good idea to pilot your questionnaire, where a group of people complete it as if they were your target respondents. If you have the time and resources, you could pilot it with a group of people very similar to your intended respondents. Often, however, researchers only have the resources to gather some colleagues together and ask them to help evaluate it. The trial run of your questionnaire should help you find out:

- where people have difficulties in answering certain questions;
- whether people find some questions ambiguous or vague;
- whether people can follow the instructions for how to answer the different types of questions;
- whether the pre-defined responses cover all desired answers;
- how long it takes people to complete it – is this a reasonable time?

To find out what people think of your questionnaire, you can ask them to think aloud while completing it (verbal protocol analysis – see Chapter 14), interview them after they've completed it, or issue them with yet another questionnaire.

Validity and reliability

A good researcher will consider a questionnaire's *content validity, construct validity* and *reliability*.

- **Content validity**: as noted already, is concerned with whether the questions are a well-balanced sample of the domain to be covered. For example, if you wanted to evaluate student satisfaction with the way a course had been taught, you would need to make sure you asked questions about *all* the approaches to teaching that had been used: lectures, seminars, laboratory-based practical work, computer-based support systems, and so on. You would also have to think about the concept of 'student satisfaction' and what aspects it incorporates (for example, effort demanded of students, punctuality of teacher, relevance to employment, match to expectations). Use of the literature, previously used questionnaires and a panel of experts can help you address content validity.
- **Construct validity**: is concerned with whether we are measuring what we think we are measuring via our questions. For example, a multiple-choice test might be designed to assess students' reasoning skills, but might really measure how quickly they can read. To test construct validity, it may be necessary to correlate responses against other responses in the questionnaire or other information. For example:
  - If you think that dissatisfaction with an IT department correlates with a high number of calls to the IT help-desk, you could look to see if respondents who stated they were dissatisfied did indeed make many calls to the help desk.
  - Students' performance in a multiple-choice test could be correlated with their subsequent performance in an end-of-year examination, to see if those who scored well in the test also did well in the examination. (Of course, this assumes that the exam itself has construct validity.)
- **Reliability**: is concerned with whether a questionnaire would yield the same results if given repeatedly to the same respondents. Unfortunately, this is usually difficult to assess – respondents could change their views over time, or remember the answers they gave last time and simply repeat them, or even deliberately decide to give the opposite view this time. The simplest approach to reliability is the *split-half method*. The questions in the questionnaire are divided into two equivalent groups. The score of a respondent in one half is compared with the score in the other half – if the questionnaire is reliable the two scores should be the same.

There are various sophisticated statistical tests to help you assess construct validity and reliability, but they are beyond the scope of this book. See the 'Further Reading' section.

The Internet and Questionnaires

The Internet offers the possibility of sending questionnaires to people across the world, without having to worry about postage costs and delivery times. Questionnaires can be emailed to people – either within the text of an email message or as a file attachment to the message. Alternatively, a questionnaire can be placed on the web as a web form. Examples of web questionnaires can often be found on organizations' websites, where webmasters ask for user evaluation of the site.

So far little is known about the best kind of questionnaire designs for use via the Internet – an opportunity for some research. It is thought that Internet-delivered questionnaires need to be shorter than paper and pencil questionnaires because:

- Most people are slower at typing and mouse clicks than they are at writing and putting ticks in boxes. Respondents may therefore become tired and bored before reaching the end of an email or web questionnaire, giving less thought to their answers or even abandoning the exercise altogether.
- Many web users like to surf quickly from page to page and are reluctant to spend long on any single page when there might be more interesting things elsewhere on the web.
- For respondents on 'pay-as-you-go' connections, the longer your online form takes to complete, the more it costs them.
- The longer the web questionnaire takes to complete, the greater the risk of the respondents' network connections going down. If their work so far is lost, they will probably give up rather than start again.

Email questionnaires can be completed section by section and only submitted when the respondent is ready. For web questionnaires, you should try to provide the same facility by allowing respondents to save their half-completed forms and only submit when they are ready.

Email responses normally show the respondents' email address – thus reducing their anonymity. Potential respondents may therefore be unwilling to answer questions on sensitive topics via email. Web forms, on the other hand, can be completed and submitted anonymously. But this brings with it further difficulties: what is to stop someone answering your questionnaire many times, thus distorting your results? You could implement some kind of control, for example, protecting your web questionnaire via a password. But if each respondent is issued with a unique password that they must use, they will worry that they are not anonymous to you.

Web forms allow the use of drop-down menus or radio buttons for the pre-defined responses, It is not yet known whether one is preferable to the other for web questionnaires, although empirical research will, no doubt, eventually inform us. One danger with drop-down menus is that the respondent may make a choice but accidentally use the mouse scroll button again, rolling the option choice to an unintended answer.

If your questionnaire is sent as an email attachment, some potential respondents will not open it for fear of viruses. You therefore need to assure them in your covering email message that you have checked it is virus-free. You should also make sure it is readable by most potential respondents – don't assume everyone uses Microsoft® Word®. Similarly, for a web-based questionnaire, you need to test it on different platforms and browsers, to make sure each potential respondent is able to read it and complete it in the way you intended.

Examples of Questionnaires in IS and Computing Research

There has been much use of questionnaires in IS research. They are mostly associated with surveys, the most popular research strategy in IS research. In computing, they are often used within a design and creation strategy for user evaluation of a computer system, although it must be said that many such user evaluation questionnaires are poorly designed. Examples of work in IS and computing of questionnaire-based research include:

- An investigation via questionnaire into technology adoption and sustained use of it, which suggests that the often-cited technology acceptance model (Davis, 1989) needs adaptation to take account of gender differences (Venkatesh & Morris, 2000).
- A study into the business knowledge of IT professionals and its contribution to their relationships with business clients (Bassellier & Benbasat, 2004).
- The development of a questionnaire to assess the usability of websites, based on a set of guidelines produced by Microsoft® (Agarwal & Venkatesh, 2002).
- An experiment that involved system users completing questionnaires, in order to investigate whether the rich representation of information via multimedia can better support the needs of decision-makers than textual representation alone (Lim & Benbasat, 2000).

Evaluating Questionnaire-based Research

Advantages of questionnaire-based research include:

- Questionnaires are often more economical than other data generation methods. A large amount of data can be generated for relatively low costs of materials and time.
- The use of pre-defined answers (as in closed questions) makes questionnaires easy for respondents to complete and easy for researchers to analyse.

- There are few geographical limits to where they can be used – they can be sent out via post, telephone and email.
- Self-administration questionnaires require no special social skills of the researcher.

Disadvantages of questionnaire-based research include:

- Pre-defined answers can cause frustration in potential respondents, so that they refuse to answer, and can bias respondents to the researcher's way of seeing things.
- A researcher cannot normally query disparities between answers or check the truthfulness of answers.
- A researcher cannot correct misunderstandings, probe for more detail, or offer explanations or help.
- Self-administered questionnaires are unsuitable for those with poor literacy skills or visual handicaps.

You can use the 'Evaluation Guide' below to help you analyse and evaluate questionnaire-based research. If there is insufficient information for you to answer some questions, you should not completely reject the research report, but you should treat the findings with caution and be wary about treating the report as evidence.

EVALUATION GUIDE: QUESTIONNAIRES

1 What was the research topic? Were questionnaires an appropriate data generation method for this topic?
2 Was the questionnaire self-administered or researcher-administered? Was this appropriate for this research topic?
3 Is a copy of the questionnaire provided? If yes, does it meet the guidelines given in this chapter for layout and structure? If no, how does that affect your confidence in the research?
4 What question types were used? Open, closed or both? Was this appropriate?
5 Are the questions and possible responses clear, unambiguous, the appropriate format and in the right order?
6 Do the researchers say whether they pre-tested and piloted the questionnaire? If not, how does that affect your confidence in the research?
7 Do the researchers discuss content validity, construct validity and reliability of their questionnaire? If not, how does that affect your confidence in the research?
8 What limitations in their use of questionnaires do the researchers recognize?
9 Can you identify other flaws or omissions in the researchers' reporting of their use of questionnaires?
10 Overall, how effectively do you think the questionnaire-based approach has been reported and used?

PRACTICAL WORK

1   Questionnaires are often associated with surveys by post. However, they don't have to be sent out and returned by post. Other mechanisms include:

   a   **Delivery and collection questionnaire**: the researcher delivers the question-naire to each respondent and returns later to collect it.
   b   **Telephone-based questionnaire**: the researcher telephones the respondents, asks them each question on the questionnaire and notes the responses.
   c   **Email-based questionnaire**: the researcher emails the questionnaire to respondents and receives the completed forms back via email.
   d   **Web-based questionnaire**: the researcher places a questionnaire on the web and respondents are asked to complete and submit it electronically.
       Assess the advantages and disadvantages of each of these mechanisms.

2   You have been asked to find out how potential applicants to your university evaluate its website.

   a   List the kinds of questions you might ask them.
   b   Write some questions you could use in a questionnaire to be sent to the potential applicants, illustrating *all* the different types of question explained in this chapter.
   c   Analyse whether you have some questions that you would use if the questionnaire were to be sent out by post, but would not use if it were to be placed on the web for completion.

3   Practise analysing and evaluating research based on questionnaires. Study a piece of research that used them as a data generation method. (Concentrate on the design and use of the questionnaires rather than the researchers' statistical analysis of the data.) Answer the questions in the 'Evaluation Guide' above, using the material in this chapter to help you.

FURTHER READING

Although focused on market research, Peterson (2000) gives much advice on question-naire design that is equally applicable to research in IS and computing. His book is clearly written, with many examples of good and poor questions. He also suggests sources for commonly reused questions. Oppenheim (1992) also gives useful advice on surveys and questionnaire design.

   ISWorld (www.isworld.org) contains a living document (Newsted, Huff, Munro, & Schwarz, 1998) with a tutorial on surveys and questionnaires, useful references and a searchable data bank on questionnaires and the items within them that have been used in IS research. The data bank provides either the actual questions used, or links to the appropriate reference. Straub (1989) argues that too little attention has been paid to the validation of question-naires. He explains reliability and the different types of validity in greater detail than is ▶

▶ possible in this book, and illustrates how they can be achieved via a questionnaire that he used to investigate computer abuse carried out by individuals against organizations.

Hewson, Yule, Laurent and Vogel (2003) discuss Internet-based questionnaires and provide sample code (both html and Javascript) for questionnaires that are to be hosted on either a Unix server or an ASP-based Microsoft® Windows® server. They also suggest some online resources that give guidance on the development of questionnaire-based surveys.

References

Agarwal, R., & Venkatesh, V. (2002). Assessing a firm's web presence: A heuristic evaluation procedure for the measurement of usability. *Information Systems Research, 13*(2), 168–186.

Bassellier, G., & Benbasat, I. (2004). Business competence of information technology professionals: Conceptual development and influence on IT-business partnerships. *MIS Quarterly, 28*(4), 673–694.

Davis, F.D. (1989). Perceived usefulness, perceived ease of use, and user acceptance of information technology. *MIS Quarterly, 13*(3), 319–340.

Hewson, C., Yule, P., Laurent, D., & Vogel, C. (2003). *Internet research methods. A practical guide for the social and behavioural sciences.* London: Sage.

Lim, K.H., & Benbasat, I. (2000). The effect of multimedia on perceived equivocality and perceived usefulness of information systems. *MIS Quarterly, 24*(3), 449–471.

Newsted, P., Huff, S., Munro, M., & Schwarz, A. (1998). Survey instruments in information systems. *MISQ Discovery, 22*(4), 553–554. Retrieved 3 February 2005 from www.isworld.org/surveyinstruments.surveyinstrument.htm

Oppenheim, A.N. (1992). *Questionnaire design, interviewing and attitude measurement* (2nd ed.). London: Continuum.

Peterson, R.A. (2000). *Constructing effective questionnaires.* London: Sage.

Straub, D.W. (1989). Validating instruments in MIS research. *MIS Quarterly, 13*, 147–169.

Venkatesh, V., & Morris, M.G. (2000). Why don't men ever stop to ask for directions? Gender, social influence and their role in technology acceptance and usage behaviour. *MIS Quarterly, 24*(1), 115–139.

16 Documents

In this chapter you will learn about:

- documents as a method of generating data for your research;
- how to use documents in research;
- how the Internet can be used for document-based research;
- how documents have been used in previous IS and computing research;
- the advantages and disadvantages of document-based research;
- how to analyse and evaluate document-based research.

Defining Documents

Documents can be treated as another source of data, an alternative to interviews, observations and questionnaires. We can divide them into two types: *found documents* and *researcher-generated documents*.

- **Found documents** already exist prior to the research, such as the documents found in most organizations: production schedules, profit and loss accounts, internal telephone directories, job descriptions, procedure manuals, and so on.
- **Researcher-generated documents** are put together solely for the purposes of the research task, and would not otherwise have existed. For example, a researcher undertaking an ethnography (see Chapter 12) would probably take photographs and make field notes about what they observed and thought. These images and notes become an important source of data when the researcher analyses, interprets and writes up their study. Similarly, a researcher who is designing and creating a new IT artefact (see Chapter 8) would produce many models and diagrams (for

example, storyboards, use case scenarios or data flow diagrams). These documents are important in illustrating and justifying the design process. A researcher can also design a document but ask someone else to complete it. For example, someone working on a help-desk might be asked to keep a log for a month recording the different kinds of requests dealt with and the time taken to respond satisfactorily.

Organizations produce a large number of documents that might be useful sources of data, such as:

- formal records, for example, personnel records, sales figures, shareholder reports and minutes of meetings;
- informal communications, for example, notes, memos and emails;
- public records, for example, electoral (voter) registers and registers of births, marriages and deaths.

Individuals also produce and use documents, such as:

- personal papers and communications, for example, diaries, logs, letters, phone texts and emails;
- documents from our everyday lives, for example, bus tickets, shopping lists, till receipts and credit card bills;
- gravestone inscriptions;
- graffiti and tee-shirt slogans.

Publications are also a form of document-based data, such as:

- academic literature, for example, books, journal articles and conference papers (a literature review [see Chapter 6] is a form of document-based research);
- popular literature, for example, newspaper articles, magazine pieces and brochures;
- guides, for example, programmer manuals and software guides.

Previous research can also provide a form of documentary data that you might reuse in your own research. Such data is called *secondary data* (perhaps a better term would be *second-hand data*). Examples include:

- research data and field notes from studies, which have been intentionally archived for the benefit of future scholars;
- government or other publicly funded surveys, for example, government censuses, unemployment counts and labour market surveys;
- internal organizational research, for example, job-satisfaction surveys and suggestion schemes.

The meaning of 'documents' has also now been extended to encompass more than just written materials. A document is taken to mean any symbolic representation that can be recorded and retrieved for analysis. We therefore sometimes refer to *multimedia documents*, which, as well as the textual documents outlined above, include:

- visual sources of data, for example, pictures, photographs, diagrams, animations, comic strips, signposts, videos and models;
- aural sources, for example, sounds and music.
- electronic sources, for example, screenshots, websites, computer games and the archives of online communities.

Such multimedia documents have not been used in research as much as textual documents. However, since a large part of IS and computing is concerned with the design and use of digital multimedia, perhaps we can except to see more use of multimedia documents for research in these disciplines in future.

Veda is interested in the fact that there are far fewer women than men in the computing industry, and has decided to use multimedia documents in her research. She will examine the websites and annual reports of some computing professional bodies, such as the BCS and the ACM. She plans to analyse the text of these documents for any evidence of implied gender bias. She will also analyse visual data such as the photographs and images used, to see whether more men than women are featured, and whether any messages are conveyed about the respective roles of men and women in computing.

CASE STUDY
Example of
document use

Planning and Conducting Document-based Research

Documents can be used within any of the research strategies discussed in this book: design and creation, surveys, case studies, ethnographies, experiments and action research. For example, within a design and creation research strategy (see Chapter 8), company memos can provide information about the client's rationale for requiring a new computer system, or company reports can illustrate the kind of output end-users will expect from a new system. In case studies and ethnographies, documents can be used to corroborate or question data obtained from other data generation methods. For example, an interviewee might tell you they think their organization has 500 employees, but personnel reports might show it has 600 employees. Surveys of documents are also possible, such as a literature research or a survey of particular types of website. This section looks at some of the issues to consider when using documents as part of your research strategy.

Obtaining access to documents

It can be far easier to obtain document-based data than it is to plan and conduct interviews or design and issue questionnaires. Many documents can be obtained simply by visiting the library or using the web. Often researchers can therefore obtain useful documentary data without having to negotiate consent, make appointments or ponder ethical problems. However, this applies only to documentary data that is in the public domain, for example, government-published reports, company annual reports and public archives of previous research. Sometimes a fee is payable to access previous research. For example, market research companies publish their findings, but charge a high price, often beyond the budget of many researchers.

Other documents may be sensitive and confidential, for example, internal company memos or police records. Such documents are not so easily obtainable. You need to negotiate with those who hold the data, and often also with those described in the documentary data, to allow you access as a bona fide researcher. You need to convince the 'owners' of the data that you will respect its confidentiality and not use it in any way that might harm people or the organization. Depending on the data protection laws in your country, you may find that you are not allowed access to any individual's files, unless that individual chooses to obtain them and show them to you.

There might also be some documents that you know to exist, and that would be very useful to your research, but they are regarded as too secret to show even a genuine academic researcher, such as a company's strategic plans, or a second set of financial accounts that are concealed from the tax office. You will probably only be able to get access to such secret documents if you use covert participant observation (see Chapter 14).

For 'found' data, you also have to deal with copyright issues. You will probably have to obtain written permission to reproduce an image (or piece of music) in your research from whoever owns the copyright. This might be the person who created it, or the person who commissioned it. Sometimes a fee is payable, which can be quite large for images drawn from advertisements or the media. You should therefore make clear that you want to reproduce the image for your small-scale academic research and will not gain financially from it – this can result in lower or waived fees. If, after trying hard, you fail to find the copyright owner, you need to add a statement to your paper or thesis that says something like, 'Rigorous efforts have been made to trace the copyright holders of the images used and obtain permission to reproduce them. Where they have not been traced, the author invites further information and will seek to remedy the situation'.

Using secondary data and research data archives

There is a well-established tradition of reusing data in research. For example, figures provided in government and other publicly funded statistical reports can be used as data in your own research. Often the raw data is made available as well as statistical analysis of it – you can reuse either the original data or the statistical findings.

Museums, art galleries and libraries act as archives of images and documents. Increasingly research data archives are also being set up, which catalogue the data generated in previous studies, archive it, publicize its existence and encourage other researchers to reuse it. Many of these are accessible online, often without fee. Until recently, most of these research archives concentrated on quantitative data, usually gathered via surveys and questionnaires. Qualitative data has not been archived to the same extent. For example, Corti and Thompson (2004) cite a study in 1991 that found that 90 per cent of qualitative data from academic research was either lost or at risk – sitting in researchers' homes or offices, inaccessible to others and likely to be lost after the researchers retire. However, some archives of qualitative data do now exist, for example, Qualidata at the University of Essex (UK), and at the time of writing, several countries are considering whether to set up national qualitative data archives including Germany, Switzerland and Canada.

Possible uses of secondary data include:

- Reusing data that someone else has already collected, such as survey data from questionnaires or interview transcripts, saving you the bother of generating such data yourself.
- Using data about interviewees to enable re-contact and follow-up interviews, to be compared with the interview responses given earlier.
- Re-analysing the data – asking different questions of it from the original researchers, using different statistical techniques to look for new correlations or patterns, looking for different themes in qualitative data or applying a different theoretical framework.
- Finding out from researchers' field notes about their research methodology – which you can use or modify in your own research.
- Verifying or challenging the research, so supporting or questioning its credibility. You could examine the data obtained by an earlier researcher and trace how it was analysed and interpreted. You might, for example, find evidence of unacknowledged bias or assumptions in the original researcher's work.

Evaluating documents

It is important to evaluate 'found' documents, to see if they are authentic, and to assess how far you can trust them. You should consider the author – did they have a particular view that might shape how a report was written or a picture taken? And you should consider the context and timescale in which a document was produced – quickly, immediately after a witnessed event? Or more leisurely, based on information gleaned only indirectly from others who were present?

You should also consider what the purpose was for which the documents were originally created – to encourage shareholders to buy more shares? To make senior managers think a department is being very active? The purpose *you* want to put the documents to (your research) will probably be quite different. You therefore need to assess whether the documents really are relevant and appropriate to your research.

Always remember that documents present only a partial view or account of something aimed at a particular audience for a particular purpose. For example, many formal organizational records are intended to show and enhance accountability. They are supposed to provide a detailed, systematic and accurate picture of some aspect of the organization. However, they only show what is agreed should be put 'on the record'. The minutes of a meeting, for example, often report only (apparent) consensus decisions. They do not report on what may have been an acrimonious debate prior to any decision being taken. Nor do they usually show whether people are happy with the decisions taken.

Diaries and field notes usually present someone's personal account of events and their thoughts on them. They too are a partial account and cannot be taken as an objective report of what occurred. Photographs and videos are also one person's framing of a situation, and in this digital age can easily be modified afterwards.

Even government statistics cannot be believed uncritically – governments often have a political purpose in mind and want to present their findings in the best possible light for them. For all statistics you should ask:

- Whether counting and measuring the object under investigation is easy and straightforward. For example, counting the population of a country may be hampered by unknown numbers of homeless people and by some people failing to register with the authorities to avoid paying taxes.
- Whether someone or an organization has a vested interest in the statistics produced. For example, sales figures, number of households without access to the Internet, average time to answer the telephone, number of help-desk calls handled per week – all have consequences for individuals or organizations, who may be tempted to measure and record in a way that produces the 'right' outcome.
- Whether the statistics depend on a series of individual decisions and judgements. For example, Prior (2004) describes the series of judgements that have to be made by doctors about cause of death and by computer data personnel about coding categories for these causes of death. Such decisions in each country lead to statistics that are eventually collated and published in the World Health Organization's annual manual of world health statistics and mortality rates. This manual appears extremely factual and authoritative, but is ultimately based on individuals' expertise, discretion and judgement, not 'facts'. The more judgement and decisions that have to be made in gathering and collating statistical data, the less reliable are the final results.

Analysing documents

Two broad approaches are possible for analysing documents: documents as *vessels* and documents as *objects*.

- **Documents as vessels**: documents are seen as receptacles that hold content (data). That content can be analysed – with suitable scepticism about the reliability of the content and the author (see above). Content analysis is a quantitative technique that counts the number of times something occurs in a set of documents (for example, warnings about cost over-runs on a computer project). Alternatively, themes analysis is a qualitative technique that examines the different topics covered within a selection of documents. For images, semiotic analysis looks at the symbolism embodied in the image. (Data analysis is discussed further in Chapters 17 and 18.)
- **Documents as objects**: documents are treated as entities in their own right. You look at who produces them, who consumes them, and how they are developed, exchanged and circulated. For example, by looking at the distribution lists of company memos or emails, you can deduce the network of communications in that company and work out who is in or out of particular groups and therefore learn something about the politics of that organization.

The Internet and Document-based Research

The Internet is ideally suited to document-based research, since so much of it is in the form of (electronic) documents: personal and company webpages, emails, discussion list archives, bulletin boards, online auctions, and so on. To study the Internet often requires the study of documents.

All the previous warnings about the need to evaluate documentary sources carefully also apply to the Internet – where the scope for misleading documents is probably even larger than in the offline world. Similarly, Internet-based documents are just as much a partial, selective representation of something as their equivalents offline. For example, what people type as their opinion in a discussion forum is not necessarily what they really think. An Internet document, like any offline document, is also produced with a particular audience and purpose in mind: to make a person or a company look good, to inflame a debate, and so on.

You also need to consider the ethics of using Internet documents. For example, as earlier chapters have explained, although postings to discussion forums seem to be in the public domain, because anyone can access them over the web, the authors and intended readers often perceive them as private communications, and can be hurt or angry if you use them in your research. (See Chapter 5 for more discussion of Internet ethics.)

Software can be used to produce more documents about the Internet. For example, cookies and server logs can be used to discover when and how people visit a website and move around it. These documents can be 'found' – many organizations keep statistics about visits to their website. Or they can be researcher-generated – with the necessary permissions and ethical considerations, for example, you could write a program to track people's web usage.

One problem in analysing Internet-based documents is their transitory nature – often the next time you try to visit a site it's changed, or disappeared entirely. It's worth making a copy of the webpages you are researching, so that you can look at it again later. Of course, the copy should only be for the purposes of your own research, you should not reproduce it anywhere or otherwise infringe the copyright. If you need to copy a whole website, software programs are available that can do this for you (for example, WebReaper, available from: www.webreaper.net, which is free for non-commercial use), although you might find that companies have installed protection mechanisms to prevent the programs downloading their site to your hard disk. If you do need to find a version of a website that has now disappeared, you could ask the owner of the site, or you could try the Internet Archive (www.archive.org), which is free to the general public.

Examples of Documents in IS and Computing Research

In most disciplines, documents have not been used in research as much as interviews, observations and questionnaires, and IS and computing are no exception. However, taking a document-based approach could be particularly relevant for readers of this book, since so much of IS and computing is already concerned with the generation and handling of documents. For example:

- New computer-based systems are developed to automate and speed up paper-based systems (that is, document systems).
- Most information systems produce documents (either paper-based or electronic).
- Much IS and computing research is now concerned with the development and use of websites (that is, multimedia document systems).
- New computer-based scanning and visualization techniques can contribute to research in other disciplines such as medicine and archaeology (that is, electronic images as documents for analysis).

Document analysis is often used within ethnographies, case studies and action research (see Chapters 10–12). Examples of IS and computing research that has used document analysis as its main focus include:

- a proposal for a development methodology for hypermedia information systems that employs a workflow model based on corporate documents (Lee & Suh, 2001);
- a study using logs and questionnaires to examine how people seek information from websites, leading to the identification of 'bouncers', 'checkers' and 'returnees' (Nicholas, Huntington, Williams, & Dobrowolski, 2004);

- an analysis of electronic textbooks on the web, assessing how appearance and design can affect users' sense of engagement (Wilson, Landoni, & Gibb, 2003);
- studies of how websites are used as tools for self-representation (Seale, 2001; Wynn & Katz, 1997);
- an exploration of the effect of computer graphic systems on the visual culture of engineering designers, who use drawings to organize resources, political support and power (Henderson, 1999).

Evaluating Document-based Research

Advantages of document-based research include:

- Much documentary data can be obtained quickly, cheaply and conveniently, without the need for appointments and permission, and with fewer ethical problems to consider than other data generation methods.
- Since many documents have already been produced for another reason, they are readily available and can be collected unobtrusively.
- Using secondary data from regularly published reports allows longitudinal studies, which might not be possible otherwise because of the time commitment required from the researcher.
- Documents are often permanent, and many are in the public domain, meaning that other researchers can easily check and scrutinize the research based on them, helping to give your work credibility.

Disadvantages of document-based research include:

- You need to evaluate carefully any document including its author, source, purpose and how it was produced.
- They cannot be relied upon to give an objective picture of reality. Nor can any other data generation method, but the official, authoritative-looking nature of many documents means that researchers sometimes forget this.
- Access to some types of documents is expensive or impossible, or, particularly for Internet-based documents, only temporary.
- Secondary data has often been collected and analysed for a different purpose and might not map well onto your research questions.
- Regularly published surveys can change their categorization methods, so longitudinal comparisons are not possible. For example, governments change the way they define and calculate unemployment and inflation.

You can use the 'Evaluation Guide' to help you analyse and evaluate document-based research. If there is insufficient information for you to answer the questions, you should not completely reject the research report, but you should treat the findings with some caution and be wary about relying on the report for evidence.

EVALUATION GUIDE: DOCUMENTS

1   What was the research topic? Were documents an appropriate data generation method for this topic?

2   What kinds of documents were used? (Textual or multimedia, quantitative data or qualitative data, organizational or personal, and so on)

3   Did the researchers use 'found' documents? If so, do they explain how they gained access to them?

4   Did the researchers use 'researcher-generated' documents? If so, do they explain how they were designed and used?

5   Do the researchers justify the appropriateness of their chosen documents and explain how they assessed their credibility, reliability and possible bias?

6   Are the documents analysed as vessels of content or as objects, or both?

7   Are extracts from the documents used in the report of the research?

8   What limitations in their use of documents do the researchers recognize?

9   Can you identify other flaws or omissions in the researchers' reporting of their use of documents?

10 Overall, how effectively do you think the document-based approach has been reported and used?

PRACTICAL WORK

1   Suggest documentary data sources you could use to find out:

   a   the number of households in your country that have access to broadband;
   b   the rate of absenteeism in a systems development department in an organization, as compared to the other departments;
   c   a company's annual expenditure on hardware and software;
   d   the growth in recent years of the web;
   e   how decisions about the design of a company's corporate website are made;
   f   how a conspiracy theory spreads throughout the world.

2   Produce a list of criteria you could use to check the authenticity and trustworthiness of (a) a shopping website and (b) a website purporting to provide factual information. Now visit some websites and assess them against your criteria. Have they done everything they can to make you trust them and their content? Now consider whether you would need to amend your criteria if they were to be used for assessing offline documents.

3   Try to keep a copy of all the documents you handle during the next week (memos, emails, shopping till receipts, travel tickets, and so on). What could a future historian learn about you and your life from these documents?

4   Study a piece of research that used documents as a data generation method. Answer the questions in the 'Evaluation Guide' above, using the material in this chapter to help you. If there is insufficient information for you to answer the questions, you should not completely reject the research report, but you should treat the findings with some caution.

FURTHER READING

Prior (2004) argues that the study of documents should play a greater role in academic research. In particular the 'documents as objects' viewpoint is an under-researched area, yet important in our document-driven age. He (2003) gives plenty of advice on using documents. Advice on the use of multimedia documents such as images and sound can be found in Bauer and Gaskell (2000), Prosser (1998) and Rose (2001). Guidance on using secondary data and data archives is to be found in Corti and Thompson (2004), Kiecolt and Nathan (1986) and Stewart and Kamins (1993).

The University of California, San Diego, maintains an online list of social science data catalogues and archives across the world, which could be useful to IS and computing researchers (odwin.ucsd.edu/idata/). The Internet Archive (www.archive.org) is an ongoing project to build a digital library to prevent Internet and other digital material being lost, aiming to offer permanent and free access to researchers and the general public. It holds a collection of archived webpages from 1996 onwards, as well as other collections of digital material (for example, those related to September 11, 2001, and those documenting the development of the Arpanet, the forerunner of the Internet). It also contains bibliographic resources that suggest how the archive might be used for research and discuss copyright and ethical issues associated with digital libraries.

References

Bauer, M.W., & Gaskell, G. (Eds.). (2000). *Qualitative researching with text, image and sound: A practical handbook*. London: Sage.

Corti, L., & Thompson, P. (2004). Secondary analysis of archived data. In C. Seale, G. Gobo, J.F. Gubrium, & D. Silverman (Eds.), *Qualitative Research Practice* (pp. 327–343). London: Sage.

Henderson, K. (1999). *On-line and on paper: Visual representations, visual culture and computer graphics in design engineering*. Cambridge, MA: MIT Press.

Kiecolt, K.J., & Nathan, L.E. (1986). *Secondary analysis of survey data*. London: Sage.

Lee, H., & Suh, W. (2001). A workflow-based methodology for developing hypermedia information systems. *Journal of Organizational Computing and Electronic Commerce, 11*(2), 77–106.

Nicholas, D., Huntington, P., Williams, P., & Dobrowolski, T. (2004). Re-appraising information seeking behaviour in a digital environment: Bouncers, checkers, returnees and the like. *Journal of Documentation, 60*(1), 24–43.

Prior, L. (2003). *Using documents in social research*. London: Sage.

Prior, L. (2004). Documents. In C. Seale, G. Gobo, J.F. Gubrium & D. Silverman (Eds.), *Qualitative Research Practice* (pp. 375–390). London: Sage.

Prosser, J. (Ed.) (1998). *Image-based research: A sourcebook for qualitative researchers*. London: Sage.

Rose, G. (2001). *Visual methodologies: An introduction to the interpretation of visual materials*. London: Sage.

Seale, J.K. (2001). The same but different: The use of the personal home page by adults with Down syndrome as a tool for self-presentation. *British Journal of Educational Technology, 32*(3), 343–352.

Stewart, D.W., & Kamins, M.A. (1993). *Secondary research, second edition. Information sources and methods*. London: Sage.

Wilson, R., Landoni, M., & Gibb, F. (2003). The WEB Book experiments in electronic textbook design. *Journal of Documentation, 59*(4), 454–477.

Wynn, E., & Katz, J. (1997). Hyperbole over cyberspace: Self-presentation and social boundaries in Internet home pages and discourse. *The Information Society, 13*, 297–327.

17 Quantitative Data Analysis

In this chapter you will learn about:

- the different kinds of quantitative data;
- how to prepare your quantitative data for analysis;
- using visual aids for quantitative data analysis;
- using statistics for quantitative data analysis;
- how to analyse and evaluate research based on quantitative data analysis.

Defining Quantitative Data Analysis

Quantitative data means data, or evidence, based on numbers. It is the main type of data generated by experiments and surveys (see Chapters 7 and 9), although it can be generated by other research strategies too. It is primarily used and analysed by positivist researchers (see Chapter 19), but is sometimes generated by interpretive and critical researchers too (see Chapter 20). Examples of numeric data include:

- number of people expressing satisfaction with an organization's IT help-desk;
- a company's annual turnover for each of the last 5 years;
- time in seconds to process a data file;
- number of characters in a computer animation;
- number of people accessing the Internet for more than 20 hours per week;
- number of hot links on a website.

The idea of data analysis is to look for patterns in the data and draw conclusions. There is a wide range of established techniques for analysing quantitative data. A simple analysis would use tables, charts or graphs – these enable the researcher or reader to *see* some patterns. At the next level of complexity, simple descriptive statistical techniques allow more patterns to be found such as the average value of a set of instrument readings. More complex statistical techniques enable you to establish whether patterns you see in the data really do exist and are not just the result of chance. You should read this chapter before you even start producing any quantitative data – so that you can be sure to generate the appropriate kinds of data for the analytical techniques you plan to use.

For small-scale projects, you might only need the simple quantitative analysis techniques. For larger projects – such as a survey with many respondents that involves a questionnaire, where you want to see if responses to one question are associated with a particular kind of response to another question – you need the more complex analysis techniques.

Many researchers shy away from numerical analysis because they don't like mathematics and statistics. The good news is, however, that there are computer-based programs available to do the analysis for you. These range from table and charting tools found in word processing programs and spreadsheet programs such as Microsoft® Excel® to, for the more complex statistical techniques, specialized programs such as Minitab and SPSS. These software tools take away the need for laborious number crunching by hand and you don't even have to know the formulas they use to produce their results. However, the bad news is that reviewers and examiners are sometimes suspicious of papers and theses that use many complex statistical techniques. Some writers have noted that the increasing use of sophisticated statistical techniques might not be due to the increasing statistical knowledge of researchers – rather it could be due to the increasing availability of computer programs that do the statistical analysis for them. Reviewers and examiners question whether researchers use statistical techniques without understanding them, and therefore sometimes use them inappropriately. You would be well advised to make sure you do understand what each technique does and when it can be used, while leaving the actual number crunching to a computer.

This chapter summarizes some techniques available for quantitative data analysis and indicates when and how they can be used. It should help you to employ tables and charts to visualize your data, use appropriate means to describe it, and choose some methods to examine trends and relationships within it. It does not provide a tutorial on each technique (there's not enough room). If you plan to use statistical techniques in your research project, you should also study one of the many specialized books available – some are suggested in the 'Further Reading' section.

Types of Quantitative Data

First, we need to know the different kinds of data used in quantitative data analysis – because different analysis techniques are suited to different kinds of data.

We are particularly concerned with four different types: nominal, ordinal, interval and ratio data.

Nominal data

Nominal data is that which describes categories and has no actual numeric value. For example, a questionnaire might ask about the respondents' gender ('Circle 1 for female, 2 for male'). The response is categorized by a number, but it would not be meaningful to carry out arithmetical operations on the set of responses (for example, what would 'average gender' mean?). There is no numerical value or order to the numbers used for the categories ('Circle 1 for male, 2 for female', or 'Circle 15 for male, 20 for female' would both work just as well). The only analysis possible is the frequency – how many respondents circled one code number and how many respondents circled another code number. This type of data is sometimes called *categorical data*.

Ordinal data

With ordinal data, numbers are allocated to a quantitative scale. For example, students could be ranked in terms of their examination results, 1, 2, 3, for example. This time, unlike nominal data, there is an order to the designated code numbers so some arithmetical operations are possible – we can tell which student did better than another student. However, the arithmetical operations are limited. We don't know *how much better* the first placed student was than the second, or the tenth, and so on. A common use of ordinal data is in categorizing responses to Likert scale-based questions, where numbers are assigned to the range of responses. For example, the responses 'Disagree strongly', 'Disagree', 'Neither agree nor disagree', 'Agree', 'Agree strongly' might be coded 1, 2, 3, 4 and 5, respectively). Again you can see there is an order to the designated code numbers for each response – 5 means greater agreement than 4, for instance. But we cannot know by how much 'Strongly agree' (5) is greater than 'Agree' (4). For ordinal data, the categories are ranked, but we don't know the differences or intervals, between each rank. This type of data is sometimes called *ranked data*.

Interval data

Interval data is like ordinal data, but now measurements are made against a quantitative scale where the differences, or intervals, between points of the scale are consistently the same size, that is, the ranking of the categories is *proportionate*. You can therefore state the difference between any two data values precisely. For example, the difference, or interval, between the years 2000 and 2004 is the same as that between 1914 and 1918. For such data addition or subtraction can be used (but not multiplication or division).

Ratio data

Ratio data is like interval data, but there is a true zero to the measurement scale being used. For example, people's age, weight, or height, or companies' number of subsidiaries, head count of employees or annual turnover. Someone's age can be 0, annual turnover can be 0, and so on, whereas for interval data such as calendar years there is no true zero – there is no year 0 before which there was no history. With ratio data, because there is a true zero, we know that not only is, say, 4 the same interval from 2 as 6 is from 4, but also 4 is twice as big as 2 and 6 is three times as big. Because there is a true zero on any scale used for ratio data, addition, subtraction, multiplication and division can all be used. (If you don't see the reasoning for the importance of having a true zero on a scale, don't worry – just accept it.)

Further data categories

Two other categories of data that you might need to know are: discrete and continuous data.

- **Discrete data:** each measurement leads to a whole number, not a fraction of a number. For example, 'number of children' will lead to a whole number response, no sensible person will answer, say, '0.75'.
- **Continuous data:** the possible measurements don't come in neat chunks but could be measured to greater and greater accuracy, for example, age can be measured in years, days, minutes, seconds, milliseconds or even smaller units. If data is continuous, the researcher needs to decide the level of accuracy needed. For example, 'age last birthday' might be adequate.

Data Coding

Some of your data may already be in numeric form – measurements you have taken, number-based responses to questions you posed, and so on. Other data needs to be coded into a number if you want to enter data quickly and easily and carry out quantitative data analysis on it. For example, if you used a questionnaire you need to:

- code each predefined answer option you included;
- code each theme which appears in respondents' answers to open questions.

The coding scheme you design must contain codes that are *mutually exclusive*, that is, there is no overlap between one code and another bringing the danger that you could code some data in more than one way. It must also be *exhaustive* – that is, cover every pre-defined option and every theme that you find in the data. It must also be *consistently applied* – that is, if more than one person works on the data coding, each must apply the scheme in the same way.

You should create a *code book*, where you note each code used and the kind of data to which it applies. You also need to include codes for missing data – whether the reason for the missing data is because a respondent ignored a question, or a question was not applicable to some respondents, or some other reason.

If using a software program you need to input your quantitative data. Usually this is done into a table, with columns for the variables (the measurements taken, observations made or questions answered) and one row for one case (one questionnaire, one experiment, and so on). You should then check for errors – slip-ups are easy when inputting data. Watch out for:

- values that are unlikely, for example, 'age' is 120;
- codes that don't exist in your code book;
- illogical relationships, for example, if a person is coded as having a PhD but is also coded as never having been to university, there is probably an error;
- filtering rules that have not been followed in a questionnaire, for example, if a 'yes' response to question 7 triggered the request to jump to question 12, the values for responses to questions 8–11 should all be coded as missing data; an error has occurred if they are not coded in this way.

Having coded your data, you are now ready to start your quantitative analysis, using one or more of the techniques described in the next two sections.

Visual Aids for Quantitative Data Analysis

The simplest form of analysis uses tables and charts to present the data in a visual way that allows you to explore it and 'see' values and patterns in it. These tables and charts can also be included in the write-up of your research, so the reader sees what you see. Typically, we use tables and charts to show: specific values, highest and lowest values of a variable, frequencies, proportions, distributions and trends, as the following examples show.

Tables

Tables are suitable for use with all types of data, and are easily produced using word processing software. For example, Figure 17.1 shows the actual values obtained for 'Number of people allocated to each systems development project team'.

You could use another table to plot the frequency of project team sizes – see Figure 17.2. This shows a pattern – some sizes of teams are more common than others. Note that the researcher chose how to group the projects – a different table would have been produced if the display categories were based on 0–2 members, 3–4 members, 5–6 members, and so on. Remember that whenever you create groups from your data you are moving away from the raw data and imposing your own meaning upon it.

Project	No. allocated		Project	No. allocated
Robin	2		Lily	5
Swallow	3		Iris	9
Swan	5		Spider	2
Eagle	2		Ant	5
Osprey	3		Bear	2
Sparrow	0		Lynx	10
Finch	1		Wolf	5
Mallard	1		Coyote	4
Pelican	13		Deer	2
Rose	4		Fox	8
Daisy	5		Tiger	9

Figure 17.1   Number of people allocated to systems development projects

No. of people allocated	No. of projects
0–3	10
4–7	7
8–11	4
> 11	1

Figure 17.2   Frequency of project team size

Bar charts

Bar charts are often used for displaying frequencies. For example, the data in Figure 17.2 is displayed in a bar chart in Figure 17.3. More complex bar charts are also possible. For example, Figure 17.4 shows the number of days lost through sickness for three teams. However, the more data you try to show in one chart, the harder it can be for the reader to understand it. Be careful not to overload the reader.

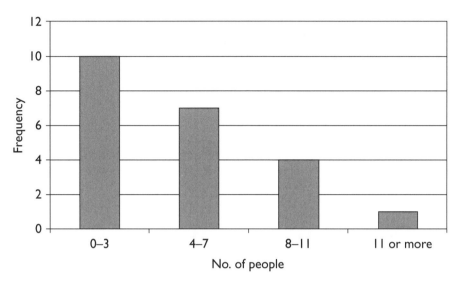

Figure 17.3 Allocation to project teams

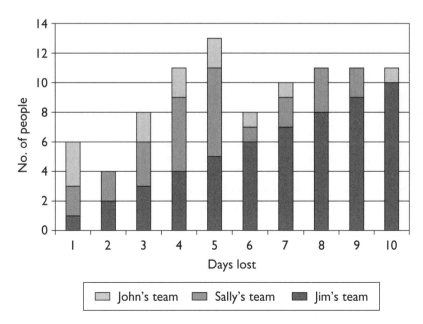

Figure 17.4 Days lost through sickness

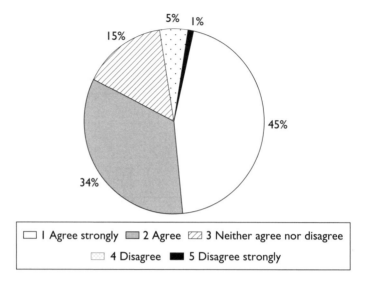

Figure 17.5   Percentage of people agreeing that a web presence is essential

Pie charts

Pie charts are good for showing proportions as in Figure 17.5. For ease of reading, usually you should have not more than seven segments.

Scatter graph

A scatter graph can be used to show a relationship between two variables. You plot your data as points on a graph, where the x-axis represents the values of one variable, and the y-axis represents the values of the other variable. If no line can be seen around which the data points tend to cluster, then there is no relationship between the variables. The more closely the points tend to cluster around a line, the closer a relationship there is between the variables. If, as the values for one variable increase, so do the values for the other, you have a positive relationship between the variables. If, as the values for one variable increase, the values for the other decrease, you have a negative relationship. Figure 17.6 suggests a positive relationship between salary and hours spent per working day accessing the Internet. Remember that normally you will need many values for each variable to be able to reveal any relationship between them.

Line graphs

Line graphs are used for showing trends in data, as in Figure 17.7, which indicates the changing turnover of a company over several years.

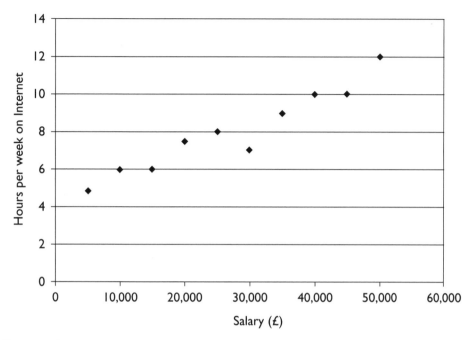

Figure 17.6   Relationship between salary and Internet access

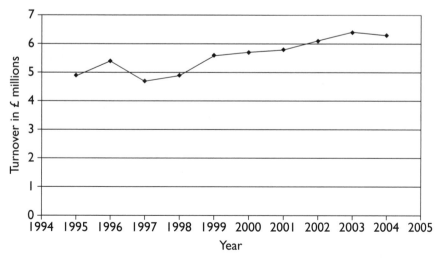

Figure 17.7   Annual turnover, 1995–2004 inclusive

Whatever kind of chart you choose to use make sure that:

- It is easy to read.
- It has a title.
- It gives information about the units represented in the columns of a bar chart or table, the segments of a pie chart or the axes of a graph.
- It displays enough information to make it worthwhile, but doesn't overload the reader with too much detailed information.

Using Statistics for Quantitative Data Analysis

Tables and charts help us to organize our empirical data, or evidence, and identify interesting aspects of it. However, they are dependent on the researcher's individual interpretations of the data, aided by tables and charts whose formats the researcher decides. Statistical techniques, on the other hand, offer more universal means and criteria for evaluating key points and making generalized conclusions based on the evidence. For example, a scatter graph might show that the value of one variable *seems* to be linked to another variable. Statistical analysis can tell us whether there is indeed such a link, or whether the pattern observed in a graph is just down to chance. In this section, we therefore look at a range of statistical measures. Some are simple and can be calculated fairly easily, others are more complicated and need a computer program to do the calculations.

Describing the central tendency

It can be useful to know about the central tendency of the data, that is, where the majority of the values tends to be found. We have three statistical measures for describing the central tendency: the mean, median and mode.

Mean
The *mean* is the measure most people are referring to when they speak of the 'average' in everyday language. It is found by totalling all the values found and dividing by the number of cases. For example, from a set of exam results:

Smith	77
Watson	73
Singh	69
Hassan	64
Jones	52

The mean is 67.

The mean can only be used with real numbers; it can't be used with nominal data. It would be silly, for example, to have a coding scheme with the codes for job roles as:

Senior manager	1
Junior manager	2
Systems developer	3
Call centre operative	4

and then to declare the mean job role was 3.7.

The mean forms the basis for various statistical tests and is widely used. However, it does have disadvantages. If you only have a few results, the mean is not very meaningful. Also, if your data has some extreme instances, they can distort the value of the mean. For example, you might find that the salary of most people is in the range £15,000–£50,000, but one person earns £200,000 and two £100,000. These three 'outliers' in your data will make the mean higher than it otherwise would have been. A few outliers cause less of a distortion problem if you have a large data sample. They are also less problematic if you have outliers at both the high and low end of the range, so they tend to cancel each other out.

Median

The *median* is the mid point in a range of scores or data results. To find it, we list the values in order (either highest to lowest, or lowest to highest, it doesn't matter) and read off the middle value. For example, for a set of examination results:

Smith	77
Watson	73
Singh	69
Hassan	64
Jones	52

The median is 69.

If you have an even number of values, you take the average of the two middle values. For example:

Smith	77
Watson	73
Richards	71
Singh	69
Hassan	64
Jones	52

The median is 70.

The median gives us the point where 50 per cent of the cases in our data set lie to one side of it, and 50 per cent to the other. It can be used with ordinal, interval and ratio data, but not nominal data. It is also unaffected by outliers in your data, meaning that it's a better measure than the mean of the central tendency of your data if you have some extreme cases.

Mode

The *mode* is the value that is most common in your data set. It is found simply by finding which value occurs most frequently in your data set. For example, in the results:

52, 52, 64, 64, 69, 71, 73, 73, 73, 77
The mode is 73.

(If two values share the same frequency of occurrence, then you have two modes, or a *bimodal distribution*.)

The mode can be used with all four types of data: nominal, ordinal, interval and ratio. It can be used where the other two measures (mode and mean) are inappropriate. For example, we can talk about the most commonly used word processing program (the mode), where it wouldn't make sense to talk about the median or mean word processor. It is unaffected by outliers in the data, like the median, but, again like the median, it is not used in further statistical tests.

Describing the distribution

As well as knowing the central tendency of the data, we might want to know how widespread the values in a data set are, and how evenly spread they are, that is, we need to find out about the distribution or *dispersion* of the data. We have three statistical methods for describing the distribution of values in a data set: the range, fractiles and standard deviation.

Range

The range tells us how far apart the highest and lowest data values are. For example, in the data set:

52, 52, 64, 64, 69, 71, 73, 73, 73, 77

the highest value is 77 and the lowest 52, and the range is 25. The range is a general guide to the values within one data set. However, it can be misleading about the spread, because it is affected by extreme values. For example, if we have a data set containing nine values:

1, 3, 7, 9, 11, 12, 13, 19, 39

the range is 38, yet, seven of the eight values are within a range of just 18. If using the range to describe your data, watch out for extreme values and make sure you don't give a misleading impression.

Fractiles

Fractiles help us divide up the data values we have. We've already met the median – the point where 50 per cent of the data values lie to one side of it and 50 per cent to the other (see above). In effect, the median divides the spread of data into two. But we could divide the spread into smaller parts:

- Quartiles divide the spread into four, so each quartile contains one quarter of the data values in the set.
- Deciles divide the spread into ten.
- Percentiles divide the spread into 100.

One use of fractiles is to enable us to focus on the middle part of the data for further analysis and omit the extreme values or outliers. If we concentrate on quartiles 2 and 3, for instance, we are looking at exactly half of the data values (by definition), and those values are the ones that are around the middle of the spread.

On the other hand, we might want to focus on the values at the high and low end of the range, for example to compare incomes of those in the top decile (the top tenth, who earn more than the other nine-tenths of respondents in a poll) with those in the bottom decile (the lowest tenth of earners).

Percentiles let us think in terms of percentages. If a score is at the 80th percentile, for instance, it means that the score is at or above 80 per cent of the scores in the distribution. (So the median is also known as the 50th percentile.)

Standard deviation

The SD is probably the most used measure of distribution. It tells us the average amount of variability in a set of scores – or, to put it another way, the *average distance of each data value from the mean.*

Standard Deviation

The *larger* the SD is, the larger the average distance each data value is from the mean.
The *smaller* the SD is, the smaller the average distance each data value is from the mean.

To find the SD, we find the difference between each individual score and the mean, square each difference, sum all these squares together, divide the sum by (size of the sample −1), and find the square root of the result.

Or, of course, we tell a spreadsheet or statistics program to do the calculation for us. If the mean of a set of student exam results was 60, and the SD 5, that tells us that the results were clustered around the 60 mark much more closely than for the class where the mean was 60 and the SD 25.

If we end up with a SD of 0, that means there is no variability at all in the scores, they are all identical. This will rarely happen. If you get an SD of 0, look to see if you have made a mistake in inputting the data or in using your statistics software.

The SD is useful for telling us about the distribution of the values in a data set, and is used in further statistical analysis. However, since it uses the mean, the SD can only be calculated for data values that are true numbers – interval and ratio data, not nominal nor, strictly speaking, ordinal data. Like the mean, it is sensitive to extreme scores (outliers). If you are using the SD of a data set that has some extreme values in it, note that in your report.

Finding relationships in the data

As well as knowing about the spread and distribution of the values in a data set, we might want to see if there is an association or relationship between the values for one variable and another, or between one data set and another. For example, we might want to look at our completed questionnaires to see if the responses to 'How much is your annual salary, to the nearest pound?' are in some way linked to the responses to 'How many hours a week do you spend on the Internet?' Do those who earn more spend more time on the Internet, or less, than those who earn lower salaries? Let's briefly look at some statistical tests for exploring relationships.

Correlation coefficients

To find out the strength of any apparent link, or correlation, between two variables, we need to calculate the *correlation coefficient* for them. Two statistical measures that find a correlation coefficient are:

- **Spearman's rank correlation coefficient** – this works with ordinal data;
- **Pearson's product moment correlation coefficient** – this works with interval and ratio data.

The formulas for both are complex, but most statistics programs will calculate them for you. The result of this calculation will be a value between −1 and +1.

- a positive coefficient (for example, 0.7) means there is a positive relationship between two variables – as one goes up the other also goes up;
- a negative coefficient (e.g. −0.6) means there is a negative relationship between the two variables – as one goes down the other goes up;
- a zero coefficient means there is no relationship between the variables;
- any correlation coefficient between 0.3 and 0.7 (plus or minus) is regarded as demonstrating a reasonable correlation;
- the closer the coefficient is to 1 (minus or plus), the stronger, or more perfect, the relationship is between the two variables;
- it is rare to find a perfect correlation, but not impossible.

Warning: Correlation Coefficients

Just because you identify a relationship between two variables, you cannot assume that one *causes* the other. There might be some other factor involved. If you want to investigate patterns in terms of cause and effect, so that from the values of one variable you can predict the value of another variable, you will need to use *regression analysis* – which is beyond the scope of this book.

The null hypothesis and tests of significance

If we think there is a relationship between the values for one variable and those for another, we would like to know whether that link should be taken seriously as a 'true' or genuine relationship, or whether it is down to chance, that is, a one-off fluke. In other words, we need a test for statistical significance – are our results worth being taken seriously?

Researchers start off with the assumption that there is *no* relationship – any apparent link is a fluke. This is called the *null hypothesis* – we start from the premise that there is no true relationship between some variables (even though our data tends to suggest there is), and will stick to that view unless persuaded otherwise. For example:

- There will be no difference between the average scores of novice and experienced data entry personnel on the ABC reactions test.
- There is no relationship between mathematical ability and programming ability.
- There is no association between size of website and number of website hits.

Statistical tests of significance give us a figure which is an estimate of the likelihood that an apparent relationship is down to chance. It is expressed as a probability (p), for example, $p < 0.04$. The null hypothesis is considered to stand if the probability of the relationship being down to chance is calculated to be greater than 1 in 20 ($p > 0.05$). If, on the other hand, it's estimated that the probability of such a relationship occurring by chance is less than 1 in 20 ($p < 0.05$), the connection is regarded as statistically significant.

Chi-square test

This statistical test looks at *whether two variables are associated to a significant level* – that is, it's unlikely an apparent relationship is down to chance. It works with all kinds of data: nominal, ordinal, interval and ratio – so you'll often see it used. It compares what is observed in the data, and what could be expected by chance.

Suppose in a test of 200 students 65 of them obtained an excellent score (70–100 marks), 70 a satisfactory score (40–69 marks) and 65 a poor score (0–39 marks). We

Score	Male	Female	Total
Excellent	27	38	65
Satisfactory	30	40	70
Poor	43	22	65
Total	100	100	200

Figure 17.8   Table of students' test scores

Score	Male	Female	Total
Excellent	32.5	32.5	65
Satisfactory	35	35	70
Poor	32.5	32.5	65
Total	100	100	200

Figure 17.9   Table of expected results

wonder whether gender of the students is related to the ability to do well (or not) in the test. We therefore create a table that relates the two variables as in Figure 17.8:

In our sample of 200 students, we can see that, on average, males performed worse than females. Can we draw the conclusion that the same is true for the broader student population from which our sample was drawn? Or did we just happen to get an unrepresentative sample of students? How likely is it that we used an untypical sample of students drawn, by chance, from a student population where there is *no* relationship between gender and performance?

We can use the chi-square test to find out the likelihood of us having an unrepresentative sample by chance. If there was *no* association between gender and performance in the test, we would expect the table to look like Figure 17.9. The chi-square test performs a set of calculations using the difference between the expected values as shown in Figure 17.9 and the actual values as shown in Figure 17.8. For our example, a computer program would calculate chi-square as 10.07.

'So what?' you might say. Well, we can look up the value we obtained in a table of critical values for chi-square, and find out whether we can have confidence that the observed relationship in the sample is not down to chance. But to do this we also need

Significance level	Degrees of freedom							
	1	2	3	4	5	6	7	8
$p < 0.1$	2.71	4.00	6.25	7.78	9.24	10.64	12.02	13.36
$p < 0.05$	3.84	5.99	7.81	9.49	11.07	12.59	14.07	15.51
$p < 0.01$	6.63	9.21	11.34	13.28	15.09	16.81	18.48	20.09
$p < 0.001$	10.83	13.82	16.27	18.47	20.52	22.46	24.32	26.12

Figure 17.10 Extract of a table of critical values for the chi-square test

to know the characteristics of the table used, based on the numbers of columns and rows that had data values in them (don't include the 'total' row and column, as these are just a check, not data). This is known as the table's *degrees of freedom*. In Figure 17.8 we have three rows and two columns. The degrees of freedom is $(R–1) \times (C–1)$ where R is the number of rows and C the number of columns. So we have $(3–1) \times (2–1) = 2$ degrees of freedom. Tables of critical values for chi-squared typically show degrees of freedom against probability. Figure 17.10 gives an extract of such a table. Looking down the column for 2 degrees of freedom, we see that for significance at the 0.05 level, chi-squared would have to be at least 5.99 and for significance at the 0.001 level it would have to be at least 9.21. So we can assert that the probability of getting by chance a sample with the association we've found between gender and performance is less than 1 in 100 ($p < 0.01$). As we normally look for at least $p < 0.05$, the connection is regarded as statistically significant.

Of course, the chi-square test can't tell us *why* there is a link between gender and performance, it just confirms that the association we've observed between them is statistically significant.

The chi-square test can only be used where there is a sufficiently large data set (at least 30 in the sample), and a minimum value of 5 in each table cell.

T-tests

Sometimes we want to compare two sets of data to see if there is a significant difference between them. For example, a teacher might want to compare the results of a class of students where they have tried a new teaching method, with those of the previous year's class, taught the old way. Perhaps this year the mean is 66 and last year it was 62. Can the teacher be certain that the difference in means is down to the new teaching method, and not just chance variation in the performance of class members?

The null hypothesis would state that there is no significant difference between the means for the two groups. To see whether there is in fact a statistically significant difference we can use the *independent groups* t-*test*. To use it, the samples must be independent, that is, each student was tested only once. The independent groups *t*-test uses the mean and SD of the two sets of data to calculate a figure that tells us the likelihood that any differences between the two sets of data are down to chance. We can then look up this figure in a table of critical values for *t*, to see whether the two groups' performance is significantly different, that is, whether the probability of the observed difference being down to chance is less than 1 in 20 ($p < 0.05$).

This test can be used with small sample sizes (< 30), and the samples do not have to be the same size – so it will not matter if there were more students enrolled in the previous year than the current year.

Alternatively, you might have a situation where the same participants have been tested twice. For example, you might want to measure student performance at the beginning of a course, and then give the same test to the students at the end. For each student you would have pairs of data – the before and after scores. To see whether any apparent difference in scores is significantly different, you could use the *dependent or matched pairs* t-*test*. This looks at the means from each group (before and after) and the differences between the scores.

This section could only summarize some common statistical tests, and there are many more tests. If you are considering including statistical analysis in your research project, I suggest you look at the 'Further Reading' section to get more guidance. You'll also probably find it useful to enrol on a statistics course.

Interpretation of Data Analysis Results

Having subjected your data to some numerical analysis, don't assume you have finished. You now have to interpret your results. This means putting your own meaning onto your data. You should think about:

- What do your results show?
- What do they imply?
- How do they relate to other reported research in the literature about your research topic?
- Do you findings agree or disagree with those of other researchers or people in authority?
- What do you think is important in your results?
- What relevance do they have for other researchers?
- What relevance do they have for people in the real world beyond universities?

Typically, researchers writing up quantitative data analysis have a 'Results' section, followed by a 'Discussion' section where they interpret the results.

Evaluating Quantitative Data Analysis

Of course, if you have generated quantitative data, you will have to use quantitative data analysis. But if you are still at the planning stage of your research, you should think about the advantages and disadvantages of quantitative work.

Advantages of quantitative data analysis include:

- It provides (seeming) scientific respectability. Some people believe generating and analysing quantitative data is the only valid form of research.
- The analysis is based on well-established techniques, and tests of significance give you confidence in your findings.
- The analysis is based on measured quantities, not subjective impressions, and statistical tests can be checked by others.
- Large volumes of data can be analysed quickly using software programs.

Disadvantages of quantitative data analysis include:

- Many people dislike working with numbers.
- There is a danger of doing ever more sophisticated statistical tests, using computers, without understanding them properly, while losing sight of the original purpose of the research project.
- The analysis can only be as good as the data initially generated. By focusing on what can be measured, important non-quantitative aspects of the research topic may be missed.
- You have to be clear about what statistical test you will use, and what kinds of quantitative data they require, before you even start data generation.
- It is not as scientifically objective as it appears. Many decisions taken by the researcher can influence the results, such as the scales on the x-and y-axis, and the size of groups used in frequency counts.

You can use the 'Evaluation Guide' to help you analyse and evaluate research that employs quantitative data analysis. If there is insufficient information for you to answer the questions, or you do not understand the numerical analysis, you should not completely reject the research report, but you should treat the findings with some caution and be wary about relying on the report for evidence.

EVALUATION GUIDE: QUANTITATIVE DATA ANALYSIS

1   What kinds of quantitative data were analysed (for example, nominal, ordinal)?
2   Do the researchers use appropriate visual aids to explain their data and data analysis?
3   What means do the researchers use, if any, for describing the central tendency, distribution and relationships in the data?
4   Do the researchers justify their choice of statistical measures and tests, or assume that the reader will know what they are and why they are used?
5   Do the researchers discuss the null hypothesis?
6   How much of the report is concerned with analysis, and how much with interpretation of the results? Do you think the balance is appropriate?
7   Are the researchers' conclusions justified on the basis of the data they have presented?
8   What limitations in their quantitative data analysis do the researchers recognize?
9   Can you identify other flaws or omissions in the researchers' use of quantitative data analysis?
10   Overall, how effectively do you think quantitative data analysis has been reported and used?

PRACTICAL WORK

1   Here's a set of measures concerned with the time taken (in seconds) to complete a computer-based task:
     61, 64, 61, 65, 65, 67, 54, 77, 65, 67, 72, 59, 65, 61, 70, 71, 61, 65, 64, 69, 58, 66

   a   Find the mean, median, mode, range and SD.
   b   Use a range of visual techniques to explore the data and discover patterns within it.
   c   Now investigate how changing the axes used in a graph or the way you group the data into frequencies can change the way the data appears.

2   Investigate what resources are available at your university to help with quantitative data analysis, for example, software, training courses, expert members of staff.
3   This chapter could only cover a few statistical tests. Investigate what other tests exist and how they are used, for example: ANOVA, multiple regression, the Mann–Whitney test, Shapiro–Wilk test and Kolmogorov–Smirnov test.
4   Practise analysing and evaluating research that uses quantitative data analysis. Study a piece of research that used it. Answer the questions in the 'Evaluation Guide' above, using the material in this chapter to help you.

FURTHER READING

There are many books on statistics. An easy-to read introduction is given by Salkind (2004). Field and Hole (2003) also explain well the use of statistics, particularly for quantitative data derived from experiments rather than surveys. Both these texts walk you through using the SPSS software program to do statistical analysis. Other useful texts include Coolodge (2000), Field (2000) and Kerr, Hall and Kozub (2002). Finally, Kitchenham et al. (2001; 2002) give advice on using statistics in empirical software engineering.

References

Coolodge, F.L. (2000). *Statistics. A gentle introduction*. London: Sage.

Field, A. (2000). *Discovering statistics using SPSS for Windows. Advanced techniques for beginners*. London: Sage.

Field, A., & Hole, G. (2003). *How to design and report experiments*. London: Sage.

Kerr, A.W., Hall, H.K., & Kozub, S.A. (2002). *Doing statistics with SPSS*. London: Sage.

Kitchenham, B.A., Pfleeger, S.L., Pickard, L.M., Jones, P.W., Hoaglin, D.C., El-Emam, K., et al. (2001). *Preliminary guidelines for empirical research in software engineering*. Ottawa: National Research Council of Canada.

Kitchenham, B.A., Pfleeger, S.L., Pickard, L.M., Jones, P.W., Hoaglin, D.C., El-Emam, K., et al. (2002). Preliminary guidelines for empirical research in software engineering. *IEEE Transactions on Software Engineering, 28*(8), 721–734.

Salkind, N.J. (2004). *Statistics for people who (think they) hate statistics* (2nd ed.). London: Sage.

18 Qualitative Data Analysis

In this chapter you will learn about:

- how to prepare your qualitative data for analysis;
- how to analyse both textual and non-textual qualitative data;
- the grounded theory approach to qualitative data analysis;
- computer tools to support qualitative data analysis;
- how to analyse and evaluate research based on qualitative data analysis.

Introduction

Qualitative data includes all non-numeric data – words, images, sounds, and so on – found in such things as interview tapes, researchers' diaries, company documents, websites and developers' models. It is the main type of data, or evidence, generated by case studies, action research and ethnography (see Chapters 10–12). It is also the main kind of data used and analysed by interpretive and critical researchers (see Chapter 20), but can be generated by positivist researchers too (see Chapter 19). If you have generated some qualitative data, you now need to analyse it.

You *can* use quantitative (numerical) analysis on qualitative data. For example you could:

- Count the number of times a particular word or phrase occurs in some text. For example, during interviews with systems developers, how often do they refer to 'the user'(assuming that one can stand for all) and how often to 'the users' (recognizing multiple users, possibly with differing views)?
- Count the number of words or pages allocated to different topics on a website. For example, on a website belonging to a political party, how many pages are allocated to explaining its policies, and how many to criticizing opposing political parties?

However, most qualitative data analysis involves abstracting from the research data the verbal, visual or aural themes and patterns that you think are important to your research topic. This chapter explains how you might do this.

Qualitative researchers have been criticized for not providing enough information about data analysis: how they worked from their raw data to their conclusions. Often it is as if the conclusions appeared by magic. This chapter will help you think about and reflect upon data analysis, so that you *can* describe your analysis process to others.

Unfortunately, qualitative data analysis is not always a straightforward task. There are no hard and fast rules about how to do it. Whereas quantitative data analysis can draw upon well-established mathematical and statistical procedures (see Chapter 17), qualitative analysis has fewer procedures and is more dependent on the skill of the researcher to see patterns and themes within the data. There is also a danger of researchers feeling swamped by the amount of qualitative data they have collected. Words take up more space than numbers, have different meanings for different people and have to be studied in the context of other words that were said at the same time. Just a 1-week field study can result in hundreds of pages of typed notes, so it is difficult to know where to begin and how to manage the data. This chapter therefore describes some techniques to help you manage and analyse your qualitative data.

❝ The slippery meaning(s) of words

'But "glory" doesn't mean "a nice knock-down argument",' Alice objected.

'When *I* use a word,' Humpty Dumpty said in a rather scornful tone, 'it means just what I choose it to mean – neither more nor less.'

(Lewis Carroll, *Through the Looking Glass*, [1872], Chapter 6)

❞

Analysing Textual data

Data preparation

First of all, you need to get your data into a form ready for analysis. As far as possible, get all your materials in a similar format – all on the same sized sheets of paper, for instance. This can help with filing and sifting through the material. Audio tapes may have to be transcribed – remember that 1 hour of tape can require 4–5 hours for transcribing. If you decide not to transcribe the full content of each tape, you do at least need to index each one, so that you can easily find the sections you do need to transcribe. Where possible, prepare your transcripts and any other data so that you have wide margins in which you can write. Many researchers use the left-hand margin for location codes (see below), and a wider right-hand margin for their own notes on themes found in the data.

You also need to plan an efficient filing system for your data. Whether you use an online or offline system, you need to decide where you will store the data and the folders and the file name conventions to use. Then you need to work out a system for locating particular segments of data. For example, the location code: *Smith-13/11/04-12-5* might mean the words said by Smith in an interview on 13 November 2004, found on page 12 and line 5 of the typed transcript.

Most of your raw data will probably be irreplaceable. So make at least one duplicate copy of all your data (photocopy *everything* if you are using hardcopy, despite the time and cost, and if possible also make duplicates of audio and video tapes). Then *always* work with the duplicate copy. If a duplicate copy gets spoiled in some way, or you've written too much on it and want a clean start, make *another* duplicate copy and use that. Don't risk spoiling or harming your original data in any way. Of course, if you're doing data analysis with the aid of a computer, you will need to keep backups of your analysis work too.

Data analysis

Start off by reading through all of your data to try to get a general impression. Now, start to identify key themes in the data. Initially you could use just three themes:

- Segments that bear no relation to your overall research purpose so are not needed (at least for the current study).
- Segments that provide general descriptive information that you will need in order to describe the research context for your readers (for example, history of a company, number of employees, location, time your respondents have spent in their current job role).
- Segments that appear to be relevant to your research question(s).

Now you can focus on the third of the types described above – the sections that are relevant to your research question(s). You need to categorize each segment or *unit* of data (a unit might be a word, sentence, paragraph or even a page), by writing in the margin a heading, sub-heading or other label that describes the theme presented by that unit of data. For an example of such analysis, see Figure 18.1 from a piece of research concerned with looking at the use of metaphors during information systems development.

To start with, your choice of categories is not crucial – you'll have plenty of time to change them later. It's just important to categorize each unit somehow. The categories can come from:

Developer 1: But as the business grows they seem very – well, as if they don't really want to change the way they work. And I think part of their success is the way that they work, because they're so unstructured, because it doesn't take any red tape or paperwork and anything else, and because they will work till midnight if somebody wants six generators by 2 days after tomorrow or whatever. And I don't think you can easily automate a system that's like that.	*Growth – organism metaphor. Culture metaphor.*
Developer 2: No. (…) I think there's a fairly classic thing, you know these family-owned businesses start off small, even though they've got a large turnover, you know it's still small in terms of the number of employees. And they grow but they want to keep that unstructured way, but there comes a point, if they actually want the business to grow, as opposed to be stable and just maintain its position (and people say well you can't do that anyway these days, don't they?), there comes a point when they have to recognize that the unstructured way isn't going to continue to work.	*Organism metaphor – growth. Culture metaphor. Culture – needs to change.*
Developer 1: I think this is like slow recognition, but you can't – it's dawning on them, but they don't want to believe it. And you can't make them believe it. Because if you start getting dogmatic and – you know, saying 'You really should –' and 'You have to do this' then nothing's going to work, is it? Nothing that you try and do is going to work at all.	*Culture – can't enforce change of culture.*

Figure 18.1   Theme analysis

- Existing theories you have found in the literature or have developed yourself, (in Figure 18.1, the categories are derived from Morgan's [1997] work on metaphors for organizations). This is known as a *deductive approach*. Be careful, however, not to be too committed to a given theory, so that you overlook other themes in the data.
- Categories observed in the data, such as those used by your respondents or the authors of the documents you are studying, or that occur to you as you read the material. This is known as an *inductive approach*. The idea is that you have a completely open mind and just allow the data to 'speak' to you. However, in practice no one can completely empty their mind of all previous experiences, learning and prejudices – so be aware of your own thought tendencies.

Now you can start to refine your categories – some will be too large and need to be broken down into smaller sub-categories; others will occur only rarely and might be combined with other categories. Keep an up-to-date list of the categories you use – modifying it each time you change your categories.

Keep working though your data, reading it many times and categorizing the themes that you see. If you don't have too many categories, you can use highlighter pens on the text – one colour per category, so that you can see more easily where each one occurs.

Next, you start to look for themes and inter-connections between segments and categories. You might find it useful to take all the data segments categorized under one theme and see if some pattern is present across all of them. If researchers are using hard copies of the data, they often literally cut and paste together all the segments that relate to one theme (remembering to include each segment's location code, so they know where it came from) and then read and analyse the new document they have created. Of course, cutting and pasting is easy to do if you are analysing your text on a computer – but many researchers like to be able to spread out and see together all the documents they are working on, which is not possible on a computer.

You might also find it helpful to use visual aids such as tables or diagrams to analyse the data. For example, in the study mentioned earlier that looked at the use of metaphors during information systems development, a table was used to correlate use of particular metaphors at observed meetings against the date – see Figure 18.2. This shows much use of metaphors at the beginning, but then a large gap where none were used – the researcher then looked for reasons for this gap.

Similarly, Figure 18.3 uses a table where views about satisfaction with an information system have been grouped according to the job role of each interviewee. The table makes it easy to see that the all the developers were highly satisfied, but the administrative users were not. Such a pattern might not have been spotted if the researcher had stuck to analysing the interview transcripts in, say, chronological order. Having spotted the pattern, the researcher can now look for further related themes in the data, for example:

- whether people in other job roles share the same satisfaction rating;
- the different criteria used by different people for deciding whether a system is satisfactory.

Figure 18.4 uses a visual format to show a taxonomy of computer users, as discovered in a transcript of an interview with a technician who worked on an organization's IT help-desk.

Next you start to go beyond the patterns you see in the data and try to explain them. You build up a theory about what your data 'says' – linking it to any theories you might have included in your original conceptual framework, to what the literature

	18/11/03	25/11/03	2/12/03	9/12/03	13/1/04	20/1/04	27/1/04	3/2/04	24/2/04	3/3/04	10/3/04	5/5/04
Machine	*	*	*	*	*	*						
Organism	*	*	*	*		*						*
Brain												
Culture	*	*	*	*								*
Political system			*	*								
Psychic prison			*									
Flux & transformation			*									
Domination			*									
24 hour clock			*									
Football team						*						
Conductor & orchestra							*					*
Ecosystem												

Figure 18.2   Using a table to analyse data – use of metaphors over time

says, or to the broader political or social context. You can test your emerging theory by looking for contradictory evidence within your data – things that challenge or question the interpretation you have started to put on the data. Where possible, you should also go back to the field to look for further data that supports or contradicts your emerging explanation – qualitative data analysis is often carried out in parallel with doing the fieldwork that generates the qualitative data. It is important not to settle on the first explanation that seems to fit – look for alternative explanations or problems with your proposed explanation.

You should also keep notes about your analytical process, the stages you went through, the ideas that occurred to you – these notes become a further source of data and help you explain to others how you did the analysis. Tables or other diagrams that you have used to look for patterns can also be included in your final report – they help the reader to understand your data, process and conclusions.

Job role	Interviewee	Satisfaction with computer system	Reasons given
Developers	Interviewee 11	High	First successful use of OO [object-oriented] method
	Interviewee 5	High	No overtime required
	Interviewee 9	High	Few bugs reported
Users – admin	Interviewee 4	Low	Preferred previous manual system
	Interviewee 7	Low	User interface too awkward
	Interviewee 6	Acceptable-low	New work-arounds needed
User – manager	Interviewee 1	Acceptable	Budget only slightly exceeded, delivered on time

Figure 18.3   Satisfaction with a computer system

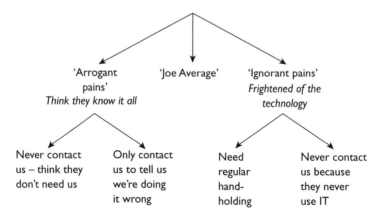

Figure 18.4   Mike's taxonomy of end-users

Analysing Non-textual Qualitative Data

Non-textual qualitative data includes audio tapes or sound clips, videos, photographs, and multimedia documents, as found on the web. In the social sciences, where much of the research with qualitative data occurs, there has been far more use of textual than non-textual data. Often visual data, such as a photograph, has been used only to support or illustrate the analysis of textual data, rather than as an independent source of data. However, non-textual data is likely to play a much more central role in IS and computing research, since the web and its multimedia documents is a highly important research arena, information systems increasingly make use of visual aspects (such as windows, radio buttons, drop-down menus) and since many computing researchers focus on the use of computer-based sound, animations, and so on.

Data preparation is similar to that for textual data. You need to get all your material into a form ready for analysis, with duplicate copies made, a location coding system (video, sound and animation clips will need to be time-coded to aid later retrieval), areas where you can write your categorization of data segments and a well-ordered filing system.

As with textual analysis, you then need to analyse the data looking for themes and patterns. Some researchers treat images as if they are a true representation of some aspect of the real world – for example, photographs are provided to illustrate an ethnographic account of life in a group of people. However, most people are now aware of how easily an image can be digitally manipulated, so place less reliance on an image as an objective picture. Instead, many researchers now look beyond the surface appearance of an image and consider it as cultural artefact or symbolic system and look at, for example:

- the cultural context in which it was created;
- the messages it conveys about gender roles, the family, loyalty, bravery, and so on;
- the symbols and signs it utilizes.

The scope for different kinds of patterns and themes can be much larger in non-textual data than in textual data. For example, if analysing a video or animation clip, you might look at:

- **Denotation**: what or who is depicted in the piece, in what genre or style?
- **Connotation**: what ideas and values are being expressed via the piece?
- **Production**: how has it been made in terms of camera angles, lighting, colour, rendering, background sounds, perspective, and so on?
- **Author**: who produced it, in what circumstances and why?
- **Viewer**: how does a viewer interpret or react to the piece?

You might find you need to produce several different transcripts of one video, animation or sound clip, each concentrating on a different aspect. For example, for a video, you could produce a transcript that concentrates on the speech of the characters, another on patterns of movement, another on gaze, another on structure, and so on. Each of these would then be analysed for themes and patterns.

Grounded Theory

Grounded theory is a particular approach to qualitative research where the intention is to do field research and then analyse the data to see what theory emerges, so that the theory is *grounded* in the field data. This is an inductive approach (see above) and contrasts with a deductive approach, where a researcher develops a theory first and then goes into the field to evaluate it. Note that grounded theory is concerned with *generating theories* – research that leads only to a descriptive account of the subject matter would not be classified as a grounded theory approach.

Unfortunately, many researchers now claim that they are using grounded theory or 'a grounded theory-type approach', when all they are doing is analysing inductively their qualitative data for themes, as described in the previous section. Grounded theory has particular practices incorporated within it, which address the selection of people and instances to include in the research, the way that data is analysed and the kind of theory that is generated.

Selection of people and instances

Researchers using grounded theory do not start out by identifying a sample of people or instances to investigate. Instead, they start off with just one person (or instance), generate the data, analyse it and on the basis of their first emerging ideas from the data then decide who or what to look at next. This process of data generation → data analysis → data generation continues indefinitely. The researchers follow a discovery trail, not knowing where they will go or when they will finish, using *theoretical sampling* of successive sites, people or sources, which are chosen in order to test or refine new theories, ideas or categories as they emerge from the data collected and analysed so far. Initially, there is a preference for unstructured interviews and observations, but as the emerging theory becomes firmer, more structured forms of data generation, such as questionnaires, are feasible. The process only finishes when it becomes clear that further data no longer triggers new modifications to the data categories and emerging theory, that is, the research has reached the point of *theoretical saturation*.

Data analysis

The grounded theory researcher should approach data analysis with an open mind – not with preconceived ideas about what will be relevant or what will be useful concepts around which to categorize the data. There are three phases of coding: open, axial and selective.

1 **Open coding**: the initial process of labelling units of data, based on terms and concepts found in the data, not those found in the literature or a pre-existing theory.
2 **Axial coding**: as a list of codes begins to emerge, the researcher moves to a higher or more abstract level of analysis and looks for relationships between the codes. It will be found that some codes can be incorporated under broader headings, and some codes are found to be more important (axial) than others.
3 **Selective coding**: the researcher focuses attention on just the core codes – those that have emerged as being vital for any explanation (theory) of the complex phenomenon being investigated. These will be combined into a theory that explains the phenomenon under investigation.

Analysis involves a *constant comparative method* – as any new code, category or concept is identified in the data, all previously coded material is revisited to see if it can now be better coded. Similarly, as any theory emerges, it is checked out against all the data collected so far. In this way, the researcher's emerging theory is always closely linked to (that is, *grounded in*) the empirical data.

Theories

Grounded theory research should lead to theories that have practical relevance for the people in the situation studied. This means that the researcher's explanations of events or situations should 'make sense' to the people involved, and ideally should help them address their practical needs.

History of development

Glaser and Strauss (1967) proposed grounded theory as an inductive approach to theory generation from qualitative data. Since then it has become a well-established approach in the social sciences, but its history of development is rather complex. After their 1967 ground-breaking book, Glaser and Strauss developed grounded theory in different ways, and now disagree rather acrimoniously on how it 'should' be done (Glaser, 1992; Strauss, 1987; Strauss & Corbin, 1994, 1997, 1998). Other authors have subsequently given their own views about it. If you want to use grounded theory, you will therefore need to know about the debate surrounding it, and be clear about which version you are using – the early one or a later one, and the version according to Glaser, Strauss, Strauss and Corbin or other 'grounded theory theorists' – see the 'Further Reading' section for guidance.

Grounded theory can be used in positivist research, but is more widely used in interpretivist and critical research (see Chapter 20). It is reasonably well known in IS research but is not yet accepted by all IS researchers. Grounded theory is little known in the computing discipline. If you want to follow a grounded theory approach, you should discuss with your supervisor the risks involved and read the relevant literature so that you can defend your work against criticisms from those unfamiliar with it.

Computer-aided Qualitative Analysis

There are software programs to help you analyse qualitative data – both freeware and commercial software products. You should find out whether your institution already has such software tools. You may find it also offers training courses on how to use them.

Many of these tools concentrate on the analysis of textual qualitative data, providing such facilities as:

- text search – to help you look for a word or phrase in the text;
- coding – to enable you to apply your own code or categories to units of text;
- data organization – to help you organize and file your data;
- writing tools – to enable you to write your own notes and self-memos;
- visual displays – to show links between data segments;
- exporting – to allow you to incorporate your analysis in another software program such as a word-processor.

Some tools also help with the analysis of audio and video tapes and images, providing such facilities as:

- transcript creation – to turn an audio file into text;
- coding – to enable you to attach your own code or categories to video or audio clips;
- data organization – to help you organize and file your digitized audio and video;
- hyperlink creation – to enable you to create links between different media types.

Some researchers find a software tool is very helpful in data analysis. Others argue that:

- It can take too long to become familiar with the software tool.
- The analysis can be restricted to the capabilities and ways of working embedded in the tool.
- They feel distanced from the raw data.

You should make your own mind up. Remember, though, that a tool cannot do the analysis for you – it can help you search and find links, but cannot identify categories, have sudden intuitive leaps or develop an explanation of the data.

Evaluating Qualitative Data Analysis

Of course, if you have generated qualitative data, you will have to use qualitative data analysis. But if you are still at the planning stage of your research, you should think about the advantages and disadvantages of qualitative work.

Advantages of qualitative data analysis include:

- The data and its analysis can be rich and detailed, including words, images, websites and sounds, all of which are very useful to IS and computing researchers. It does not study only that which can be reduced to numbers.
- There is the possibility of alternative explanations, rather than a presumption that there will be one 'correct' explanation. This means that it is possible that different researchers might reach different, but equally valid, conclusions.

Disadvantages of qualitative data analysis include:

- There is a danger of feeling overwhelmed by the volume of qualitative data that can emerge from even a small number of interviews. Researchers might feel swamped and unable to identify themes and patterns.
- Interpretation of the data is more closely tied to the researchers (their identity, backgrounds, assumptions and beliefs) than in quantitative data analysis. This means that their conclusions must be much more tentative than those from quantitative data analysis. Researchers and reviewers can find this frustrating.
- Non-textual data and its analysis does not fit easily into theses and papers, which are much better suited to text.

You can use the 'Evaluation Guide' to help you analyse and evaluate research that employs qualitative data analysis. If there is insufficient information for you to answer the questions, you should not completely reject the research report, but you should treat the findings with some caution and be wary about relying on the report for evidence.

EVALUATION GUIDE: QUALITATIVE DATA ANALYSIS

1 What kinds of qualitative data were analysed? (Text only, or non-textual too?)
2 Do the researchers claim to have used a grounded theory approach? If so, do you agree that they did?
3 What themes and relationships do the researchers identify in the data?
4 Were emerging categories and explanations checked out by returning to the field?
5 Do the researchers use tables or diagrams to explain their data?
6 Do the researchers offer alternative explanations of the data?
7 Are the researchers' conclusions justified on the basis of the data they present?
8 What limitations in their qualitative data analysis do the researchers recognize?
9 Can you identify other flaws or omissions in the researchers' use of qualitative data analysis?
10 Overall, how effectively do you think qualitative data analysis has been reported and used?

PRACTICAL WORK

1 Practise the analysis of textual data. Look at a magazine that publishes interviews with people in the public eye: film stars, sportsmen, pop singers, and so on. Analyse three such interviews, looking for:

a purely descriptive passages which give us biographical facts for example, age, number of children, years in the business;
b themes that are covered in the interviews, for example, latest film, love life, favourite colours;
c the kind of photographs that illustrate the articles;

What themes always seem to be covered in your chosen magazine? To a visiting Martian, what might this pattern say about the magazine's readers and the society in which the magazine is created?

2 Practise the analysis of images. Visit an art museum and look at all the paintings from one era, say the 18th century. Identify any recurrent themes in terms of what is depicted and how. Investigate whether the paintings from a different era share different themes.

3 Practise analysing and evaluating research that uses qualitative data analysis. Study a piece of research that used it. Answer the questions in the 'Evaluation Guide' above, using the material in this chapter to help you.

FURTHER READING

Useful books on qualitative data analysis include Silverman (2001) and Van Leeuwen and Jewitt (2001). Miles and Huberman (1994) explain many ways of using tables, matrices and diagrams to analyse and report qualitative data. Dey (2004) gives an overview of grounded theory, its history, the contradictions within it and his personal experiences in using it. Hughes and Howcroft (2000) review its use in IS, of which Orlikowski (1993) is a well-known example.

Kelle (2004) discusses computer-assisted data analysis. The CAQDAS (Computer Assisted Qualitative Data Analysis) Networking project provides details of freeware and commercial software tools for qualitative data analysis, a useful bibliography of articles on it and computer support and platforms for debate about the issues surrounding the use of computer tools (caqdas.soc.surrey.ac.uk).

Advice on the use of multimedia documents such as images and sound can be found in Bauer and Gaskell (2000), Prosser (1998) and Rose (2001).

References

Bauer, M.W., & Gaskell, G. (Eds.). (2000). *Qualitative researching with text, image and sound: A practical handbook*. London: Sage.

Dey, I. (2004). Grounded theory. In C. Seale, G. Gobo, J.F. Gubrium, & D. Silverman (Eds.), *Qualitative Research Practice* (pp. 80–93). London: Sage.

Glaser, B. (1992). *Emergence vs. forcing: Basics of grounded theory analysis*. Mill Valley, CA: Sociology Press.

Glaser, B., & Strauss, A. (1967). *The discovery of grounded theory*. Chicago, IL: Aldine.

Hughes, J., & Howcroft, D. (2000). Grounded theory: Never knowingly understood. *New Review of Information Systems Research*, (September): 181–199.

Kelle, U. (2004). Computer-assisted qualitative data analysis. In C. Seale, G. Gobo, J.F. Gubrium & D. Silverman (Eds.), *Qualitative research practice* (pp. 473–489). London: Sage.

Miles, M.B., & Huberman, A.M. (1994). *Qualitative data analysis. An expanded sourcebook* (2nd ed.). London: Sage.

Morgan, G. (1997). *Images of organization* (2nd revised ed.). Thousand Oaks, CA: Sage.

Orlikowski, W.J. (1993). CASE tools as organizational change: Investigating incremental and radical changes in systems development. *MIS Quarterly, 17*(3), 309–340.

Prosser, J. (Ed.). (1998). *Image-based research: A sourcebook for qualitative researchers*. London: Sage.

Rose, G. (2001). *Visual methodologies: An introduction to the interpretation of visual materials*. London: Sage.

Silverman, D. (2001). *Interpreting qualitative data. Methods for analysing talk, text and interaction* (2nd ed.). London: Sage.

Strauss, A. (1987). *Qualitative analysis for social scientists.* Cambridge: Cambridge University Press.

Strauss, A., & Corbin, J. (1994). Grounded theory methodology – An overview. In N.K. Denzin & Y.S. Lincoln (Eds.), *Handbook of qualitative research* (pp. 273–285). London: Sage.

Strauss, A., & Corbin, J. (1997). *Grounded theory in practice.* London: Sage.

Strauss, A., & Corbin, J. (1998). *Basics of qualitative research. Techniques and procedures for developing grounded theory* (2nd ed.). London: Sage.

Van Leeuwen, T., & Jewitt, C. (Eds.). (2001). *Handbook of visual analysis.* London: Sage.

19 Philosophical Paradigms – Positivism

In this chapter you will learn about:

- why it is necessary to know about the underlying philosophy of research;
- the scientific method;
- the philosophical paradigm called positivism – its characteristics and how we evaluate it;
- some criticisms of positivism;
- analysing and evaluating research based on positivism.

Chapter 1 introduced the 6Ps of research: *purpose, products, process, participants, paradigm* and *presentation* (see Figure 1.4). We have now studied the first four of them, and in this chapter and the next we're going to look at the fifth: the underlying *philosophical paradigm*.

'Do I Have to Study This Philosophical, Airy-fairy Stuff?'

You might be thinking that studying philosophy seems a long way from finding out about the design and use of information systems, so perhaps you can just skip this chapter and the next? Well, almost certainly not – let's see why.

Think about two of the strategies discussed in earlier chapters: experiments (Chapter 9) and ethnographies (Chapter 12). Compare the role of a researcher using a strategy based on experiments with that of a researcher producing an ethnography. In an experiment, the researcher is careful to be objective and remove any possibility that they might influence the result. In an ethnography, on the other hand, the researcher *is* the research instrument – their observations, interactions with others and interpretations form the data for the research, and they will discuss candidly in their report how they think they affected the people they were studying. With such differing researcher roles, with objectivity in one and subjectivity in the other, can experiments and ethnography both be good, acceptable, academic research?

The answer to that is, yes, they can. They differ in approach, and in how we evaluate whether they have been carried out well, because of their different underlying *philosophical paradigms*. A paradigm is a set of shared assumptions or ways of thinking about some aspect of the world. Here, we are concerned with different communities' shared way of thinking about how to do research and gain or create knowledge. Different philosophical paradigms have different views about the nature of our world (*ontology*) and the ways we can acquire knowledge about it (*epistemology*) (see the box below). This shared way of thinking is reflected in the research strategies used and accepted as appropriate in a particular research community.

DEFINITION: Ontology and epistemology

A scholarly school of thought's ontology comprises its members foundational beliefs about the empirical or 'real' world they are researching …

I now conceptualise an epistemology as a broad and high-level outline of the reasoning process by which a school of thought performs its logical and empirical work. (Lee, 2004, p. 5)

In IS, a wide range of research strategies, with different underlying philosophical paradigms, have been used to understand the use of information systems by people. IS researchers therefore have to at least be aware of the different paradigms underlying the strategies, even if they choose to work only in the traditional paradigm (positivism – see facing page). They need to understand the different philosophical paradigms discussed in this chapter and the next, their different assumptions, strategies and methods, and the different ways in which readers from the different paradigms assess the quality of research.

In the computing literature so far, there has been little discussion of the philosophical assumptions underlying research. If you want to concentrate on designing and creating IT artefacts, and not going beyond 'proof of concept' or 'proof by demonstration' (see Chapter 8), you *may* therefore be able to ignore this chapter. *However*, if you want to cite previous research studies based on strategies other than design and creation, you have to be able to evaluate their worth, which means you have to know something of their underlying philosophy and how we assess their quality. So you need to study this chapter and the next. And if you want to explore the kind of IT artefact actually required by people, or study your IT artefact in use in the real world, then you will need to use one of the other research strategies explained in this book, which means you need to understand their underlying philosophy. So you need to study these chapters. If you want to know why some researchers from IS and other disciplines criticize many computing researchers for their naivety or for being 'management lackeys', you need to study these chapters. Finally, if you want to use an alternative research tradition to that found in most computing research (a risky but potentially very fruitful endeavour), you need to study these chapters.

Philosophy is an academic discipline in its own right, with a huge literature dating back to Socrates and beyond. This chapter and the next provide an overview of three different philosophical paradigms: positivism, interpretivism and critical research. They then discuss how the different research strategies covered in this book map onto these three paradigms. Most research in IS and computing is based on one of them.

The division into positivism, interpretivism and critical research is a broad-brush approach, since each of these paradigms could be further divided. For example, positivism can be sub-divided into positivist and post-positivist approaches, interpretivism includes approaches based on a philosophy of hermeneutics, phenomenology or constructivism, and critical research can be sub-divided into a whole range of different approaches including Marxism, feminism and queer research. However, a broad-brush approach is sufficient to highlight the main features of each paradigm and demonstrate that different research communities share different assumptions about the nature of reality, the purpose of research and what counts as knowledge. Once you have decided to which of these three paradigms your research belongs, you can use the suggestions in the 'Further Reading' section at the end of this chapter and the next to find out more.

Positivism and the Scientific Method

Positivism is the oldest of the three paradigms we shall look at. It underlies what is called 'the scientific method', the approach to research in the natural sciences (such as physics, chemistry, biology and metallurgy). This scientific method has evolved over the past 400 to 500 years – from the time of Bacon, Galileo and Newton – so it has had a long time to develop and become established. Often people know of only this approach to research, and for many it is the sole 'proper' kind of research. However, as we shall see later, it is not always suited to studying the social world, that is, people and how they think of, and act in, their worlds. For such research, the other two paradigms discussed in the next chapter are often more appropriate.

The scientific method

The scientific method has two basic assumptions:

- Our world is ordered and regular, not random.
- We can investigate it objectively.

Taking the first assumption: if your pen rolls over the edge of the table, you know that it will fall downwards. This will always happen. We do not have a situation where gravity usually pulls things downwards, but sometimes, on a whim, it pushes things upwards instead and, occasionally, it will let things just hover in the middle somewhere. On planet Earth, gravity pulls things downwards. We can also measure the strength of this gravitational force, which means that we can calculate and predict how long the pen will take to fall to the ground, and its speed of descent. There is a regular law about gravity on our planet. We can also find out what the gravitational force is on other planets and other parts of the universe, and gradually acquire more and more knowledge about how gravity works and affects our universe. But to do this, we have to assume that there is a regular way in which gravity works and indeed our universe works, there is some kind of structure or order, it's not all random behaviour. The scientific method seeks to find all the regular laws or patterns in our universe. For example, researchers at the moment are trying to establish whether or not there is a law or regularly occurring pattern that:

- The measles–mumps–rubella (MMR) vaccine can cause autism.
- People who smoke cannabis are more likely to develop brain tumours.

The second assumption of positivism is that we can investigate the world, with its regular laws and patterns, objectively. This is because, it is assumed, the laws and patterns in our world exist independently of any individual's cognition (mental thought processes) – that is, what we can learn about the world does not depend on who we are or how we personally have experienced it. We can also set aside any personal feelings and be objective and rational, to find out about how the world works. Even if our research disproves a pet theory, we can accept that, because we can rise above our personal interests and emotions in the greater cause of finding out about the world.

So the aim of the scientific method, and positivism, which underlies it, is to find the universal laws, patterns and regularities. This is mainly done by experiment (see Chapter 9). Typically, researchers carry out experiments to look for evidence of cause and effect. They produce a hypothesis that A causes B, and then look for evidence derived from carefully designed experiments that confirms or refutes the hypothesis. This allows researchers to predict what will happen: 'Under circumstances X, if Y occurs then Z will follow'. Ideally, the aim should be to *refute* (that is, disprove) a hypothesis, not confirm it. This is because we can never *prove* something is *true for all time*. This is usually explained with a reference to swans:

- **Hypothesis**: all swans are white.
- **Test**: look for swans and see what colour they are.
- **Outcome**: all swans seen are white.
- **Conclusion**: hypothesis is confirmed as true, that is, all swans are white.

You could keep on looking at swans, possibly for decades, and always see white swans, so your hypothesis 'must' be true. Perhaps you will build a whole research program that relies on the 'fact' that all swans are white. But what if finally one day you see a black swan? Your research program is in ruins. How much time, effort and money you might have saved yourself if you had tested your original hypothesis better by deliberately trying to disprove it, by trying to find one swan that wasn't white. Once you had found one black swan, you would have been able to move onto some other research topic, you needn't have looked for any other black swans since just one was needed to disprove your hypothesis. In other words:

- Things can *seem* to be true for all time, and often we can find evidence that tends to confirm they are true.
- But if something is found to be false just once – it can never be true again.

This means researchers have to recognize that even though their hypothesis might seem well proven and is an established 'law' in their research community, there is always the possibility that one day someone will come along and refute the hypothesis. Any theory we have is always susceptible to being disproved and possibly replaced by another theory. So our theories and explanations should be seen as the best knowledge we have *at the moment*.

There are three basic techniques of the scientific method: reductionism, repeatability and refutation:

- **Reductionism**: this means breaking complex things down into smaller things that are more easily studied. To find out how cigarettes cause lung cancer, for example, researchers looked at the constituent parts of cigarettes (for example, nicotine and tar) and studied how they interacted with cells or tissues in the body to cause the growth of tumours. Gradually hypotheses that have been proven (for the moment) can be built up into one overall theory.
- **Repeatability**: researchers don't rely on the results of just one experiment. They repeat the experiment many times, to be sure that their first set of results was not just a fluke. Other researchers will also try to repeat the experiment to see if they obtain the same result and to make sure that the results weren't somehow influenced by the original researchers or caused by faulty equipment or measurements. For example, Newton wrote up his experiments on light and prisms and invited other scientists to repeat them to see if they got the same results.
- **Refutation**: if other researchers can't repeat an experiment and get the same result as the original researchers, then they refute the hypothesis. A hypothesis can also be refuted if a researcher is able to show by experiment that the claim that A causes B does not hold true in certain circumstances. The more a hypothesis can stand up to tests designed to refute it, the stronger it is.

The scientific method

The scientific method enables us to build up knowledge through an iterative cycle:

1   Formulate theory about some observed aspect of the world.
2   Derive hypothesis.
3   Test hypothesis objectively.
4   Observe results.
5   Confirm or refute hypothesis.
6   Accept, modify or reject theory.

Characteristics of positivism

As stated already, the philosophical paradigm called positivism underlies the scientific method. The scientific method mainly uses experiments, but positivist researchers use other research strategies too. In IS, for example, where experiments are often not feasible, many positivist researchers use surveys. What unites subscribers to the positivist paradigm is not so much the research strategy used as the shared assumptions about the nature of our world and how to find out about it. The shared worldview of those who work in the positivist paradigm has the following characteristics:

- **The world exists independently of humans**: there is a physical and social world that exists 'out there', not just in our minds, to be studied, captured and measured. There would be a law of gravity, for example, even if some natural disaster or human accident wiped out the whole population.
- **Measurement and modelling**: the researcher 'discovers' this world by making observations and measurements and producing models (hypotheses, theories) of how it works. It is assumed there will be a one-to-one correspondence between a researcher's model and the features of interest in the world, that is, ultimately there will be one model or explanation for any aspect of the world – 'the truth'.
- **Objectivity**: the researcher is neutral and objective, an impartial observer. Facts about the world can be discovered independently of the researcher's personal values and beliefs.
- **Hypothesis testing**: research is based on the empirical testing of theories and hypotheses, leading to confirmation or refutation of them.
- **Quantitative data analysis**: there is often a strong preference for mathematical modelling and proofs, and statistical analysis. The use of mathematics provides a logical, objective means of analysing observations and results.
- **Universal laws**: research looks for generalizations: universal laws, patterns or irrefutable facts that can be shown to be true regardless of the researcher and the occasion.

Warning: Terms and definitions

Some authors call positivism 'quantitative research' and interpretivism 'qualitative research'. This is inaccurate. Quantitative data is numerical (such as measurements and statistics); qualitative is non-numeric (such as company documents, interview transcripts and pictures). Either type can be used in any of the positivist, interpretivist and critical paradigms, although quantitative data *tends* to predominate in positivist research, and qualitative data *tends* to predominate in the other two paradigms.

The paradigms are really distinguished by their ontology (assumptions about the nature of physical and social 'reality') and epistemology (assumptions about the nature of knowledge and how it can be obtained).

Judging the quality of positivist research

Even if positivist researchers have based their work on all of the above features, we still need to be able to judge whether they have carried it out well, so that we are happy to accept their findings and cite their work as evidence in our own research. We have to judge the quality, or soundness, of their research, often called the *validity* of the research. Criteria for assessing the quality of positivist research can be placed under four headings: objectivity, reliability, internal validity and external validity.

- **Objectivity**: is the research free of researcher bias and distortions? Have the researchers successfully avoided influencing the results? Do the researchers have a vested interest in a particular outcome? The latter is an issue often raised if it emerges that the researchers were sponsored by an organization that stands to gain from the study's findings.
- **Reliability**: are the research instruments neutral, accurate and reliable? Will repeated use of the research instruments yield the same results (that is, repeatability)? 'Research instruments' can mean the equipment used in an experiment. But the set of questions in a questionnaire is also a research instrument – the questions need to be neutral (not leading the respondents to answer in a particular way) and unambiguous (so that all respondents will understand the question in the same way). Sometimes researchers themselves are the research instrument. For example, a team of researchers carrying out interviews would need to make sure all researchers were asking the same questions in the same manner. Data analysis techniques are also a form of research instrument. Statistical or other mathematical tests need to be used appropriately and accurately. For qualitative data, researchers using a set of agreed categories to analyse it (called a *schema*) would need to ensure that each researcher understands the categories and uses them in the same way, otherwise the results would depend on which particular researcher analysed particular sections of data.

- **Internal validity**: was the research well designed so that the researchers examined the right things, or collected the right data from the right sources? Does the research hang together as a piece of coherent and accurate work so that the data generated really does lead to the researchers' claimed findings? Are the researchers justified in saying that A causes B and a causal relationship exists 'in reality'? (See Chapter 9 for further discussion of internal validity.)
- **External validity**: are the research findings generalizable to different people, settings or times, that is, does the research have *generalizability*? Positivist research seeks *high* generalizability. It is looking for general laws or patterns, not findings unique to one particular case. The generalizability depends on how representative the research samples were, such as the subjects used in an experiment or the respondents in a survey. (See Chapter 9 for further discussion of external validity and Chapter 7 for further discussion of the selection of representative samples.)

The scientific method, and its underlying positivist philosophy, has been very successful. It has helped to shape much of modern life including the cars we drive, the computers we use, the antibiotics we take. Our daily discourse is frequently based, often unthinkingly, on a positivist worldview, with politicians and journalists demanding 'the proof' and 'the truth' and being quick to condemn research that is not objective or findings that are unique to one setting and not generalizable. However, as noted earlier, the scientific method and positivism were developed for studying the natural world, for example, in physics, chemistry and biology. Positivism is less suited to studying the social world, as we shall see in the next section.

Criticisms of Positivism

Positivism is well suited to studying aspects of the natural world: gravity, magnetism, molecular structures, electrons, and so on. However, it is less suited to researching the social world, that is, the world of people, the organizations and group structures that they build, the cultures they develop and the meanings they impose on things. Consider, for example:

- Reductionism, breaking complex things down into simpler things to be studied, sometimes is not possible, or it misses the bigger picture. If we want to study a family, for instance, we could not do this by studying first the father, then the mother and so on. We would have to take a holistic view of the whole family and all the complex relationships within it.
- Repetition is not always possible. If we want to know about how a particular computer system was accepted and adapted when rolled out in a company, for example, we can only study it once. We cannot repeat the study several times, and with different researchers.
- Generalizing is not always desirable. Concentrating on regular laws and generalizable patterns misses out on much. Sometimes, it is useful to study the particular and the unique. For example, finding out about what it's like working for

Microsoft® might be interesting, even if Microsoft® is so untypical of other organizations that the findings are not applicable to any other.

- Not everyone sees the world in the same way. If a glass is filled to its halfway mark and placed in front of a group of people, some will say it is half-full, some half-empty. There is no law that says everyone will see the glass in the same way, but it is interesting to find that people see the same thing in different ways. We therefore need ways to study how *individuals* perceive their world and interpret it.
- Regular laws and patterns may appear to be observable in the social world, but they are the construction of *people*. For example, there is a widely held view that web-based systems must be developed to a far quicker timescale than conventional systems. This is not a law of nature, it is a shared view of people designing and using web-based systems. (If all the web systems' clients were suddenly wiped out, would web engineers still tell themselves they had to develop systems quickly and there was no time for conventional modelling, documentation and testing?) We therefore also need ways to study how groups, organizations, cultures and societies perceive their world and interpret it.

Many researchers have argued that the social world has few equivalents to the 'laws of nature' in the physical world. In the social world, different people see their worlds differently, and their views and perceptions can change over time. From the late 19th century onwards, researchers have therefore developed alternative research paradigms to the scientific method and positivism, in order to research into people and their worlds: interpretivism and critical research. These are explained in the next chapter.

Evaluating Positivist Research

You can use the 'Evaluation Guide' below to analyse and evaluate positivist research. Note that, because positivism is the dominant paradigm, researchers often don't tell us that their work is based on it; you will have to deduce this. (Hint: If the research is based on experiments or a survey, it is *usually* based on positivism.)

EVALUATION GUIDE: POSITIVISM

1   Do the researchers state their research's underlying philosophical paradigm? If not, what makes you think it is based on positivism?
2   Does the research display all the characteristics of the positivist paradigm, as discussed in this chapter?
3   Does the account of the research pay attention to positivism's quality criteria: objectivity, reliability, internal validity and external validity?
4   Do you think positivism was an appropriate philosophical paradigm for the research topic?
5   Overall, how satisfied are you that the research is consistent with the tenets of positivism?

PRACTICAL WORK

1   Think of some scientific research, current or in the recent past, that has caused controversy. For example, hypotheses such as:

   a   The MMR vaccine is linked to autism.
   b   Genetically modified crops are unsafe for humans to eat.
   c   Radio and telephone masts can cause brain tumours in humans.
   d   Sugar is bad for you.
   e   We must control carbon dioxide emissions to prevent catastrophic global warming.

   Examine how the debate about this research topic is covered in the newspapers and in television programmes. Is the quality of the research asserted and challenged on the grounds of objectivity, reliability, internal validity and external validity? Or are other factors at play too, such as the power of governments or large organizations, or the reputations of the scientists involved? Does the research debate on your chosen topic illustrate the claimed value-free, objective nature of science?

2   Practise analysing and evaluating research based on positivism. Find a piece of research based on it. Answer the questions in the 'Evaluation Guide' above, using the material in this chapter to help you.

FURTHER READING

Classic texts on the nature of the scientific method and research paradigms are Kuhn (1970) and Popper (1959). Other texts that compare positivism with the other research paradigms are suggested at the end of Chapter 20.

References

Kuhn, T. (1970). *The structure of scientific revolutions*. Chicago, IL: University of Chicago Press.

Lee, A.S. (2004). Thinking about social theory and philosophy for information systems. In J. Mingers & L. Willcocks (Eds.), *Social theory and philosophy for information systems* (pp. 1–26). Chichester: Wiley.

Popper, K. (1959). *The logic of scientific enquiry*. London: Harper.

20 Alternative Philosophical Paradigms

In this chapter you will learn about:

- the philosophical paradigm called 'interpretivism' – its characteristics and how we evaluate it;
- the philosophical paradigm called 'critical research' – its characteristics and how we evaluate it;
- how positivist, interpretivist and critical research relate to the various research strategies;
- how you might decide which philosophical paradigm underpins your own work.

Introduction

In the last chapter, we started to look at the fifth of our 6Ps of research, the underlying *philosophical paradigm*, by considering the scientific method and positivism. It has been a very successful way of finding out about the natural world we live in, but does have limitations when it comes to studying the social world, that is, the ways of seeing and doing, cultures and norms, and patterns of behaviour that have been developed and modified by *people*. In this chapter, we shall therefore look at two alternative philosophical paradigms: interpretivism and critical research. Each has a different view about the nature of our world (ontology) and the ways we can acquire knowledge about it (epistemology). After providing an overview of each of these, this chapter explains how all three philosophical paradigms relate to our research strategies (surveys, experiments, ethnographies, case studies, action research, and design and creation – see Chapters 7–12). It also offers some suggestions on how to decide on the underlying paradigm for your own research project.

Interpretivism

Let's start by looking at interpretivism (see the definition below), its characteristics and how we judge the quality of a piece of interpretive research.

DEFINITION: Interpretive research

Interpretive research in IS and computing is concerned with understanding the social context of an information system: the social processes by which it is developed and construed by people and through which it influences, and is influenced by, its social setting.

Characteristics of interpretivism

Interpretive studies do not prove or disprove a hypothesis, as in positivist research, but try to identify, explore and explain how all the factors in a particular social setting (a web development team, an organization, and so on) are related and interdependent. They look at how the people perceive their world (individually or in groups) and try to understand phenomena through the meanings and values that the people assign to them. The aim is to create a rich understanding of a possibly unique context and 'an organized discovery of how human agents make sense of their perceived worlds, and how those perceptions change over time and differ from one person or group to another (Checkland & Holwell, 1998, p. 22).

The shared worldview of those who work in the interpretivist paradigm has the following characteristics:

- **Multiple subjective realities:** there is no single version of 'the truth'. What we take to be 'real' or 'knowledge' is a construction of our minds, either individually or in a group. Different groups or cultures perceive the world differently. So, for example, systems developers in a company's IT department develop a shared view about the 'right' way to do things, which might be very different from that of the systems developers in another company just down the road. Similarly, the scientific method is itself a social construction, developed by a community of researchers over several hundred years as the 'right' way to do research.
- **Dynamic, socially constructed meaning:** whatever reality is, for an individual or a group, it can only be accessed and transmitted to others through yet more social constructions such as language and shared meanings and understanding. (For example, what *are* 'market forces' or 'geeks'?) Language and shared meanings differ across groups and over time.
- **Researcher reflexivity:** researchers are not neutral. Their own assumptions, beliefs, values and actions will inevitably shape the research process and affect the situation.

Researchers must therefore be reflexive or self-reflective (both terms are used), acknowledging how they influence the research and how their interactions with those they are studying can themselves lead to a renegotiation of meanings, understanding and practices.

- **Study of people in their natural social settings**: research is aimed at understanding people in their worlds, not in the artificial world of a laboratory as in most experiments. What happens in that natural setting is studied from the perspectives of the participants and without the researchers imposing their outsiders' previous understanding or expectations onto the situation.
- **Qualitative data analysis**: there is often a strong preference for generating and analysing qualitative data – the words people use, the metaphors they employ, the images they construct.
- **Multiple interpretations**: researchers expect that they will not arrive at one fixed explanation of what occurs in their study, Instead they will offer more than one explanation, and discuss which, if any, seems the stronger because there is more evidence for it.

Judging the quality of interpretivist research

How should we judge the quality of interpretivist research? Some have tried to use the same criteria as those for positivist research, but they are not appropriate, Let's see why (Heron, 1996; Lincoln & Guba, 1985):

- **Objectivity** in positivist research is the degree to which it is free of researcher bias and distortions. Interpretivists, however, believe that there will always be bias – no observations can be made independently of how a researcher chooses to conceptualize them on the basis of prior theory (developed by people) or previous experiences. Also, the researchers usually interact with the people being studied (for example, by asking them questions), which makes it probable that they have some effect on them and the situation.
- **Reliability** of research findings in positivist research is centred on repeatability – whether the study can be replicated with similar results. This depends on the assumption that there is some truth 'out there' that can serve as a benchmark for repeat studies. Interpretivists, however, argue that what is being studied, the thing 'out there', is a social construction by individuals, and is short-lived and changing, so the same situation is unlikely to be met in a repeat study. Furthermore, since the researcher will influence the study and its findings, as explained above, another researcher is unlikely to obtain similar results.
- **Internal validity** is the extent to which findings are accurate, match reality and measure it correctly, that is, whether the researchers are justified in saying that A causes B and a causal relationship exists 'in reality'. Interpretivists, however, believe that there is no single objective reality, but multiple constructed realities – so

Table 20.1   Quality in positivist and
interpretivist research

Positivism	Interpretivism
Validity	Trustworthiness
Objectivity	Confirmability
Reliability	Dependability
Internal validity	Credibility
External validity	Transferability

Source: Lincoln and Guba (1985)

there is no ultimate benchmark against which to test any findings. Also, for studies of complex real-life situations, it is usually impossible to isolate individual variables and their associated cause and effect.

- **External validity** is the degree to which findings are generalizable to different people, settings and times, and depends on how representative the research samples are. Interpretivists, however, accept the uniqueness of contexts, individuals and the individuals' constructions, making identical findings in other contexts less likely.

Different criteria are therefore needed for judging the quality of interpretivist research. Unfortunately, the community of interpretivist researchers has not yet arrived at an agreed set of criteria – note that this is itself an example of knowledge (how to judge interpretivist research) being under a process of social construction.

Lincoln and Guba (1985) propose a set of criteria for interpretivist research that are an alternative to, but parallel to, those for positivist research (Table 20.1).

- **Trustworthiness**: instead of speaking of the research's validity, as in positivist research, interpretivists ask how much trust we can place in the research.
- **Confirmability**: have we been told enough about the study to judge whether the findings do flow from the data and the experiences in the setting? Confirmability can be assessed by a research auditor following an 'audit trail' – looking at the raw data, the summaries of it, the analysis produced, the research notes, and so on. This auditor is in effect putting themselves into the shoes of the original researcher.
- **Dependability**: how well is the research process recorded and the data documented? Is it *possible* for others to carry out an 'audit trail' to trace the whole process? Even if there never is such an audit, the researcher should carry out and document all the research in the expectation that one could take place.
- **Credibility**: was the enquiry carried out in a way that ensured that the subject of the inquiry was accurately identified and described so that the research findings are credible? This can be achieved by, for example, prolonged engagement in the problem situation by the researcher, triangulation (multiple sources of data, methods or

theories – see Chapter 3), and respondent (or 'member') checking of descriptions and interpretations, where researchers go back to their informants to check that their write-up is correct.

- **Transferability**: can the findings in one case be transferred to another? Although each research situation is in some respects unique, it could still be a single example of a broader class of things so that some generalization is possible. The researcher should give a sufficiently 'thick' (detailed) description so that the *readers* can judge whether their own situation of interest has similar features so that the findings could be relevant there too. Interpretivism is more relaxed about needing generalizations than positivism is.

These criteria are useful for researchers trying to convince positivist researchers that interpretivism can still be sound research. (They can be employed, for example, if you think your examiners are biased towards positivist research.) They have, however, been criticized, including by the original authors: 'their parallelism to positivist criteria makes them suspect' (Guba & Lincoln, 1994, p. 114). That is, they are seen as an attempt to force interpretivism into a positivist framework, which is inappropriate. For example, member checking is suggested as a means to establish credibility. But interpretivism assumes that realities are joint constructions between people, including between researchers and their respondents, so member checking becomes a new process of reality construction. As Heron (1996, p. 161) writes:

> If I, the researcher, ask you, the member, whether my account of your view is correct, and you say it is, then we have co-created a new construction which is subtly different from and supersedes your original view. When any two people agree, after suitable discussion, that they have grasped the reality of one of them, that reality is changed by the shift from a unilateral to a bilateral perspective.

Certainly interpretive researchers should document their research process and provide the field data to convince others that their account:

- is not just something they have dreamt up from the comfort of their armchair;
- is a genuine attempt to understand the people in a particular setting and how they perceive their world(s).

By paying attention to the trustworthiness criteria outlined above, and carrying out and documenting your research as if an auditor will check it afterwards, you can convince others that it was done well.

Rather than 'proof' in the positivist sense, interpretive researchers aim for *plausibility*. They are similar to lawyers in a court. Both interpretive researchers and lawyers have to make arguments and convince their audience (readers or the jury) that their descriptions, explanations and interpretations are plausible and supported by evidence (data). In both cases, that evidence can comprise data generated from interviews, observations, questionnaires and documents. Lawyers have to explain how the evidence was acquired and consider whether it might have been tainted in any way; interpretive researchers also have to explain how their data was gathered and reflect on how they themselves may have affected the data.

People accustomed to the positivist methods of traditional science criticize interpretivist research for being 'non-scientific'. But it's meant to be. However, it can still be carefully done so that others have confidence in its findings. Interpretivist research is, however, less well-established than positivist research. This means that researchers often have to include a summary of what it is and how it differs from positivist research when publishing their work. They also have to accept that reviewers may not know of interpretivism, or on principle do not accept its tenets, so that there is a danger that good interpretive research is rejected for publication because its reviewers were prejudiced against it or had insufficient knowledge to evaluate it properly. In IS, interpretive research is increasingly becoming understood and accepted. However, in computing it is still not widely known and appreciated.

Critical Research

We turn now to our final philosophical paradigm: critical research (see the definition below). This is less well-known and accepted than interpretivism.

DEFINITION:
Critical
research

Critical research in IS and computing is concerned with identifying power relations, conflicts and contradictions, and empowering people to eliminate them as sources of alienation and domination.

Researchers in the critical research paradigm assert, like interpretivists, that social reality is created and re-created by people. But they then go on to say that that social reality also possesses objective properties that tend to dominate our experiences and ways of seeing the world, such as the prevailing systems of economic, political and cultural authority. They criticize interpretivist researchers for failing to analyse the patterns of power and control that regulate and legitimize particular ways of seeing our world.

Imagine, for example, some research at a golf club – perhaps because it needs a new computer-based information system. There may be a shared view among its members that there should be separate committees for female and male members, and that the male captain should have first choice of dates to hold competitions, with the female captain choosing from the remaining dates. Interpretivist researchers would analyse the group way of seeing the world and the members' shared understanding about how to organize a golf club. Critical researchers would go further and try to explain *why* a certain way of seeing the world (rather than any other way) dominates and are seen to represent organizational reality, that is, the way the organization 'naturally' has to be. They would look at how the wider societal history of perceptions about differences between men and women and the relative importance of men and women have shaped the members' shared way of running their organization. They would do more still, and try to challenge and remove the barriers to equality in the golf club, perhaps by encouraging the women members to question the status quo and helping them to organize themselves and to effect changes. The aim of critical researchers is to focus on the power relations, conflicts and contradictions in our modern world, and help to eliminate them as causes of alienation and domination. Interpretation and understanding are not enough. Critical researchers seek to identify and challenge the conditions of domination, and the restrictions and unfairness of the status quo and taken-for-granted assumptions.

Characteristics of critical research

The critical research paradigm in IS has been dominated by the work of the 'Frankfurt School' of philosophers and especially by one of its members, Habermas. Other critical philosophers, not in the Frankfurt School, who have influenced researchers include Bourdieu, Foucault, Latour and Marx. Although there are different styles and types of critical research, five common themes have been identified (Howcroft & Trauth, 2004):

- **Emancipation**: critical researchers are committed to freeing people from the power relations that shape our organizations and society. Critical researchers do not just try to understand and explain, they also seek to *empower* people. They are therefore more activist than researchers in the other paradigms.
- **Critique of tradition**: critical researchers do not accept the status quo, but question and challenge it. Existing patterns of power and taken-for-granted assumptions are highlighted and confronted. For example, a systems developer is often seen as someone who can meet the needs of both managers and end-users in an organization. Critical researchers challenge this, arguing that managers' and employees' interests are often irreconcilable, so the developer (often unthinkingly) ends up serving as a tool for the managers, helping to increase their productivity and restricting employee resistance.
- **Non-performative intent**: critical researchers reject research projects that are aimed at improving or increasing managerial efficiency and control, where maximum outputs (for example, productivity, profits) are achieved though minimum inputs (for example, reduced manpower). Much IS and computing research, on the other hand, has been focused on meeting managers' needs for maximized profits and enhancing their control and power.
- **Critique of technological determinism**: critical researchers challenge the idea that technological development follows its own rules and people and societies must adapt to the technology. They point out that such a view allows those with vested

interests in the technology to increase their power over others. Instead, they argue that people and society can shape the technology that we develop.

- **Reflexivity**: critical researchers, like interpretivists, question the possibility of objective, value-free knowledge (as sought by positivists). They point out that research projects and areas of development and knowledge, are often shaped by those with power and vested interests. For example, governments can decide which research topics to fund and which to ignore, and journal reviewers and editors can decide which research reports get published and which rejected. Critical researchers reflect on how their methods and they themselves have influenced the knowledge outcomes emerging from their research, and how they too are influenced by societal and organizational factors and history.

Judging the quality of critical research

As for interpretivism, criteria for judging the quality of critical research are still evolving. This isn't surprising, since both are relatively recent research paradigms. After all, it took 400–500 years of debate for researchers and philosophers to agree on validity criteria for positivist research. Critical research is less practised than interpretive research and, perhaps as a consequence, there have been fewer suggestions of criteria for evaluating it.

One set of criteria we could use is based on the ideas of 'fairness' and 'authenticity' (Guba & Lincoln, 1989, pp. 245–251):

- **Fairness**: did all the stakeholders in the research have equal access to the inquiry process, the choice of questions, the responses and their interpretation?
- **Ontological authenticity**: to what extent did the research enable the informants to enlarge their personal views of their worlds?
- **Educational authenticity**: to what extent did the research enable the informants to improve their understanding and appreciation of the constructions of others?
- **Catalytic authenticity**: to what extent did the research stimulate the informants into action or decision-making?
- **Tactical authenticity**: to what extent did the research empower the informants to take action?

Whereas positivism is concerned with 'truth' and refutable hypotheses, these criteria for critical research are concerned with changes in individuals or a social situation. Again, however, these criteria are not fully accepted. Heron (1996, p. 162), for example, points to an anomaly. If the members of a research setting are to be treated fairly in terms of their shared control of the research method and interpretation, then they must also help to establish the criteria by which it is judged, which cannot be decided just by the researchers or an academic community of critical researchers. It could even be argued that *only* the members of a researched culture should decide the relevant quality criteria.

So far, much of the discussion of critical research in IS and computing has been about what it *is*, and the literature contains only a few examples of its use. Reflections on the *process* and how to judge what is 'good' or 'high-quality' critical research have not yet been much discussed – an opportunity for some of this book's readers?

Linking Research Strategies to Philosophical Paradigms

Let's look briefly at how the various strategies we studied earlier in this book relate to the three philosophical paradigms discussed in this chapter and the last.

Experiments

Experiments (see Chapter 9) are the strategy of choice in the scientific method and are based on the positivist paradigm. For a long time, they were the only acceptable strategy for many academic researchers. Experiments are designed to test hypotheses and to establish cause and effect: if X occurs then Y happens. They demand objectivity: it is assumed, and required, that experiments can be carefully designed to ensure that the researchers themselves do not influence the outcome. They use quantitative data and mathematical techniques to measure inputs and outputs and the relationships between them. Experiments are also repeated: to be sure that X really does cause Y to happen. Experiments aim for generalizations: a regularly occurring pattern, law or theory is established. Hence there is an expectation built into the research strategy: that a regularly occurring pattern or law does exist, it is up to researchers to find it and demonstrate it.

Surveys

Surveys (see Chapter 7) are also strongly associated with positivism. Surveys, like experiments, seek patterns in the world – so a researcher using surveys must assume that such patterns exist (for example, '90 per cent of IS and computing graduates earn more than the average graduate salary in their first job'). Researchers using a survey make careful choices of sampling frame and sampling techniques so that they can assert that their chosen sample is representative of a wider population, that is, what they find in the sample 'holds true for' the wider population. Surveys use quantitative data and statistical analysis to show patterns and relationships among the data. Many surveys are designed and written up as a series of hypotheses which are tested against the data. However, they cannot confirm cause and effect, as experiments do. They are weaker than experiments in the sense that they can only confirm an *association* (for example, 'Systems analysts who expressed the highest job satisfaction were more likely to be earning below the average salary for their profession'). Another strategy would be needed to explore the reasons for the association (for example, it would be wrong to infer a cause and effect situation: 'Lower salaries cause greater job satisfaction').

Some researchers use surveys in a more interpretive way. For example, a survey could be carried out among people who are *not* considered typical of a wider population, and who differ from each other. This might enable the researchers to establish the breadth of opinions about a subject. For example, they might try to find out about the many different factors thought to be relevant to successful IT systems implementation, but without attempting to draw any conclusions about the most 'popular' factors.

Ethnographies

Ethnographies (see Chapter 12) are strongly associated with the interpretive paradigm. A researcher carrying out an ethnography recognizes that different groups or cultures will perceive the world differently, and sets out to understand how one particular group perceives its world, concentrating on social constructions such as language, symbols and organizational structures. Research is aimed at understanding people in their worlds, not in the artificial world of a laboratory. Ethnographers recognize that their own background, beliefs and actions will shape the research process and affect the situation, and their reports include a discussion of their self and how they may have shaped what was observed and how they interpreted it. Ethnographers also expect to deal with multiple interpretations. Indeed, one of the key concerns of ethnographers in recent years has been to recognize that writing up their research is a creative act whereby they construct *just one* partial interpretation of a culture and also create a form of *self*-presentation and identity.

Some ethnographers go beyond the use of language and other symbolic forms to study and question what is hidden behind them – the politics, hidden agendas, power centres and unstated assumptions. They are therefore working more in the critical research paradigm. However, if all they do is discover and describe, some would argue that they are not being true critical researchers. They should also empower those who are being oppressed by the politics, and so on, to challenge the status quo.

Case studies

Case studies (see Chapter 10), like ethnographies, are often associated with the interpretive paradigm (for example, Walsham, 1995b). They provide an account of what occurs in a social setting, which may be unique to that particular situation. Case study researchers recognize their influence on what is observed and interpreted. They examine how different people and groups perceive their world, and look for multiple interpretations.

Like ethnographers, case study researchers can also be in the critical research paradigm if they look for the power structures, hidden agendas, unstated assumptions, and so on, that serve to prevent some people from reaching their full human potential. Also like ethnographers, however, they can be criticized for not addressing all the tenets of critical research if they merely describe and do not empower those who are being oppressed to challenge and remove the barriers that are holding them back.

Other researchers have argued that case study research can be positivist (for example, Benbasat, Goldstein, & Mead, 1987; Lee, 1989; Paré, 2004). Case studies can be used to confirm or refute theories in the same way as positivist research does. For example, three theories about resistance to efforts to implement management information systems were used to generate predictions about what would happen in a particular company. By examining which events did actually occur, it was possible to decide that one theory was a better predictor than the others (Lee, 1989; Markus, 1983). The case to be studied can be chosen so that it *is* typical of a wider population, allowing general patterns to be argued for. Finally, the outcome from a case study is often a theory, which can be applied in further case studies, thus supporting repeatability and generalization.

Action research

Like case studies, researchers have argued that action research (see Chapter 11), can be in any of the three paradigms.

Many action research studies are in the interpretive paradigm. Action researchers work reflexively with the people in a particular social setting, which may be unique, discover how the people in that situation perceive their world, and carry out actions that lead to increased understanding of different viewpoints, revised perceptions and changes that the people in the situation regard as improvements.

Action research can also be critical research, if the changes brought about enable people to challenge power structures and barriers to human flourishing. The 'new action research' discussed in Chapter 11 places particular emphasis on human (rather than organizational) flourishing and is therefore critically oriented.

Action research can also have a positivist underpinning (for example, Kock, McQueen, & Scott, 1997). It can test existing theories by seeing if the theories' predictions occur in the research setting. Control groups are possible, as in positivist research: the action researcher works with one group and not another, and examines the differences in outcomes. And action research can lead to theories that are testable in further studies, allowing repeatability and generalizations. However, action research is always likely to be criticized by positivists for lack of researcher objectivity: the action researcher is not an objective observer but an active participant. Any findings may therefore be attributable to the researcher rather than to any actions taken. For example, systems development methodologies, which have often been developed through action research, may appear to be useful in many different settings, but only when used by the methodology's creators. Others who read reports of a methodology may find they do not have as much success with it.

... if a reader tells the author 'I have used your methodology and it works', the author will have to reply, 'How do you know that better results might not have been obtained by an *ad hoc* approach?' If the assertion is: 'The methodology does not work', the author can reply, ungraciously but with logic, 'How do you know the poor results were not due simply to your incompetence in using the methodology?' (Checkland & Scholes, 1990, p. 299, citing Checkland, 1972)

Design and creation

Design and creation research (see Chapter 8) can also be in any of the three paradigms. However, many designers concentrate on the technical aspects of an IT artefact without considering their underlying assumptions about the nature of the world and how we can find out about it. Indeed, for some designers, the virtual worlds offered by computer systems are so exciting that they hardly consider the real world in which we live and their systems are used.

The nature of computing

I'm personally convinced that computer science has a lot in common with physics. Both are about how the world works at a rather fundamental level. The difference, of course, is that while in physics you're supposed to figure out how the world is made up, in computer science you *create* the world. Within the confines of the computer, you're the creator. You get to ultimately control everything that happens. If you're good enough, you can be God. On a small scale.

And I've probably offended roughly half the population on Earth by saying so. (Torvalds & Diamond, 2001, pp. 73–74)

Much of design research in IS and computing is based, often unthinkingly, on positivism. It is assumed that computer systems are the means to specific ends (that is, cause leading to effect), that these ends, and hence the requirements of the system, can be stated clearly and unambiguously and are uncontroversial, incontrovertible facts, agreed by everyone involved. The designer is an objective, dispassionate outsider who uses rational thinking, and tools and methods that are based on mathematics and logic, rather than human intuition or politics. Models produced by the designer are held to be 'true' representations of reality.

Some have challenged this dominant philosophy of design and creation, and shown that it can be based on the interpretive paradigm instead. Methods have been developed where the focus is on the interpretations of all the stakeholders in a situation, such as SSM (Checkland, 1981; Checkland & Scholes, 1990), ETHICS (Mumford, 1983) and Multiview (Avison & Wood-Harper, 1990). Designers work with the stakeholders to help them articulate their views and understand different perspectives about a situation and possible improvements via IT artefacts, resulting in artefacts that the stakeholders perceive as good and appropriate for all of them.

Critical researchers argue that designers of systems cannot serve the interests of both the managers and the workers. Positivist designers sleepwalk their way into being tools of the powerful, such as the managers of organizations, and help to make worse the lives of those less powerful. They also criticize interpretivist designers for naivety in failing to recognize that open dialogue about perceptions, problems and solutions is impossible given the wider context of politics and power in which everyone must operate. Critical researchers therefore seek to design IT artefacts that assist the less powerful to overcome barriers. They see the development of IT artefacts as a political undertaking.

There is one further type of design and creation research to consider: that which involves artists exploring and exhibiting the possibilities of digital technologies. Artistic endeavours are intentionally produced artefacts, but the intention can vary: for example, to produce something aesthetically pleasing, to offer therapeutic value, to provide insights, or to provoke particular emotions. By questioning why they are creating an IT artefact, and how they will know when they have been successful, artists can reach self-knowledge about how they perceive the world and how they feel they can acquire knowledge about it or influence it. That is, they can learn about their own underlying research paradigm. For example:

- Artists with positivist leanings might want to say through their art: 'This is how the world is.'
- Those with interpretivist leanings might say: 'Here are multiple ways of viewing our world.'
- And those with critical leanings might want to use the possibilities of digital technologies to empower the oppressed to challenge the status quo and overcome the barriers that prevent human flourishing.

Which Paradigm to Choose?

As we saw in the previous section, some research strategies are naturally underpinned by a particular research philosophy. For other strategies, however, the research philosophy is not so clear-cut; effectively meaning you have a choice. This choice of will depend on:

- the nature of your research question;
- your own personal beliefs and values, which shape how you perceive our world and what kind of knowledge you want to create;
- whether you want to do the kind of research that is typically done in your discipline;
- whether you are willing to take a risk and want to challenge the status quo.

Many computing researchers concentrate on creating IT artefacts and do not think about their underlying research philosophy. However, as Chapter 19 explained, when they want to justify the need for a particular IT artefact, or evaluate an artefact they have created, they are likely to need an additional research strategy, where the underlying philosophy cannot be ignored. With their strong scientific and mathematical background, many computing researchers may only feel comfortable with the scientific, positivist paradigm. But, if the empirical examination of computing artefacts is to aim at a complete picture and understanding, there should be room for studies in the interpretive and critical paradigms too. Interpretive research offers a way of understanding computing as a practice constructed and developed by humans. Critical research goes beyond understanding computing practice to challenge the power structures and taken-for-granted assumptions about why we develop IT artefacts and how we implement them. However, readers and reviewers of the computing literature, and examiners of a PhD thesis, may need help to understand the different paradigms to prevent them judging interpretive and critical studies by the quality criteria intended only for positivist studies. You might therefore decide that it is safer to adopt a positivist approach until you have gained your PhD and are established as a researcher, and to submit your first papers to journals that seem more receptive to interpretive and critical research.

In IS, the situation is different. There has been far more use of research strategies other than design and creation. The different paradigms underlying the strategies have therefore been more widely studied and discussed. Interpretivism has been increasingly adopted and accepted in IS over the last 20 or so years. You should therefore be able to find reviewers and PhD examiners who are comfortable with the evaluation of interpretive research. However, positivism still predominates, especially in the USA, and can still be a safer option. Critical research in IS is probably at the stage interpretivism was 20 years ago: a growing community of scholars know about it and argue for it, but it is not yet anywhere near mainstream. It is therefore more risky for novice researchers, and you and your supervisor will need to think carefully about appropriate examiners and conference or journal outlets for your critical research.

Researchers in many disciplines, including IS, have argued about whether one paradigm is better than another. To resolve this, some have suggested that that the different paradigms can be combined, as a compromise solution. Others have responded that each paradigm is fundamentally different from the others in the way it sees our world, so that each requires different research strategies and different quality criteria, and the paradigms are incompatible (often called *incommensurable*). If you think you want a combination of research paradigms in your research you will therefore have to study the debate on whether the different philosophical paradigms are indeed incommensurable, and justify how and why you feel you can use more than one.

Evaluating Interpretive and Critical Research

Because interpretive and critical research are not yet as well-established as positivist research, those using them will usually explain them within their paper or thesis. This means you will normally know when a study has been underpinned by one of them. However, you should still analyse and evaluate the report, to judge whether a study is in line with its claimed underlying paradigm. You can use the 'Evaluation Guide' below to help you.

EVALUATION GUIDE: INTERPRETIVISM AND CRITICAL RESEARCH

1   Do the researchers explain the paradigm sufficiently for readers unfamiliar with it?
2   Does the research display all the characteristics of its particular paradigm, as discussed in this chapter?
3   Does the account of the research meet the quality criteria for its paradigm, as discussed in this chapter?
4   Do you think the philosophical paradigm was appropriate for the research topic? Can you suggest an alternative paradigm for this topic?
5   Overall, how satisfied are you that the research is consistent with its claimed underlying paradigm?

PRACTICAL WORK

1   A researcher is interested in the use of information systems in universities. Suggest a research question and appropriate research methodology if the researcher bases her work on (a) positivism, (b) interpretivism or (c) critical research.
2   Practise analysing and evaluating research based on either the interpretivist or critical paradigm. Study a piece of research that is underpinned by one of them. Answer the questions in the 'Evaluation Guide' above, using the material in this chapter to help you.

FURTHER READING

Surveys examining the use of the different paradigms in IS include Mingers (2003), Orlikowski and Baroudi (1991) and Walsham (1995a). Currently, I know of no such study of the computing research literature. The arguments about the different paradigms and the possibility of combining them are discussed by Fitzgerald and Howcroft (1998), where the authors manage to use humour to explain what can be a very dry area. The edited volume of Denzin and Lincoln (1994) includes chapters explaining all three research paradigms and the sub-divisions within them, although the majority concentrate on interpretivism and critical research. Trauth and Jessop (2000) show how different results emerge from an assessment of an IT system (computer-supported discussion) when the 'lens' by which it is viewed shifts from positivism to interpretivism.

Klein and Myers (1999) propose a set of principles for evaluating interpretive case studies and ethnographies in IS, and use them to evaluate three previously published interpretive studies. However, as the authors acknowledge, they concentrate on principles for research founded on one philosophical basis – hermeneutics. These principles are not therefore necessarily applicable to interpretive research that is not based on hermeneutics, and they call for other interpretive researchers to propose alternative principles.

Although concerned primarily with research into corporate organizations rather than IS and computing, Alvesson and Deetz (2000) provide useful guidance on the nature and practice of critical research. Also, Alvesson and Skoldberg (2000) explain and argue for reflexive critical research and offer a four-level framework to categorise reflexivity. They show how culture, language, selective perception and ideology permeate our research activities. McGrath (2005) discusses the nature of critical research in IS and examines two key IS texts whose authors claim to have a critical agenda but pursue it in different ways (Avgerou, 2002; Walsham, 2001). She argues that critical researchers should give more information about their research method. (Avgerou and Walsham respond to her comments in the same issue of *Information Systems Journal*.)

Finally, researchers using a design and creation or action research strategy could also look at the philosophy called 'pragmatism' (for example, Dewey, 1938). Some writers have recently argued that this better explains the philosophical underpinnings of these two strategies.

References

Alvesson, M., & Deetz, S. (2000). *Doing critical management research*. London: Sage.

Alvesson, M., & Skoldberg, K. (2000). *Relexive methodology*. London: Sage.

Avgerou, C. (2002). *Information systems and global diversity*. Oxford: Oxford University Press.

Avison, D.E., & Wood-Harper, A.T. (1990). *Multiview: An exploration in information systems development*. Oxford: Blackwell Scientific.

Benbasat, I., Goldstein, D.K., & Mead, M. (1987). The case research strategy in studies of information systems. *MIS Quarterly, 11*(3), 369–386.

Checkland, P. (1972). Towards a systems-based methodology for real-world problem solving. *Journal of Systems Engineering, 3*(2), 87–116.

Checkland, P. (1981). *Systems thinking, systems practice.* Chichester: Wiley.

Checkland, P., & Holwell, S. (1998). *Information, systems, and information systems: Making sense of the field.* Chichester: Wiley.

Checkland, P., & Scholes, J. (1990). *Soft systems methodology in action.* Chichester: Wiley.

Denzin, N.K., & Lincoln, Y.S. (Eds.). (1994). *Handbook of qualitative research.* Thousand Oaks, CA: Sage.

Dewey, J. (1938). *Logic: The theory of inquiry.* New York: Henry Holt.

Fitzgerald, B., & Howcroft, D. (1998). Towards dissolution of the IS research debate: From polarisation to polarity. *Journal of Information Technology, 13*(4), 313–326.

Guba, E.G., & Lincoln, Y.S. (1989). *Fourth generation evaluation.* Newbury Park, CA: Sage.

Guba, E.G., & Lincoln, Y.S. (1994). Competing paradigms in qualitative research. In N.K. Denzin & Y.S. Lincoln (Eds.), *Handbook of qualitative research* (pp. 105–117). Thousand Oaks, CA: Sage.

Heron, J. (1996). *Co-operative inquiry: Research into the human condition.* London: Sage.

Howcroft, D., & Trauth, E.M. (2004). The choice of critical information systems research. In B. Kaplan, D. Truex, D. Wastell, T. Wood-Harper, & J. DeGross (Eds.), *Information systems research. Relevant theory and informed practice* (pp. 195–211). Boston, MA: Kluwer.

Klein, H.K., & Myers, M.D. (1999). A set of principles for conducting and evaluating interpretive field studies in information systems. *MIS Quarterly, 23*(1), 67–94.

Kock, N.F., McQueen, R.J., & Scott, J.L. (1997). Can action research be made more rigorous in a positivist sense? The contribution of an iterative approach. *Journal of Systems and Information Technology, 1*(1), 1–24.

Lee, A.S. (1989). A scientific methodology for MIS case studies. *MIS Quarterly, 13*(1), 33–52.

Lincoln, Y.S., & Guba, E.G. (1985). *Naturalistic inquiry.* Beverley Hills, CA: Sage.

Markus, M.L. (1983). Power, politics and MIS implementation. *Communications of the ACM, 26*(6), 430–445.

McGrath, K. (2005). Doing critical research in information systems: A case of theory and practice not informing each other. *Information Systems Journal, 15*(2), 85–101.

Mingers, J. (2003). The paucity of multimethod research: A review of the information systems literature. *Information Systems Journal, 13*(3), 233–249.

Mumford, E. (1983). *Designing human systems.* Manchester: Manchester Business School.

Orlikowski, W.J., & Baroudi, J.J. (1991). Studying information technology in organizations: Research approaches and assumptions. *Information Systems Research, 2*(1), 1–28.

Paré, G. (2004). Investigating information systems with positivist case study research. *Communications of AIS, 13*, 233–264.

Torvalds, L., & Diamond, D. (2001). *Just for fun. The story of an accidental revolutionary*. New York: Texere.

Trauth, E.M., & Jessop, L. (2000). Understanding computer-mediated discussions: Positivist and interpretive analyses of group support system use. *MIS Quarterly, 24*(1), 43–79.

Walsham, G. (1995a). The emergence of interpretivism in IS research. *Information Systems Research, 6*(4), 376–394.

Walsham, G. (1995b). Interpretive case studies in IS research: Nature and method. *European Journal of Information Systems, 4*, 74–81.

Walsham, G. (2001). *Making a world of difference. IT in a global context*. Chichester: Wiley.

21 | Presentation of the Research

In this chapter you will learn about:

- how to write up your research;
- how to present your research at conferences, exhibitions and demonstrations;
- what to expect at academic conferences;
- participating in a PhD viva;
- how to analyse and evaluate research presentations.

We have now looked at five of the 6Ps of research: *purpose*, *products*, *process*, *participants* and *paradigm*. In this chapter, we shall study the last of them: *presentation*. It is not enough to do the work in line with the guidance given in the previous chapters – you also have to present it to others in the research community, so that they can scrutinize and evaluate it. So researchers need a further set of skills: writing and talking about their work in the accepted academic style.

You can present your work to an academic community via a thesis or a journal article, or you can write it up as a conference paper which you then present to an academic audience. You can also display your work via a conference poster, software demonstration or exhibition. PhD students are also often expected to discuss and justify their work to their examiners at a viva, an oral examination of the research. All these ways of presenting research are discussed in this chapter.

Writing Up the Research

Whatever kind of research you have undertaken, it will need to be written up. For many researchers, a written account will be the only tangible evidence of it that others can evaluate. For design and creation researchers, there may be a computer-based system or a piece of digital art that others can assess, but such work must also be described, justified and placed in context via a textual report.

Getting started

As Chapter 2 indicated, most researchers find that the act of writing helps them to clarify their ideas, to discover what they really think. If you followed the advice of that chapter, you will have been writing about your research as you went along. Much of this will be in the form of private notes to yourself about current problems, ideas to follow up or possible interpretations of your data. However, if you have to produce a PhD thesis or other long account of the research, it is also a good idea to write some of its chapters during the research project. Reasons for this include:

- If you leave all the writing up until the last minute, you may not have enough time to produce a good thesis. In your undergraduate course, you may have been able to write essays and assignments at the last minute and still obtain a good mark. A report of academic research, however, usually requires drafting and re-drafting over weeks or even months.
- Some researchers who leave all the writing up until the end of the project can feel overwhelmed by the amount of writing to be done and the mass of data and papers to be organized and brought into order. Many research students who fail to complete their work and gain their PhD fall at this hurdle – they have read all the literature and followed their research methodology, which led to interesting findings, but they are unable to bring it all together into a thesis. Writing up as they went along would have made the final thesis production much easier.
- Writing is as much a part of the research as all the other skills and strategies discussed in this book. Only by repeatedly writing, showing your work to others and rewriting will you become good at it.

Often the literature review can be written early in a research project, while it is still fresh in your mind. (But continue to watch out for any new relevant publications that you need to add to your review.) The chapter (or report section) that explains your research methodology (your chosen combination of strategy, or strategies, and data generation methods) is also often an easy part to tackle early. You *should* know what you have done and why.

Structure and style

There are a number of conventions about the structure and style of academic papers and theses. The typical structure is:

- **Beginning part**: title, authors, abstract, keywords (so that search engines can index your work).
- **Main part**: introduction, literature review, research methodology, results, discussion of results, limitations to the research, conclusions, recommendations or implications, suggestions for further work.
- **End part**: references, appendices (for example, questionnaire used, sample of interview transcripts, program code).

You should also acknowledge those who have assisted you in your research, which might include your supervisor, the research participants, colleagues, spouse, friends or a funding body. In a thesis, the acknowledgements usually appear at the front of the thesis, often on the page following the abstract. In a journal article or conference paper, they are generally placed after the conclusions and before the references.

Accounts based on quantitative research usually keep the data results in a separate section from the discussion and interpretation of those results. Accounts based on qualitative research, on the other hand, often weave together the data obtained (for example, direct quotes from interviews) and the interpretation of the data (for example, relating it to the theory) in one section.

Reports based on design and creation research often have a different structure to the middle, main part. They have an introduction and literature review, but then follow the stages of development (for example, analysis – design – implementation – testing) before evaluating what has been achieved and drawing conclusions. If you have produced a computer-based product, you have to decide how much program code to include. The general rule is that you include in the main text those code segments that are key to the points you wish to make, for example, they illustrate an important algorithm or demonstrate the approach you adopted, and all the remaining code is placed in an appendix at the end of the report. Remember, too, that no reader should be expected to plough through reams of code unaided – you must use meaningful variable names and document the code with explanatory comments, so that the reader can understand it.

Following the conventional structure aids your readers – they can find their way around your paper easily because it matches many others that they have read. Help them further by the careful use of meaningful headings and sub-headings. You should also provide 'signposts' that tell them what is to come or what has been covered so far. For example:

- 'The last chapter explained that … This chapter now covers …'
- 'The structure of this paper is as follows: Section 2 discusses previous work on X and indicates a gap in current knowledge, Section 3 explains the research methodology, Section 4 presents the results, Section 5 interprets those results and finally Section 6 reviews the strengths and limitations of the work, draws conclusions and suggests some areas for further research.'

Research reports have conventionally been written in the third person passive. For example:

- 'An experiment was designed to ...'
- 'A questionnaire was developed and distributed to a sample of 100 students ...'

However, some now see this as old-fashioned. Others even say it is silly to pretend that an experiment or questionnaire came into existence without any apparent human involvement. So it is now becoming more common to use the first person active:

- 'We designed an experiment to ...'
- 'We developed a questionnaire and distributed it to a sample of 100 students ...'

Oddly, although the use of 'we' is now becoming acceptable, where a team of researchers is reporting its research, for single researchers 'I' is much less accepted. 'I' often seems to suggest too much subjectivity to reviewers and assessors, and so is mostly used for reporting projects where such researcher subjectivity is *expected*, such as in ethnographies (see Chapter 12) and studies in the interpretive and critical research paradigms (see Chapter 20). Some researchers avoid 'I' by writing 'the author' instead, but others see this as old-fashioned and stilted. Consult with your supervisor and colleagues about which style is acceptable in your branch of IS or computing.

Making an argument

Chapter 1 explained that another term for 'thesis' is 'argument'. When writing up a piece of research, whether a PhD submission, a journal article or a conference paper, think of it as presenting an argument. You have to assemble the evidence to convince your readers that you have created some new knowledge using an appropriate academic research process. As you plan your thesis or paper, ask yourself the following questions:

- What is my research question?
- What is my conceptual framework for understanding the question and my answer to it?
- How did I set about answering the question?
- What is the answer to the question?
- What is the evidence to justify my answer?
- So what?

The last question ('So what?') is the one that every researcher dreads reading in a reviewer's report. Don't let them ask it – think about how and why your answer could be useful to anyone else. Does it fill a gap in current knowledge or extend an existing model? Can your answer be generalized to other situations, or does it have implications for practice?

Once you can answer the six questions listed above, you should be able to construct your argument that there was a question to answer, you've answered it using an appropriate process and your answer matters.

The argument has to 'look' right: the style and structure must match those normally expected by your readers (see above). It must have a logical sequence to it, which the reader can easily discern. Of course, it must have no spelling errors or grammar mistakes – otherwise your readers will suspect that your work was undertaken in an equally slipshod fashion. Modern word processors can identify many spelling mistakes for you, but they cannot spot when you type a word that does exist, but is not the appropriate word for a particular sentence. Nor can they prevent you confusing words that can sound the same but are spelt differently and have different meanings. Make sure, for example, that you know the difference between: where/were, affect/effect, there/their, it's/its, practice/practise.

Your assertions and conclusions should always be supported by evidence; they should not appear as if from nowhere, giving the suspicion that you just dreamt them up as you were writing.

Some of the evidence to support your argument will be based on what other people have already done, derived from a literature survey and/or a review of previous software systems or digital artwork. Be sure to use the referencing convention specified by the institution, journal or conference to which you will submit your work (see Chapter 6). Further evidence comes from your empirical data and your analysis of it. For quantitative data, you can provide both raw data and statistical analysis of it, often presented via tables, graphs and pie charts (see Chapter 17). For qualitative data, you can include actual quotes from the interviewees or documents, together with matrices, tables or other visual aids that help to explain the data (see Chapter 18). Of course, all tables and figures must be clearly laid out and labelled.

Developing a writing routine

Everyone develops a preferred mode of writing. You have to find the way that suits you best. Some set themselves a target: 1500 words every day, or 500 words before they're allowed a cup of coffee. Others might not produce anything for a week, but when inspiration strikes they write for hours in a continuous flow. Write in the way that suits you: longhand first and then at a computer, or straight into a word processor? With background music playing, or in total silence? Write new work at the time of day when you are at your best. Use the time when you function less well to do the more mechanical parts such as spelling corrections and checking reference details.

The important thing is just to keep on producing words. The first draft doesn't have to be perfect. In fact, eventually you will realize that *no* account is perfect, so there is no point in trying to find the one best way of expressing your thoughts. If you use a word processor, you can easily change sentences and move sections around, until you have a version that is satisfactory. If the right words won't come, just write down some words that are close – you'll be able to improve them later. If the sentences won't come, just write fragments – you'll be able to turn them into sentences later. If you have no motivation to write the next chapter on your work plan, write another one instead, don't stick rigidly to the plan. If your thoughts are too jumbled to allow you to write *anything*, go for a walk – many people find fresh air and the regular motion of walking help calm and clear the brain.

When you have written enough for one day, a useful trick is to finish partway through a sentence or paragraph, so that you will look forward to completing it the next day, and you have an easy way back into your work.

Reviews

When you have completed a thesis chapter or a paper, leave it for a few days. When you come back to it you should be better able to tell where the structure is not clear, the evidence is not provided or the prose is too wordy. It is always a good idea to have a friend read your text too. They will see mistakes and sections lacking clarity that your eyes just skim over because you are so familiar with the material.

Your supervisor should also read and comment on your text. Don't expect them to read the first draft – supervisors are busy people and should be given a draft that has already received some polishing. On the other hand, don't insist on waiting until you have a 'perfect' draft before you show it. Your supervisor will have more experience than you in recognizing when a research paper can be better constructed or written, so utilize that experience.

If you submit your report to a conference or journal, you will normally receive back two or three anonymous reviews. It is rare for a paper to be accepted without revisions. A good review will highlight both the strengths and weaknesses of your paper, suggest how it can be improved, and even suggest other literature you can cite. Sometimes the reviewers ask for minor modifications, but other times they ask for substantial rewrites, even, sometimes, asking for more empirical research to be undertaken and incorporated into the paper. Even if they reject a paper outright, good reviewers will normally indicate how it can be improved so that it will be publishable in future. Most researchers, even well-established ones, feel hurt and slighted when a reviewer does not seem to recognize the brilliance of their paper. But after a few days reflection, they usually recognize that the reviewer had a point, and that following the advice will improve the work.

Conference Paper Presentations

If your paper is accepted for a conference, you will be expected to attend the conference and present the paper. (In the case of papers with multiple authors, only one author need attend and present.) Papers do not go into the conference proceedings unless they have been presented by someone, so don't submit a paper to a conference unless you are confident that you can obtain the funds for travel, accommodation and conference fees.

You might also have to present your work to colleagues at your own institution. Here, we will concentrate on conference presentations, but much of this section applies to in-house presentations too.

Preparing the presentation

Find out how long your presentation should be. Usually conference speakers are allotted 20 minutes to present, with 10 minutes afterwards for audience questions and discussion, but sometimes less time is allocated.

It is rare for presenters simply to read their paper to the audience – after all, the audience members are perfectly capable of reading your paper in the conference proceedings themselves. Nowadays, the norm is that you prepare some slides based on your paper (using Microsoft® PowerPoint® or some other presentation software), and you talk around the points on the slides. You might also want to include some screenshots, for example, webpages relevant to your talk, or illustrations of the user interface to the software program you are discussing.

Don't produce too many slides – you will end up either over-running your time or flashing them on and off the screen so quickly that the audience is unable to read them. As a guide, 10–14 slides are usually enough for a 20-minute presentation. You will not, therefore, be able to cover everything that is in your paper. You'll need to focus on one or two aspects. You could, for example, focus on:

- the aspect you are particularly proud of;
- an argument you want to make;
- what the audience is likely to be most interested in;
- the area where you are seeking advice from the audience.

Make sure the font size is large enough to be read by audience members at the back of the room (for example, not less than 24 point). If you want to use a complicated diagram with small type, consider making copies available as a handout, so that the audience can read it from their own printed copy while you indicate relevant parts on the screen.

You can use transparencies and an overhead projector instead of a computer-supported presentation. However, as this is becoming less common, check with the conference organizers that an overhead projector and screen will be available. One advantage of using an overhead projector is that you retain flexibility – it's easy to skip a few transparencies if you are running out of time, or add some extra ones if you are in danger of finishing too quickly.

Getting ready to speak

If you are giving a computer-supported presentation you will need to bring your file on some kind of storage medium (for example, CD, floppy disk, USB memory stick). Check beforehand with the organizers that their system will be able to read your storage medium and file format. You will be expected to load your presentation onto the conference's system – often onto the desktop of a PC. Sometimes this is done for you, but often you are expected to do it yourself, at the start of the day or in the refreshments break immediately preceding your session. If you have difficulties, technical staff are usually on hand to help. Make sure you give your file a name that can easily be found again on the computer system. Many conference speakers make the mistake of naming their file after the conference (for example, WWW_Conference_05.ppt), and, of course, everyone else in their session has named their file after the conference too, so no one can find their own presentation on the PC's desktop. A better filename would start with your own name (for example, Watson_WWW_Conference_05.ppt).

It's worth taking a few moments before your session starts, to familiarize yourself with the computer system you will be using. For example, the page-up and page-down keys might not be where you are used to finding them. If the organizers have provided a laptop, it might not have a mouse but a touch pad instead – if you're not used to using a touch pad, practise on someone else's before the conference, just in case.

Sometimes you can give a presentation using your own laptop computer. However, again check beforehand with the conference organizers that this is alright. A computer may need a network connection in order for it to be linked up to the projector, so the organizers may require you to use their computer system, which already has the necessary connection and passwords. If you do use your own laptop, at the end of your presentation don't just unplug it and rush away – make sure that the speaker following you is able to link up to the projector for their presentation.

CASE STUDY
Anticipating
problems

On arriving at a conference Joe realized he had left his presentation on a disk sitting on the desk in his office. But he did not panic. Before leaving his university he had emailed himself a copy of his presentation. He used the facilities provided by the conference to access his email over the Internet and quickly obtained another copy.

Make sure that you arrive at your session not less than 10 minutes before it is due to start. Introduce yourself to the session chair and the other speakers (one session usually has three or four paper presentations). Sit somewhere where you can quickly and easily reach the podium when it is your turn to present.

Doing the presentation

Speak slowly, clearly and loudly. It's always useful to have a copy of your slides in your hands, with notes about what you want to say, so that you have some prompts and so that you know which slide will appear next and won't be taken by surprise. As you talk, try not to look at the screen all the time – you'll have your back to the audience. Similarly, try not to spend the whole time looking down at your notes, or at the computer screen. Instead, look around the room and maintain eye contact with one person for a few seconds before moving on to another person. If you are really nervous, especially if this is your first presentation, say so. Most audiences will be sympathetic (and remember that even the most seasoned presenter still gets nervous, even if they won't admit it to anyone but themselves).

The session chair will probably indicate when you have only a few minutes remaining of your allotted time. It is essential that you keep to time – other presenters are waiting to speak and the audience members may be keen to get to another presentation, or the lunch table.

Don't be put off if people arrive after you've started your presentation, or leave before you've finished. Many conference sessions run in parallel, so conference delegates move between the different sessions to attend the presentations they're particularly interested in. On the other hand, when you are one of the *speakers* in a session, it is considered impolite to your fellow presenters if you do not stay for the whole session. So don't rush off as soon as you've finished your bit. Stay and at least try to look interested in what the other speakers are saying, even though you can't concentrate because the adrenaline is still flowing and your heartbeat still racing.

After you have finished presenting your paper, the session chair will ask the audience for questions. Don't be disheartened if no one asks any questions – it can be hard for audience members to absorb quickly what you have said and formulate a question. Often people will wait until a later refreshment break to speak to you more privately and make comments and suggestions. A good session chair will have prepared some questions anyway, in case no one from the audience speaks up.

Sometimes each presentation is followed by a short talk from a discussant. This is someone who has read the paper beforehand and presents a summary of the key points and raises some questions. A good discussant can enable both the speaker and the audience to gain more from the time available for questions and answers. However, poor discussants can focus on one part of the paper and move the emphasis away from what the speaker wanted. If you can, try to speak to your discussant before your presentation and find out what issues they intend raising.

If you don't know how to answer a question, don't be afraid to say so. Try one of the following, for example:

- 'That's an interesting aspect I hadn't thought of. But I'd like more time to think about it, so I'm not going to be able to respond right now. Sorry.'
- 'Thank you. That's a useful suggestion. Can you give me some references on that later?'
- 'I'd like to discuss that point with you in much more detail, but now probably isn't the time. Perhaps over coffee later?'

You can also turn things round and put the audience on the spot rather than yourself, by making clear in your presentation where you are looking for help or advice from the audience. Leaving a set of questions on display as your last slide can help you 'manage' audience responses.

You might also come across audience members who really want to make a presentation themselves and display their own expertise. They will talk for a long time, expressing opinions, mentioning barely related studies, describing their own work, saying what you could have done instead, and so on. A good chair will intervene and ask such a person to come to the point. If that doesn't happen, just wait patiently and console yourself that at least this person is reducing the time available for other people to ask you awkward questions. If, at the end of the long spiel, you're no longer sure what the question was, say so – most of your audience will be equally lost.

Posters and Exhibitions

Sometimes a conference programme committee might offer you the opportunity to display a poster about your work, rather than presenting a paper. A room will be made available where all the posters are displayed around the walls and conference delegates browse along them at will. The conference programme will also contain one or two slots where you are expected to stand next to your poster and discuss its content.

You will need to check with the conference organizers how much space you are allocated – some conferences will limit you to perhaps one A1 sheet, others allow two or three. At its simplest, a poster can be hard copies of some PowerPoint slides, stuck onto a larger sheet of paper. Other posters are very glossy affairs, using high-colour printing. Your university publicity department *might* be able to help you produce a professional-looking poster.

Ideally your poster should be eye-catching and summarize your current area of research. Try to use graphics rather than a lot of text – delegates won't want to spend a long time reading a poster. Remember that your poster needs a title, legibility from a distance and your full contact details.

If you are presenting digital art at an exhibition, the format will, of course, depend on the nature of your work. Often you will be expected to provide a short textual explanation of each piece – make sure they can be read easily from a distance. You should also write a personal statement reflecting on your work, its ideas and its influences, which will probably be put into the exhibition programme or catalogue. The exhibition organizers will also probably expect you to attend at pre-arranged times to discuss your work with the visitors.

Software Demonstrations

If you have produced some software as part of your research, such as a program or website, you will often be expected to demonstrate it. Here, then, are some tips for doing this:

- Make sure that your software runs exactly as you expect on the machine designated for the demonstration. Many researchers discover only at the last minute that their software requires particular plug-ins or a particular version of a database – which are not installed on the designated machine. If presenting at your own institution, check your software runs correctly on the required machine at least a week before-hand, and double-check the day before – as computer technicians the world over have a habit of upgrading machines just when you want them to stay the same.
- If planning to run your demonstration from your laptop computer, make sure the battery is fully charged. Some institutions will not allow you to plug anything into their electricity supply unless it has been fully safety-tested first.
- If possible, be at the machine, with all files open and programs running, before your audience or examiners arrive. They do not want to wait while you boot up a machine, type in passwords and so on.
- Present your work in a logical, structured way. Don't move your mouse hither and thither around the screen, trying to show all the functions as quickly as possible. If your work involves interaction with a database, for example, you could show how a record is created, modified and then deleted.
- If your software malfunctions at some point, do not swear. Nor should you spend the next 10 minutes inspecting the source code for the bug. Apologise, say it was working correctly yesterday, and move onto some other part of the program. Only if the audience or examiners express an interest, should you go back to the faulty part. If you *can't* move onto another part of the program, be prepared to talk clearly and succinctly about what the program *should have* done.

Presenting Yourself

As well as presenting your paper, poster, artwork or software, you are also presenting an image of yourself to your research community. Among the conference delegates or exhibition visitors, you may find people who can help you with your research, or potential PhD examiners, or editors of journals you might want to submit to or do reviews for. You want them to see you as professional, interesting and interested in the research of others.

It's worth asking your supervisor or colleagues what are the appropriate clothes to wear to a particular conference. For example, at conferences where many delegates are from business schools, you might find that many of them wear suits and ties and look like management consultants. On the other hand, delegates at a multimedia or web systems conference might wear more casual clothes. Many conferences include a formal conference dinner, where delegates normally wear something a little smarter than they have worn during the day, but not very formal – tuxedos and ball-gowns would be way over the top.

Many conference delegates will attend few of the presentations – they use the occasion to network with others. You too should seize the opportunity to get to know fellow researchers and become known by them. This means that you have to be prepared to talk to people you don't know, often without anyone introducing you, at the conference welcome reception and refreshment breaks. Some standard opening lines include:

- 'How are you enjoying the conference?'
- 'What area of research are you working on?'
- 'I've just heard an interesting presentation on … . Were you there?'
- 'What did you think of this morning's keynote talk?'
- 'I see you're from X University. Do you know Y who works in the Business School there?'
- 'Are you just attending this conference, or are you planning to stay on for a few days' sightseeing?'

PhD Vivas

For PhD students, probably the most important presentation is the viva – where you are expected to 'defend the thesis'. The format of the viva varies from country to country. For example:

- In the UK, you will be faced with an internal examiner from your university, and one or two external examiners from other universities. The viva takes place in private and lasts, normally, between 1 and 3 hours.
- In some other countries, you face a panel of examiners, some of whom may be from a completely different academic discipline, and the viva takes place in public, perhaps with your family in the audience.

Whatever form the viva takes, it is an opportunity for you to explain and justify your work.

Prepare for your viva by re-reading your thesis as if you were an external examiner. Decide what questions an examiner might ask, and prepare suitable answers. Typical questions include:

- 'What debates/issues/problems does your research address?'
- 'Why did you choose this research strategy/these data generation methods/this case?'

- 'What would you do differently if starting again?'
- 'What do you consider to be your main contribution to knowledge?'
- 'What did you enjoy most in your work?'
- 'How would you turn your thesis into one or more journal articles?'

The examiners could ask you questions to establish that you are indeed the author of the thesis. For example:

- 'Could you explain the overall structure of your thesis?'

They can ask detailed questions about the content:

- 'On page 72 you say that … Could you explain that further?'

Or they can ask questions about the broader context of your work:

- 'How do you think your topic fits into the current research into … ?'

As you re-read your thesis make a note of all the typographical errors you overlooked before – there will always be some. Then when an examiner points some out you can show that you are already aware of them.

Defending a thesis does not mean rebutting all criticisms. It means being able to justify what you did and what you have written and the conclusions you have drawn, but also being able to recognize where there are limitations in your work. Where possible, answer the examiners' questions with reference to your thesis, for example:

- 'I explain my research strategy in Chapter 3, where I argue that action research was an appropriate strategy because …'
- 'Yes, Smith's work is interesting, but his approach is not really applicable in my work, as I point out on page 20.'
- 'Yes, it would have been useful to have observed the system in use for a longer period, but changes in the organization meant that wasn't possible. In the section on "Further Work", I propose observing the system in use in another organization.'

If the examiners ask why you have not cited an author who you've never heard of, don't panic. Try:

- 'I'm not familiar with his work. Do you feel reference to his work would further strengthen my thesis or invalidate it in some way?'

If you have the opportunity to watch or participate in a mock viva, take it. It will give you useful insight into what to expect on the day. Finally, remember: although most PhD students are nervous about their viva, once it's underway most find that they enjoy it. It's an opportunity to talk about work where you are, for the moment, the world authority!

Evaluating Presentations

You can use the two 'Evaluation Guides' below to help you analyse and evaluate written reports of research and oral presentations at conferences.

EVALUATION GUIDE: WRITTEN PRESENTATIONS

1   Is the prose written in a clear style, without spelling and grammatical errors?
2   Does the report have a clearly signposted structure and logical sequence?
3   Have the necessary conventions been followed, appropriate to the discipline and intended readers?
4   Does the abstract effectively summarize the content of the paper?
5   Are the references complete and in the style expected for your discipline?
6   Are all tables, diagrams and other illustrations properly labelled?
7   Do the tables and diagrams enhance the visual appeal of the paper and also aid the reader's comprehension of the research?
8   Is there any material that should be in an appendix rather than the main body, and vice versa?
9   Is evidence provided for each assertion or conclusion?
10 Overall, how effectively do you think the research has been presented?

EVALUATION GUIDE: ORAL PRESENTATIONS

1   Is the speaker ready to start when it is their turn? Is any technological support handled with confidence?
2   Is the speaker's dress and behaviour appropriate for the setting?
3   Is the research presented clearly and audibly, with good use of eye contact?
4   Does the presentation have an obvious structure and logical sequence?
5   Does the speaker use an appropriate number of visual aids?
6   Are the visual aids legible to audience members, and do they assist the listeners' comprehension of the research?
7   Does the speaker speak confidently and complete the presentation within the allotted time without apparent rushing?
8   Does the speaker handle audience questions well?
9   Does the speaker show courtesy to other speakers in the session?
10 Overall, how effectively do you think the research has been presented?

PRACTICAL WORK

1   When we make an argument, we have to avoid 'logical fallacies'. Find out what is meant by this (there is information on the web). Identify some examples of logical fallacies in the press or broadcast media.
2   Prepare an oral presentation. Base it either on some of your own work, or on a paper you have read that is relevant to your research. Give the presentation to some of your colleagues and ask them to assess it, using the 'Evaluation Guide' above to help them. Reflect upon how you might improve your presentations in future.
3   Practise analysing and evaluating written presentations. Find a research paper that is relevant to your work and answer the questions in the 'Evaluation Guide' for written presentations above, using the material in this chapter to help you.
4   Practise analysing and evaluating oral presentations. Attend the presentation of a research paper – either within your department or at a workshop or conference. Answer the questions in the 'Evaluation Guide' for oral presentations above, using the material in this chapter to help you.

FURTHER READING

Useful and humorous guides to writing up research include Becker (1986) and Day (1998). Wolcott (2001) is a short, well-written guide to writing up qualitative research and Collier (1996) analyses how research is presented in scientific and technical communications. Tierney (1995) gives practical advice on oral presentations. Loseke and Cahill (2004) give useful insights into the publishing process, including why manuscripts are rejected. Although they focus on the publication of qualitative social science research, especially ethnographies, much of their advice is also relevant to IS and computing researchers, whatever their research approach.

Books aimed specifically at doctoral students writing their PhD thesis include Bolker (1998), Davis and Parker (1997) and Dunleavy (2003). Hockey (1999) discusses the difficulties faced by artists and designers who focus on making and creating, but must still present their research through text. Booth, Colomb and Williams (2003) are especially good on building an argument and revising drafts, and Murray (2003) gives valuable advice on surviving a viva.

Lee (1995) offers advice to academic reviewers, which will give you an idea of what you might expect when you submit a paper. Mingers (2002), a well-established IS researcher, describes his experiences in trying to get one particular journal article accepted by the reviewers and published. Finally, for light relief, Lodge (1985) satirizes the world of academic conferences.

References

Becker, H.S. (1986). *Writing for social scientists: How to start and finish your thesis, book, or article*. Chicago, IL: University of Chicago Press.
Bolker, J. (1998). *Writing your dissertation in fifteen minutes a day*. New York: Owl Books.

Booth, W., Colomb, G.G., & Williams, J.M. (2003). *The craft of research* (2nd ed.). Chicago, IL: University of Chicago Press.

Collier, J.H. (1996). *Scientific and technical communication. Theory, practice, and policy*. London: Sage.

Davis, G.B., & Parker, C.A. (1997). *Writing the doctoral dissertation* (2nd ed.). New York: Barron's.

Day, R.A. (1998). *How to write and publish a scientific paper*. Westport, CT: Greenwood Press.

Dunleavy, P. (2003). *Authoring a PhD thesis: How to plan, draft, write and finish a doctoral dissertation*. Basingstoke: Palgrave Macmillan.

Hockey, J. (1999). Writing and making: Problems encountered by practice-based research degree students. *Point, 7*(Spring/Summer), 38–43.

Lee, A.S. (1995). Reviewing a manuscript for publication. *Journal of Operations Management, 13*(1), 87–92.

Lodge, D. (1985). *Small world. An academic romance* (paperback ed.). London: Penguin.

Loseke, D.R., & Cahill, S.E. (2004). Publishing qualitative manuscripts: Lessons learned. In C. Seale, G. Gobo, J.F. Gubrium, & D. Silverman (Eds.), *Qualitative research practice* (pp. 577–591). London: Sage.

Mingers, J. (2002). The long and winding road: Publishing papers in top journals. *Communications of AIS, 8*, 330–339.

Murray, R. (2003). *How to survive your viva: Defending a thesis in an oral examination*. Maidenhead: Open University Press.

Tierney, E. (1995). *How to make effective presentations*. London: Sage.

Wolcott, H.F. (2001). *Writing up qualitative research*. London: Sage.

Final Words

This book has explained what we mean by research and discussed a variety of strategies, data generation methods and philosophies. It should be seen however, as a *guide* – not a cookbook for research. There is always a danger that novice researchers, just like novice programmers or systems developers, will feel they have to follow a method rigidly in order to 'do the thing right'. More experienced researchers, programmers and developers come to realize that a method is not always to be interpreted literally, but can be adapted and modified to suit the particular research context. Having read this book, you should therefore:

- put into practice the suggestions given, but be ready to deviate where necessary – but of course know *why* you are deviating;
- talk to experienced researchers about how they do research, the false trails they follow, the uncertainties they experience – so you come to realize that no one can ever be a perfect researcher;
- give accounts of how you do your research, so that others can learn from your experiences;
- contribute to the literature on research methodology – particularly on research into IS and computing – so that the next edition of this book can cite your work too.

Finally, I hope this book helps to make your research enjoyable, and I wish you good luck in your future projects.

Index